SUPPERTIME SURVIVAL

The Complete Weekly Meal Planner

Happy, healthy eating!
Lynn Roblin

LYNN ROBLIN RD

AND

BEV CALLAGHAN RD

In Good Health!
B Callaghan

MACMILLAN CANADA
Toronto

Canadian Cataloguing in Publication Data

Roblin, Lynn, date.

Suppertime Survival
Includes Index

ISBN 0-7715-7355-3

1. Suppers. 2. Cooking. 3. Menus.
I. Callaghan, Bev. II. Title.
TX738.R63 1996 641.5'3 C95-933084-4

1 2 3 4 5 TG 00 99 98 97 96

Cover and text design by Sharon Foster Design
Front cover photo by Doug Bradshaw Photography
Interior photos opposite pages 58 and 154 by Michael Mahovlich
Back cover photo by Al Peacock
Children's clothes by Kids Only, Canada

Macmillan Canada wishes to thank the Canada Council, the Ontario Ministry of Culture and Communications and the Ontario Arts Council for supporting its publishing program.

Macmillan Canada
A Division of Canada Publishing Corporation
Toronto, Ontario, Canada

Printed in Canada

Acknowledgements

Suppertime Survival is the result of an idea we first discussed when we were trying to survive supper with a growing family. With the support of our families and the many people who believed in our idea, Suppertime Survival has become a reality. Writing this book has sometimes seemed like an overwhelming task but together we have not only produced a book that we are extremely proud of but we have strengthened our friendship and developed a working relationship that can survive much more than supper!

We would like to thank the following people for their special contributions to Suppertime Survival:

Our husbands, Blair Roblin and Frank Callaghan, for their endless patience with us, and the kids, and for their unwavering support throughout the entire writing of this book. We couldn't have done it without them!

Our children, Amelia, Cameron, Heather and Erin Roblin and Sarah, Lisa and Maggie Callaghan for understanding, as best they could, when Mom was too busy to play.

The terrific team at Macmillan Canada for all of their guidance, support and enthusiasm for this project in particular Denise Schon for giving us the opportunity to write this book and our editor, Susan Girvan, for keeping us on track and always maintaining her sense of humour!

The team at Info Access (1988) Inc. for the Nutrient Analysis and Rainbow Data in particular Barbara Selley RD and Sharyn Joliat RD for their expert advice and general support of the entire project.

Barbara McHughan, our terrific friend, for typing the recipe manuscripts, inputting our copy edit and keeping us company late at night!

Mary Gauntlett for her steadfast support, her assistance with the recipe testing and her helpful recipe suggestions.

Our countless friends and neighbours for all their help with the never-ending task of testing recipes and for always lending a hand with our kids when we were in a pinch!

Our professional reviewers:
For their technical and practical advice: Meredith Jackson RD, Mary Fodor O'Brien RD, Judy Midgette RD, Lydia Dumais RD and Margie Armstrong.

Our lawyer Fraser Mann at Borden & Elliot for his help getting this project off the ground.

The Beef Information Centre for their photograph of *Curried Beef in a Pita.*

The Dairy Farmers of Canada for their photograph of *Greek Pasta Salad.*

The Ontario Chicken Producers' Marketing Board for their photograph of *Quick Marinated Barbecued Chicken.*

The Ontario Egg Producers' Marketing Board for their photograph of *Basil Zucchini Strata.*

Our photographers, Douglas Bradshaw for our fabulous cover photograph and Michael Mahovlich for the great photographs of our *Baked Fish with Oven-Fried Potato Cubes* and *Extra-Speedy Spaghetti Supper.*

LYNN ROBLIN AND BEV CALLAGHAN
MARCH 1996

This book is dedicated to our husbands, Blair Roblin
and Frank Callaghan
and our children,
Amelia, Cameron, Heather and Erin Roblin
& Sarah, Lisa and Maggie Callaghan.

Our true source of inspiration!

Introduction

Suppertime is one of the busiest times of the day. You might be arriving home late or preparing dinner before you dash out. If you have children, you may be picking them up from childcare or dropping them off at one of their many activities. If you have had a long day at home with young children, you may just be trying to survive the "arsenic hours." Whatever the case, you still need to deal with those nagging questions, "What's for supper?" and "When do we eat?"

We know that getting a healthy and appealing supper on the table during a busy week can be a challenging task. As busy parents, we needed something to help us cope with the dreaded daily dinner dilemma. *Suppertime Survival* evolved and it has truly helped us survive suppertime with as little fuss as possible.

Suppertime Survival can help even the busiest families enjoy healthy meals with a minimum of planning and preparation. A Suppertime Survival Meal Planner is included to help you plan your weekly suppers. You can choose from more than 60 delicious supper meals in this book. The meal planner and supper meals are working for us and we know they can work for you!

Simple and Easy

All of the recipes and supper meals in *Suppertime Survival* are easy to follow and use ingredients that are readily available. No special techniques or fancy preparation methods are required and the number of pots and pans used is kept to a minimum, for faster cleanup. Convenience foods such as prepared pasta sauces, canned soups, prepared salsa or salad dressings, frozen vegetables and canned beans have been used to speed up preparation time and keep the ingredient list short. Cooking has never been simpler.

Time Efficient

The supper meals in *Suppertime Survival* are divided into four sections depending on how much time you have available to prepare them. There are meals that take 30 minutes from start to finish, meals that can bake in the oven while you relax or play with the kids, make-ahead meals and meals for those days when you just don't feel like cooking.

Balancing Meals with Canada's Food Guide to Healthy Eating

Each supper meal in *Suppertime Survival* has a Rainbow Balance Chart to go with it. This chart is divided into the four food groups contained in Canada's Food Guide to Healthy Eating (Grain Products, Vegetables & Fruit, Milk Products, Meat & Alternatives). The Rainbow Balance Chart shows the number of servings from each food group that each supper meal contains. If a supper meal is missing a serving from one of the food groups, we give you suggestions on how to "Fill in the Rainbow" to balance each supper meal.

Feeding Families Through the Stages

Cooking for a family can be a tricky business! Trying to balance everyone's likes and dislikes with his or her different nutritional needs and activity levels can sometimes seem overwhelming. To cope with this, we provided a variety of supper meals that can fit in with everyone's various needs and schedules. Questions about feeding babies and suggestions on how to manage mealtime madness with small children are covered. We also tackle the important issue of healthy weights for the entire family.

Other Important Information

We know that making healthy food choices can be difficult. *Suppertime Survival* will help you put together a well-stocked kitchen, offer advice on steering smartly through the grocery aisles, and provide you with important information on how to prepare and store foods safely.

Suppertime Survival also includes a chapter called Eating on the Run because we know many people are often away from home at mealtimes. We talk about how to fit fast foods into your day and suggest some Meals to Go based on some of our *Suppertime Survival* meals.

Where to go for help

Registered Dietitians (RD) are the most reliable and qualified source of nutrition information. They can answer your nutrition questions and help you plan a healthier way of eating. Registered Dietitians work in public health departments, health centres, hospitals, universities, food industries and in private practice. If you have specific nutrition questions or health concerns that affect your family's food choices, we recommend that you contact your local health unit or hospital to locate a Registered Dietitian in your community.

We know *Suppertime Survival* can help you

We are both Registered Dietitians and we have tried to provide you with the most up-to-date and reliable nutrition information possible. Our goal is to help you survive suppertime, while providing nutritionally balanced supper meals for your family. Many different families have tested our supper meals and are already surviving supper with great results. We know that your family will soon be surviving supper too.

Lynn Roblin RD, and Bev Callaghan RD,
March, 1996

Chapter 1

SUPPERTIME SURVIVAL

A family sharing a relaxing meal together sounds wonderful, but fast lane living doesn't often allow for this. We live varied and busy lives. Family members come and go at all hours of the day, including mealtime. Sometimes it's easier to opt for a quick food fix at the closest fast food outlet or grab a prepared entrée from the grocery store than to prepare a meal from scratch.

There is nothing wrong with this style of eating—occasionally. But over time, if convenience and fast foods are eaten too often, your family will be eating more fat and salt and less fibre and essential nutrients than they need. Therefore it's important for your family to enjoy nutritionally balanced meals most of the time. That means eating meals that include a wide variety of grain products, vegetables, fruit, milk products, lean meats and meat alternatives such as eggs, dried peas, beans and lentils. Having more of these foods doesn't take as much effort as you might think.

STEPS TO SUCCESSFUL SUPPERS

One of the biggest suppertime challenges is simply deciding what's for supper. That depends on the amount of time you have for supper, your family's food preferences and the foods you have on hand. Here's how to make supper happen easily in your home!

Step #1: Review Your Family's Activity Schedule

Deciding what's for supper really means figuring out what you can realistically make and serve in the time you have available on a given day of the week.

- Take a look at your family's activities
- Decide how much time you have to make a meal.
- Choose a complete supper meal from one of the categories.

Quick fixes: These meals take 30 minutes or less to prepare and are perfect for people who can prepare a meal—but want it fast. Try Speedy Vegetable and Chicken Stir-Fry (page 44), Beef Stroganoff (page 28), Zucchini and Red Pepper Frittata (page 50) or Spanish Rice with Lentils (page 42).

Make and Bakes: These meals take about 20 minutes to prepare and about 15 to 75 minutes to bake. They give you time to do other activities while supper cooks. Try the simple and nutritious Pork Tenderloin with Roasted Sweet Potatoes (page 68), Family Tuna Noodle Casserole (page 62) and Spinach Frittata Fingers (page 70). This section also includes barbecue recipes, which cook up quickly but require time to marinate.

Make-Ahead Meals: These meals take 30 minutes or more to prepare but the time invested is worth it. Most of these meals can be put into the freezer and pulled out on days when you don't have time to cook or when you are out and about during meal preparation time. We have perfected a recipe for Batch Ground Meat and Vegetables (page 88) that you can use to create meals in minutes. Try the Extra-Speedy Spaghetti Supper (page 92), Fusilli with Vegetarian Pasta Sauce (page 124) and Warm Taco Salad (page 102). "Souper" suppers are soups that can be made quickly or ahead of time such as Carrot Ginger Soup (page 117) and Broccoli Soup (page 116). Team these soups with a sandwich for a light, nutritious supper.

Bail-Out Meals: These meals take 15 to 20 minutes to prepare and are great for days when you get home late or just don't feel like spending time in the kitchen. Fast Fish in the Microwave (page 138) and Bail-Out Bean Burritos (page 134) are great choices.

Meals to Go: These meals are usually made ahead of time or use planned leftovers. They can be eaten while on the run, in the car, or while hanging out at an arena or pool. Chapter 4 (Eating on the Run) includes a selection of portable meals taken from other recipe sections. Curried Beef in a Pita (page 36) are a big hit with families and can be eaten easily in the car or on the playing field. These meals are healthier alternatives to typical fast food fare, but you need to plan and prepare them ahead of time.

Make dinner once!

Make one supper meal that the whole family can enjoy and avoid becoming a short-order cook. There is nothing more frustrating than being in the kitchen for two hours catering to everyone's likes and dislikes. Serve meals that you know are acceptable, but be sure to include a variety of different meals over the week.

- If you have a picky eater, the solution may be as simple as presenting family foods to them differently. For example, if your child won't eat foods that are mixed together, you can still make a mixed dish such as a stir-fry. Set aside some of the vegetables and cooked meat before adding the sauce, and serve with plain rice. That way your child can enjoy basically the same foods as the rest of the family.
- If some family members get home after everyone else has eaten, put their supper on a plate and keep in the refrigerator. They can heat up their meal later in the microwave.
- Serve part of supper before supper! Preschoolers often cannot wait until everyone is home and ready to eat supper, and many schoolage kids are starving when they get home from school. Snacks are acceptable and can even help boost nutrient intakes if the right choices are made. Set guidelines about the kinds of snacks allowed; for example, only food from one of the four food groups before supper. A fruit platter or raw vegetables on the table before supper will disappear quickly when kids are hungry and helps them get more of these nutrient-packed foods into their day.

Step #2: Plan Ahead

Planning ahead makes dealing with supper easier to handle. If you do, you can guarantee your family a better variety of nutritonally balanced supper meals throughout the week.

Think about what to serve for supper ahead of time so that you are not in a mad panic when suppertime rolls around. Take a few moments earlier in the day to think about supper, or even better, plan a whole week's worth of suppers.

Prepare your shopping list at the same time as you plan your weekly meals. This helps to cut down your visits to the grocery store and ensures that you have the ingredients you need on hand.

Review the meals and recipes that you plan to make and add any ingredients that you need to your shopping list. To determine how much food to buy, check the serving sizes suggested by Canada's Food Guide to Healthy Eating.

A simple tool called the Suppertime Survival Weekly Meal Planner (opposite) can help you do just that. Use it to record your supper meals for one week at a time. Keep the supper meal planner in a visible place, such as on the refrigerator, so that other people in your household, including teens and child-care providers, can help with meal preparation. Leave recipes and instructions out so that supper can be started without you.

How to use the Meal Planner

- For variety and maximum nutrient exposure, choose supper meals that feature different foods each night and include plenty of grains, vegetables and fruit.
- Vary the kinds of meat and alternatives you use over the week. For example, choose different egg, bean, meat, fish or poultry meals.
- Add foods that you need to complete each meal. For example, include servings from the Milk Products group if they are not part of a supper recipe. Ideally, a balanced supper meal should include something from each of the four food groups in Canada's Food Guide to Healthy Eating. Sometimes including only three out of the four food groups is all that is needed if servings from the missing group have been met at other meals and snacks.
- Plan to use leftovers and combine them with other foods for a new meal.

Desserts are optional and depend on what foods you still need to balance your daily food intake according to the food guide. Fruit, fruit crisps, oatmeal cookies, fig bars, digestive cookies, rice pudding, sherbet, sorbet, low-fat yogurt, milk pudding, light ice cream and ice milk are easy desserts that are higher in nutrients and lower in fat than cakes, pies and pastries.

SUPPERTIME SURVIVAL WEEKLY MEAL PLANNER

Day / Activity	Supper Meal	Shopping List
Monday		
Tuesday		
Wednesday		
Thursday		
Friday		
Saturday		
Sunday		

Example of SUPPERTIME SURVIVAL MEAL PLANNER

Day / Activity	Supper Meal	Shopping List
Monday picking kids up at 5, meeting at 7	Make Ahead Easy On Ya Lasagna (pg 98)* Veggies and Dip (pg 91) Garlic Bread (pg 127) *Prepare in advance for a quick weeknight supper	Batch Ground Meat and Vegetables (pg 88) or ground beef prepared tomato sauce part skim mozarella cheese low-fat plain yogurt, cottage cheese (low fat), spinach, carrots, green pepper, cucumber, bread
Tuesday at the arena until 6	Bail Out Fast Fish in Microwave (page 138) Quicky Couscous (pg 53) Zucchini Salsa Sauté (page 139) light vanilla ice cream chocolate syrup	fish fillets couscous salsa zucchini, green pepper ice cream
Wednesday	Make and Bake Tangy BBQ Chicken with Rice (page 72) Corn on the Cob milk Pear Crisp (page 86)	chicken breasts barbecue sauce corn on the cob canned pears
Thursday choir at 6:30	Quick Fix Spanish Rice with Lentils (page 42) fruit yogurt	canned tomatoes canned lentils onion green peppers fruit yogurt,
Friday A. home from gym at 6, C. out to game at 6:30	Meal to Go Spinach Frittata Fingers (pg 70) bagel fruit milk	eggs spinach red pepper Cheddar cheese cottage cheese bagels

Suppertime Survival does include some dessert recipes:
Baked Apples
Blair's Rice Pudding
Chocolate Angel Food Cake
Fresh Berries with Vanilla Yogurt Topping
Pear Crisp

Suppertime Survival Tips

Most people don't have the luxury of having supper ready the instant they walk in the door. No matter how organized the person responsible for preparing supper is, you still need time to change gears, deal with family demands and set yourself up for any suppertime activities. Here are some tips to get you started.

- Prepare meals or part of meals ahead of time. Vegetables and dip can easily be made the night before. Double recipes for soups, casseroles and baked pasta dishes, and freeze the extras for a quick meal on a busy night. The Make-Ahead Meals section has great meal suggestions that include batch cooking recipes.
- Try speed-scratch cooking to get meals on the table faster. That means using convenience products as well as fresh ingredients to create quicker meals. Extra-Speedy Spaghetti Supper (page 92), Speedy Vegetable and Chicken Stir-Fry (page 44) and Black Bean, Corn and Couscous Salad (page 136) are good examples of speed-scratch cooking.
- Take items that need to be defrosted out of the freezer the night before and let them defrost in the refrigerator. Leaving frozen food or meat on the counter to defrost during the day is not a safe practice and can cause food poisoning.
- Stock your pantry, fridge and freezer with items that you frequently use so that you can always pull a meal together at the last minute.

DO YOU HAVE A SMART KITCHEN?

A smart kitchen is one that is well stocked with staples and includes the tools you need to prepare meals simply and successfully. This section includes suggestions for basic shelf ingredients as well as a list of the baking dishes and utensils you need to prepare most of the meals in *Suppertime Survival.*

BASIC SHELF INGREDIENTS

Keep a ready supply of these staples in your Smart Kitchen and you can pull together balanced supper meals in record time.

Grain Products

All-purpose flour
Unprocessed wheat bran
Cornmeal
Cornstarch

Whole wheat bread
Whole wheat rolls/buns
Whole wheat pita bread
Flour tortillas
Flatbread rounds
Small bagels

Dry bread crumbs
Cornflakes or cornflake crumbs

Brown rice
Long grain rice

Pasta:
Quick-cooking couscous
Fusilli
Penne
Small pasta shells
Ready-cut macaroni
Spaghettini or spaghetti

Vegetables & Fruit

Lemon juice
Unsweetened applesauce
Vegetable juice cocktail

Frozen:
Unsweetened orange juice concentrate
Unsweetened fruit juice concentrate
Baby carrots
Corn
Spinach
Mixed vegetables (carrots/corn/peas)
Vegetable medley (broccoli/cauliflower/carrots)

Canned:
Mandarin oranges
Sliced peaches
Pineapple tidbits
Tomatoes
Tomato paste

Milk Products

Cheddar cheese
Grated Parmesan cheese
Part-skim mozzarella cheese
Plain yogurt (1 or 2% M.F.)
2%, 1% or skim milk

Meat & Alternatives

Large eggs
Frozen fish fillets (individually frozen)
Canned tuna packed in water
Vacuum-packed sliced pepperoni
Peanut butter

Canned:
Baked beans in tomato sauce
Black beans
Refried beans
Red kidney beans
Chick-peas or garbanzo beans
Lentils

Convenience Products

Canned:
Condensed tomato soup
Condensed cream of broccoli soup
Condensed Italian-style tomato soup
Condensed golden mushroom soup

Prepared salsa
Prepared tomato-based pasta sauce
Prepared pizza sauce
Calorie-reduced vinaigrette salad dressing
Frozen cheese ravioli
Frozen meat tortellini

Other foods

Soft margarine
Olive oil
Vegetable oil
Light mayonnaise

Sodium-reduced soy sauce
Honey
Fancy molasses
Granulated sugar
Brown sugar
Syrup
Worcestershire sauce
Tabasco sauce
Barbecue sauce
Ketchup
Dijon mustard
Mustard
Honey mustard
Balsamic vinegar
Cider vinegar
Unseasoned rice vinegar
Chicken bouillon cubes/sachets
Vegetable bouillon cubes/sachets
Packaged vegetable dip seasoning mix

A variety of herbs and spices including:
Dried basil
Black pepper
Chili powder
Curry powder
Ground cinnamon
Ground cumin
Ground coriander
Garlic powder
Ground ginger
Ground nutmeg
Dried oregano leaves
Dried rosemary
Dried thyme leaves
Dry mustard

Utensils and baking dishes used in Suppertime Survival

A Smart Kitchen does not depend on a lot of fancy gadgets and gizmos to run smoothly! *Suppertime Survival* meals use as few pots, pans and baking dishes as possible to help keep your kitchen fairly uncluttered. If you outfit your kitchen with the following utensils and baking dishes, you will have everything you need to prepare most of the supper meals in this book.

UTENSILS

Set of 3 mixing bowls (small, medium, large), preferably microwaveable and dishwasher-safe

Set of 4 glass liquid measuring cups (1 cup/250 mL, 2 cup/500 mL, 4 cup/1 L, 8 to 10 cup/2 to 2.5 L)

Set of 4 plastic or metal dry measuring cups (imperial or metric)

Set of 4 or 5 plastic or metal measuring spoons (imperial or metric)

1 large 10-inch (25 cm) metal balloon whisk (Buy a heavy-duty one that will last for years!)

1 or 2 wooden spoons

1 slotted spoon

1 can opener (essential for survival cooking!)

1 large colander (for draining pasta and vegetables)

1 or 2 plastic spatulas

1 or 2 small paring knives (Keep them sharp! Dull knives can be dangerous.)

1 large chopping knife

1 bread knife

1 hand-held grater

1 potato masher

Cutting board

Meat thermometer

Skewers and a kitchen fork for testing doneness

Bamboo skewers or metal skewers for kabobs

Plenty of plastic storage containers in 1-cup (250 mL), 2-cup (500 mL) and 4-cup (1 L) sizes (for storing all those meals that are going to save the day at 6:00 p.m.)

Pots, Pans and Baking Dishes

1 large nonstick skillet

1 small nonstick skillet

1 set of metal saucepans with lids (small, medium, and large, including a Dutch oven)

2 cookie sheets 15½ x 10 inches (40 x 25 cm)

1 or 2 glass baking dishes (9- x 13-inch/3 L)

1 or 2 glass pie plates (10-inch/25 cm)

Chapter 2

Balanced Eating with Canada's Food Guide

For some families, supper is the only meal of the day that they share together. For others, it may be a meal that is eaten on the run or as family members pass through the kitchen at different times. Whatever the case, supper is an important meal of the day and should contribute significantly to everyone's total daily nutrient needs.

WHAT IS A BALANCED MEAL?

Nowhere is it written that supper has to be a hot meal or include meat and two vegetables. Anything goes at suppertime, provided that it contains a variety of foods from different food groups and isn't too high in fat or heavy on the extras. French fries, for instance, do not count as a balanced meal. But French toast, syrup, strawberries, cantaloupe and milk are worthy candidates. So are pizza, fruit juice and carrot sticks. Canned baked beans with toast, orange slices and milk also make the grade.

A meal that includes something from each of the four food groups in Canada's Food Guide to Healthy Eating can be called a balanced meal. The easiest way to make sure that your family's meals are nutritionally balanced is to follow Canada's Food Guide To Healthy Eating.

Canada's Food Guide to Healthy Eating is a simple tool that outlines the kinds and amounts of foods your family should eat to get the nutrients they need every day. A copy of the Food Guide is opposite page 26.

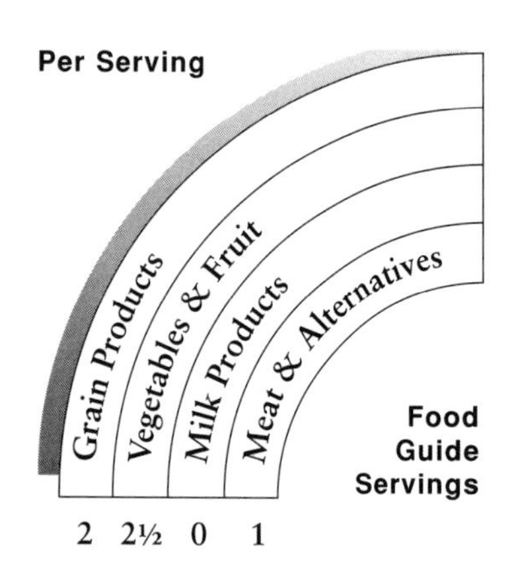

Filling in the Rainbow

Complete this meal with a serving from the Milk Products group if necessary to balance the rest of the day.

Each *Suppertime Survival* meal includes a Rainbow Balance Chart to show you how that meal fits with Canada's Food Guide to Healthy Eating. This chart indicates the number of servings of food from each food group in one serving of the complete supper meal. Our goal was to develop supper meals that included something from each food group and additional servings from the Grain Products and Vegetables & Fruit groups.

In some cases, a meal may be missing a serving from one of the four food groups. When this happens, we provide suggestions to help you complete the supper meal. We've called this Filling in the Rainbow. For example, Speedy Vegetable and Chicken Stir-Fry with Rice (page 44) provides 2 servings from the Grain Products group, 2½ servings from the Vegetables & Fruit group and 1 serving from the Meat & Alternatives group. This meal does not provide a serving from the Milk Products group.

It is not absolutely essential to have something from each group at every meal. Sometimes family members may have already satisfied their requirements for a food group earlier in the day, especially with the Milk Products or Meat & Alternatives groups. We don't need to eat as many servings of food from these two food groups. Therefore, adding extra servings of Milk Products or Meat & Alternatives may not be necessary to complete a meal.

BALANCING SUPPER WITH THE REST OF THE DAY

You can compare your family's food choices to Canada's Food Guide to Healthy Eating using the questions on page 156.

What's left for you to do is consider what your family has eaten earlier in the day at other meals and snacks. That way you can use the supper meal to balance out the rest of your family's day.

Grain Products:
5-12 servings per day

Grain products contain iron, B vitamins and fibre. They are also a source of energy for growing and active family members.

Most people have little trouble getting enough grain products into their day. Cereal and toast for breakfast, a low-fat muffin for a snack and a sandwich at lunch add up to five servings from the Grain Products group. A cup of pasta or rice at suppertime will complete the daily requirements for most family members. Active family members and teens can easily add extra grain products to their day to satisfy their energy requirements.

VEGETABLES & FRUIT:
5-10 servings per day

Eating more vegetables and fruit is a great way to get more fibre in your family's day. Vegetables and fruit are also packed with vitamins, especially those with antioxidant properties such as vitamins C and A (beta-carotene). They also provide folic acid which is important for forming blood cells and nervous tissue, and is particularly important for women considering pregnancy. Dark green and dark orange vegetables and orange fruit contain the highest amount of these important nutrients.

Getting enough of the Vegetables & Fruit group into every family member's day may be more difficult, especially for children who would prefer not to eat vegetables. Get them off to a good start early in the day by including fruit at breakfast and more vegetables or fruit for snacks and at lunchtime. If you can knock off a few Vegetables & Fruit servings early in the day, you won't have to play catch-up with this food group at suppertime. A glass of juice plus sliced fruit on cereal or French toast for breakfast, a piece of fruit in the lunch bag, and raw vegetables for a snack before supper add up to four servings from the Vegetables & Fruit group. A few more servings from this group at suppertime will help fill in the rainbow for the day. Active people and teens can satisfy their energy needs with more servings of Vegetables & Fruit throughout the day.

MILK PRODUCTS:
2-4 servings per day

Milk products are a very important source of calcium and vitamins A, D and riboflavin. Calcium is especially important for women and growing children as it helps develop and maintain strong bones and teeth. If you are concerned about the amount of fat your family consumes, use skim, 1% or 2% milk, except for children under the age of two, who should drink whole milk. Preparing family meals with lower-fat milk products also helps decrease fat intakes.

Children 4-9 years: 2-3 servings per day

Youth 10-16 years: 3-4 servings per day

Adults: 2-4 servings per day

Pregnant and Breast-feeding women: 3-4 servings per day

The minimum number of servings from the Milk Products group is 2 servings per day. Many adults may have satisfied their need for foods from this group by the time supper rolls around. Children and teens, on the other hand, may still need additional milk servings at suppertime. That's why many of the *Suppertime Survival* meals suggest that you complete the meal with a glass of milk or a serving from the Milk Products group.

MEAT & ALTERNATIVES:
2-3 servings per day

Meat & Alternatives provide protein, iron and B vitamins. Red meats, pork and poultry provide heme-iron, which is important for preventing anemia in children and women who are pregnant or menstruating. To lower your family's fat intake, trim visible fats and skins on meat and poultry and include more fish and fat-reduced meat and poultry products. Include more beans, peas and lentils, which are low in fat and high in folic acid, carbohydrates and fibre.

Most families have little difficulty getting enough servings from this food group. One egg, a slice of lean ham, a peanut butter or tuna sandwich each count as one serving from the Meat & Alternatives group. Sometimes family members get enough servings from this food group before suppertime. Therefore a supper meal that does do not include a serving from the Meat & Alternatives group would be perfectly acceptable. We have included some of these kinds of meals in *Suppertime Survival*, for example Greek Pasta Salad (page 38) or Fusilli with Vegetarian Pasta Sauce (page 124).

Many of the *Suppertime Survival* meals include meat, fish and poultry. In keeping with the recommendations made in the Food Guide, we've developed recipes that provide 2 to 3 oz (50 to 100 g) of meat per serving (a serving about the size of a deck of cards). In some cases, meat is used as an ingredient in meals (ground beef in Homemade Spaghetti Supper (page 90), Beef Stroganoff (page 94) or Warm Taco Salad (page 102)). These meals provide ½ serving from the Meat & Alternatives group. This is acceptable, especially if other choices from the Meat & Alternatives group are eaten earlier in the day.

Suppertime Survival Vegetarian Meals

For families who are trying to enjoy more meatless meals, *Suppertime Survival* includes plenty of great-tasting choices. Family members who are switching to a more vegetarian way of eating should be concerned with planning meals that provide adequate amounts of iron, zinc and protein.

Asparagus Frittata
Bail-Out Bean Burritos
Basil Zucchini Strata
Black Bean, Corn and Couscous Salad
Broccoli Soup
Carrot Ginger Soup
Creamy Macaroni and Cheese
French Toast with Peaches and Syrup
Fusilli with Vegetarian Pasta Sauce
Greek Pasta Salad
Lentil and Pasta Soup
Mediterranean Pizza
Ravioli with Prepared Pasta Sauce
Spanish Rice with Lentils
Spicy Garden Gazpacho
Spinach Frittata Fingers
Sweet Beans and Toast
Three-Bean Chili with Couscous
Vegetarian Lasagna
Zucchini and Red Pepper Frittata

Other Foods

Use foods that are high in fat or calories in moderation.

Foods and beverages that are not part of any food group are called Other Foods. Butter, margarine, oil, salad dressing, sugar, jam, honey, syrup, candies, pickles, ketchup, mustard, and snack foods such as chips and pretzels are just some of the Other Foods that we eat. Beverages such as soft drinks, alcohol, tea and coffee are also considered Other Foods. Other Foods help us enjoy eating and don't need to be excluded from our diet.

When trying to balance the rest of your family's day, consider the total amount of Other Foods they eat: butter or margarine on toast, mayonnaise on sandwiches, salad dressings on salads, and snack foods such as chips, candy or chocolate bars. It is important to eat in moderation when choosing foods that are high in fat, calories and salt and low in nutrients. Alcohol should be avoided by pregnant and breast-feeding women.

ABOUT THE INGREDIENTS USED IN SUPPERTIME SURVIVAL MEALS

Canada's Food Guide to Healthy Eating provides recommendations to help make healthy eating easy for families. We've used these recommendations as a basis for choosing ingredients and developing the supper meals and recipes included in *Suppertime Survival.* This means that, wherever possible, we have chosen a variety of foods that are lower in fat, higher in carbohydrates and fibre, and higher in nutrients.

Grain Products: Whole grain and enriched products such as whole wheat bread, buns and pita bread, enriched pasta, and Perfect Microwave Rice (page 44), which includes a mixture of brown and long grain white rice.

Vegetables & Fruit: Dark green and orange vegetables and orange fruit such as sweet potatoes, carrots, cantaloupe, sweet peppers, green peas, broccoli, kiwifruit, berries, oranges and orange juice. Convenience products such as canned vegetables and fruit, and frozen vegetables.

Milk Products: Regular Cheddar cheese, part-skim mozzarella cheese, plain yogurt (less than 2% M.F.), 2% milk, light ricotta cheese (5% M.F.) light sour cream (5% M.F.), and cottage cheese (2% M.F.).

Meat & Alternatives: Lean cuts of meat, trimmed of fat, with skins removed; lean fish and tuna packed in water; large eggs; canned beans, chick-peas and lentils.

Other Foods: Soft margarine, vegetable (canola) oil, olive oil, light mayonnaise, calorie-reduced salad dressing, sodium-reduced soy sauce, bouillon cubes and fresh or dried herbs and spices.

Recommended range of servings suggested for each food group, per day

5-12 servings of Grain Products
5-10 servings of Vegetables & Fruit
2-4 servings of Milk Products
 children 4-9 years: 2 - 3
 youths 10-16 years: 3 - 4
 adults: 2 - 4
 Pregnant and breast-feeding women: 3 - 4
2-3 servings of Meat & Alternatives

HOW MUCH FOOD IS ENOUGH?

Not everyone needs the same amount of food. The Food Guide suggests a range of servings because everyone has different energy (calorie) and nutrient needs. Teens have high energy needs and can therefore eat more food. They can choose the higher end of the serving range (an active male teen can have 12 servings of Grain Products). Younger children and inactive older people don't need to eat as much food and can choose from the smaller end of the range (five servings of Grain Products). Women and teenage girls have high requirements for certain nutrients such as calcium, iron and folic acid. They should choose at least the minimum recommended servings from each of the four food groups in order to satisfy their nutrient needs.

As people get older, many start to eat less food and may actually consume less than the range of foods recommended. Energy needs do decrease as people get older but their need for most nutrients stays about the same.

What is a child-size serving?

There is a wide variation in portions of foods consumed by preschoolers. That's why a child-size serving is anywhere from one-half to the full size for foods in each food group, as indicated in Canada's Food Guide to Healthy Eating. Generally the size of portion increases with age. For example, a two-year-old may eat a half-slice of bread, whereas a four-year-old is more likely to eat a whole slice. Both of these can be counted as one child-size serving of Grain Products.

EXAMPLES OF ONE CHILD-SIZE SERVING

Grain Products

½ - 1 slice of bread
15-30 g cold cereal*
75-175 mL (⅓-¾ cup) hot cereal
¼-½ bagel, pita or bun
½-1 muffin
50-125 mL (¼-½ cup) pasta or rice
4-8 soda crackers

*Approximate volumes for one serving: flaked cereal 125-250 mL (½-1 cup); puffed cereal 250-500 mL (1-2 cups); granola or dense-type cereal 30-75 mL (2 tbsp-⅓ cup).

Vegetables & Fruit

½-1 medium-size vegetable or fruit
50-125 mL (¼-½ cup) fresh, frozen or canned vegetables or fruit
125-250 mL (½-1 cup) salad
50-125 mL (¼-½ cup) juice

Milk Products

25-50 g (1 to 2 oz) cheese
75-175 g (⅓-¾ cup) yogurt
Preschoolers should consume a total of 500 mL (2 cups) of milk every day.

Meat & Alternatives

25-50 g (1-2 oz) meat, fish or poultry
1 egg
50-125 mL (¼-½ cup) beans
50-100 g (¼-⅓ cup) tofu
15-30 mL (1-2 tbsp) peanut butter

Reprinted from: Canada's Food Guide to Healthy Eating Focus on Preschoolers. Background for Educators and Communicators. Minister of Supply and Services Canada, 1995.

Chapter 3

SUPPERTIME SURVIVAL MEALS AND RECIPES

Quick Fixes

These meals can be prepared in less than 30 minutes from start to finish.

Each supper meal makes four, five or six servings.

Desserts:

Asparagus Frittata

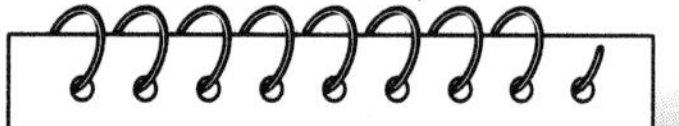

Shopping List

eggs
asparagus
part-skim mozzarella cheese
whole grain bread/rolls

To trim asparagus, gently bend the stalk until the woody end snaps off.

If you like frittatas, try Bacon and Potato Frittata (page 131) and Zucchini and Red Pepper Frittata (page 50).

This is a real treat when fresh asparagus is in season. The provolone cheese is a nice flavour change from the part-skim mozzarella. Substitute other light cheeses if you wish. Be sure to use a nonstick skillet to prevent the frittata from sticking to the pan. Wrap handle with foil, if necessary, to prevent it from burning when the frittata is placed under the broiler.

6	eggs	6
3 tbsp	water	50 mL
1 tbsp	olive oil	15 mL
1 lb	fresh medium asparagus, trimmed and cut into 2-inch (5 cm) slices (about 3 cups/750 mL)	500 g
1 tbsp	lemon juice	15 mL
	Pepper	
1 cup	shredded part-skim mozzarella or light provolone cheese	250 mL

1. Preheat broiler.
2. In medium bowl, whisk eggs with water; set aside.
3. In skillet, heat oil over medium heat; add asparagus and sauté for 4 to 6 minutes or until tender-crisp. Stir in lemon juice and pepper.
4. Pour eggs on top of asparagus. Sprinkle cheese on top; reduce heat to low and cook for 3 to 4 minutes or until bottom is lightly browned yet centre is still not set.
5. Broil for 1 to 3 minutes or until puffed and golden, watching closely as top will brown quickly.

Makes 4 servings

Grain Products
Choose whole grain and enriched products more often.

Vegetables & Fruit
Choose dark green and orange vegetables and orange fruit more often.

Milk Products
Choose lower-fat milk products more often.

Meat & Alternatives
Choose leaner meats, poultry and fish, as well as dried peas, beans and lentils more often.

Canada

Different People Need Different Amounts of Food

The amount of food you need every day from the 4 food groups and other foods depends on your age, body size, activity level, whether you are male or female and if you are pregnant or breast-feeding. That's why the Food Guide gives a lower and higher number of servings for each food group. For example, young children can choose the lower number of servings, while male teenagers can go to the higher number. Most other people can choose servings somewhere in between.

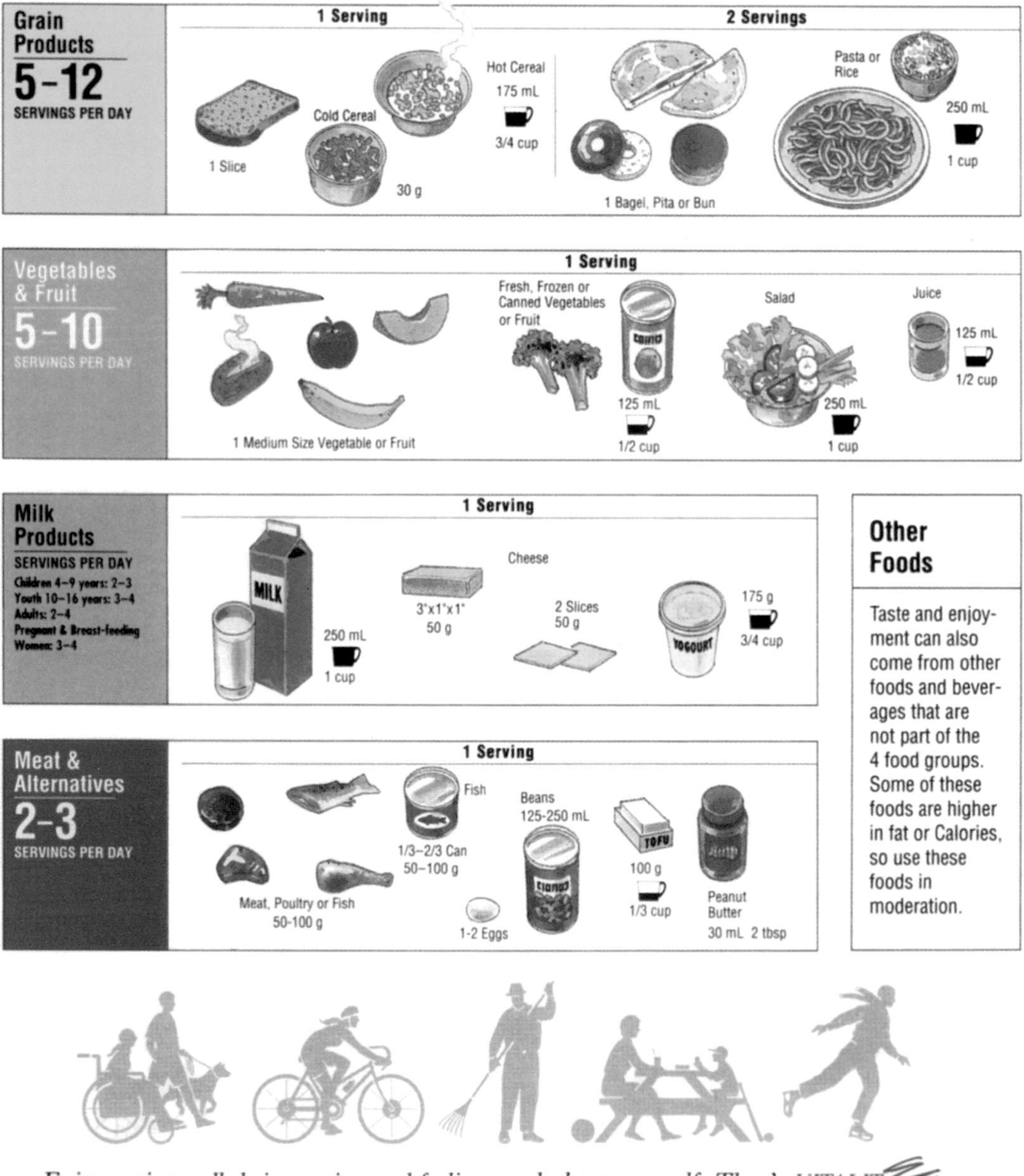

Enjoy eating well, being active and feeling good about yourself. That's VITALIT

ISBN 0-662-19648-1

For 1 serving of Asparagus Frittata

Use 2 eggs, 1 tbsp (15 mL) water, 1 tsp (5 mL) olive oil, 6 asparagus stalks, 1 tsp (5 mL) lemon juice, pepper and ¼ cup (50 mL) shredded part-skim mozzarella cheese. Use small non-stick skillet and sauté asparagus for 3 to 4 minutes or until tender-crisp. Broil for 1 to 2 minutes.

Per serving

Calories	241
Protein	19g
Fat	16g
Carbohydrate	5g
Dietary fibre	1g

Excellent source of riboflavin, folic acid, vitamin B12

Good source of vitamin A, niacin, calcium, zinc

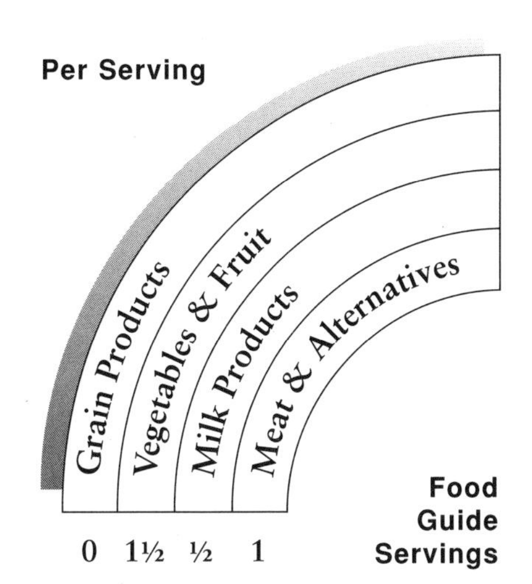

Filling in the Rainbow

Complete this meal with whole grain bread or rolls.

1 Grain Products serving = 1 slice whole wheat bread or 1 small dinner roll

Active kids, teens, men and women may need 2-3 Grain Products to balance their day.

Beef Stroganoff with Noodles

This is a great family meal that can be easily adapted for week-night entertaining. Tempt the gourmet crowd by substituting brown, oyster or portobello mushrooms for some of the white mushrooms. For an even simpler family supper, try Ground Beef Stroganoff (page 94).

1 tbsp	vegetable oil	15 mL
1 lb	lean inside round or sirloin steak, cut into 3- x ½-inch (8 x 1 cm) strips	500 g
¾ lb	mushrooms, sliced (about 4 cups/1 L)	375 g
1	medium onion, sliced	1
1	package (12 oz/375 g) broad egg noodles	1
½ cup	water	125 mL
2 tbsp	sherry	25 mL
1	can (10 oz/284 mL) condensed golden mushroom soup	1
	Pepper	
1 cup	light sour cream (5% M.F.)	250 mL
2 tbsp	chopped fresh parsley (optional)	25 mL

1. In large nonstick skillet, heat oil over medium-high heat; add steak and sauté for 3 to 4 minutes or until no longer pink. Remove from pan and set aside.
2. Add mushrooms and onion to skillet; sauté for 6 to 8 minutes or until moisture has evaporated.
3. Meanwhile, in large pot of boiling water, cook noodles according to package directions; drain.

Shopping List
lean inside round steak
mushrooms
broad egg noodles
condensed golden mushroom soup
light sour cream

Choose a lean cut of beef such as inside round (3 g of fat per 3 oz/90 g cooked serving) or lean sirloin steak (6 g of fat per 3 oz/90 g cooked serving).

Store fresh mushrooms in the refrigerator, in a paper bag, for up to 2 days. Wipe clean with a damp cloth just before using. If mushrooms are very sandy, quickly rinse them under warm running water and pat dry. Never soak fresh mushrooms in water as they will become soggy.

To save time, buy pre-packaged sliced mushrooms.

4. Meanwhile, add water, sherry, soup and pepper to skillet; reduce heat and simmer for 2 minutes. Return meat to pan and simmer for 1 minute or until heated through.
5. Turn off heat. Stir in sour cream, and parsley (if using); heat through but do not boil. Serve over noodles.

Makes 6 servings

Per serving

Per serving	
Calories	447
Protein	31g
Fat	10g
Carbohydrate	56g
Dietary fibre	5g

Excellent source of thiamine, riboflavin, niacin, vitamin B12, iron, zinc

Good source of vitamin B6

High source of dietary fibre

For a simple and elegant dessert, try Fresh Berries with Vanilla Yogurt Topping (sidebar recipe page 52)

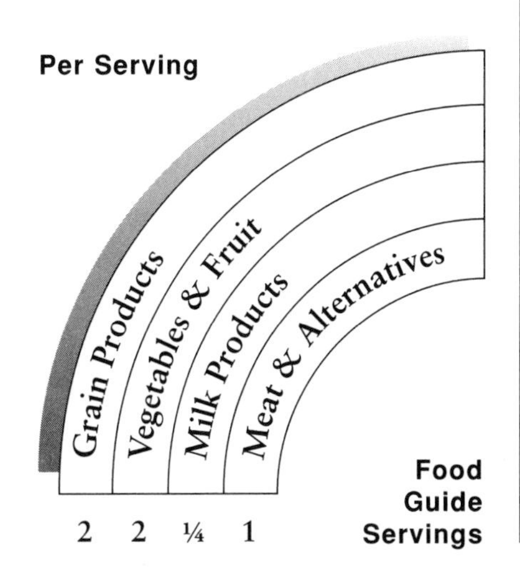

Filling in the Rainbow

Balance this meal with something from the Milk Products group if you need to top up your milk servings for the day.

Chicken Fajitas

These are fun for everyone. Try using different colours of peppers when they are readily available.

Marinade

2 tbsp	lime or lemon juice	25 mL
1 tbsp	Worcestershire sauce	15 mL
½ tsp	each dried oregano, ground cumin and ground coriander	2 mL
¼ tsp	each garlic powder and pepper	1 mL
1 lb	boneless skinless chicken breasts, cut into 3- x ½-inch (8 x 1 cm) strips	500 g

Filling

2 tsp	vegetable oil	10 mL
1	medium onion, sliced	1
1	medium sweet green pepper, sliced	1
1	medium sweet red pepper, sliced	1
10	8-inch (20 cm) flour tortillas	10
1 cup	low-fat plain yogurt	250 mL
1 cup	prepared salsa	250 mL

1. In bowl, combine lime juice, Worcestershire sauce, oregano, cumin, coriander, garlic powder and pepper. Add chicken, stirring to coat. Marinate for 10 minutes or up to 1 hour in refrigerator.
2. In large nonstick skillet, heat oil over medium-high heat; add chicken mixture and stir-fry for 2 to 3 minutes. Add onion and peppers; stir-fry for 3 to 4 minutes until chicken is no longer pink inside.

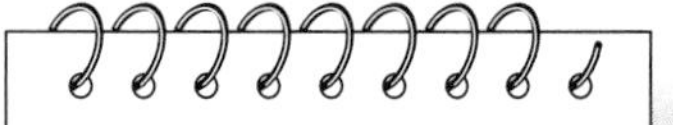

Shopping List

lime
boneless skinless chicken breasts
green and red peppers
flour tortillas
low-fat plain yogurt
prepared salsa

To warm tortillas, microwave on Low for 1 to 2 minutes.

To get the most juice out of your lime, pierce lime with a skewer and microwave on High for 30 seconds before squeezing out juice. One lime yields about 2 tbsp (25 mL) juice.

FOOD SAFETY TIP

After you prepare raw chicken or poultry, wash all utensils and cutting boards in hot soapy water or in the dishwasher.

For dessert, cool your tastebuds with a serving of lime or mango sherbet.

3. Warm tortillas. Divide chicken mixture evenly among tortillas; top with yogurt and salsa. Fold up sides.

Makes 5 servings, 2 fajitas each

Per serving

Calories	456
Protein	32g
Fat	9g
Carbohydrate	62g
Dietary fibre	4g

Excellent source of vitamin C, riboflavin, niacin, vitamin B6, vitamin B12, iron

Good source of vitamin A, calcium

High source of dietary fibre

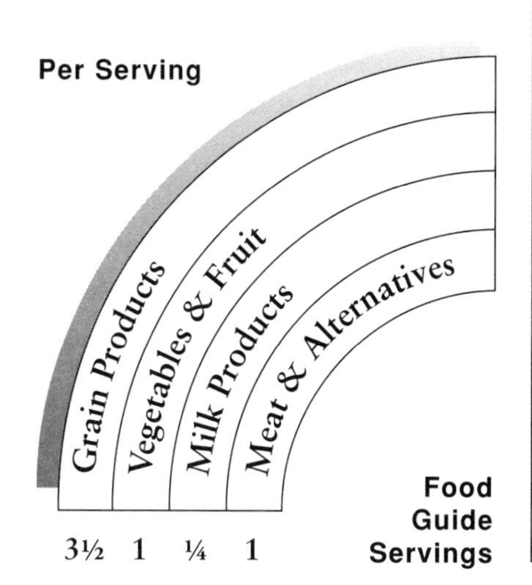

Filling in the Rainbow

This meal has something from each of the four food groups but a glass of milk will give you a full serving from the Milk Products group.

Confetti Chicken with Rice

This dish is a one-pot wonder! It is quick to prepare, tastes great and best of all is a cinch to clean up. To cut back on fat, omit the sausage, increase chicken to ¾ lb (375 g) and add ½ tsp (2 mL) each dried savory and thyme.

1 tsp	olive oil	5 mL
1	clove garlic, minced or ¼ tsp (1 mL) garlic powder	1
½ lb	sweet or hot Italian sausage (about 2 large sausages), casings removed and meat crumbled	250 g
½ lb	boneless skinless chicken breasts, cut into 1-inch (2.5 cm) cubes	250 g
2 cups	mixed chopped onions, chopped celery and diced carrots (in any combination)	500 mL
1 cup	frozen corn niblets (optional)	250 mL
¾ cup	long grain rice	175 mL
1	can (28 oz/796 mL) tomatoes, broken up	1
	Pepper	
¼ cup	grated Parmesan cheese	50 mL

1. In large saucepan or Dutch oven, heat oil over medium-high heat; add garlic, sausage and chicken and sauté for 3 to 5 minutes or until lightly browned.
2. Add chopped vegetables, corn (if using), rice, tomatoes and pepper. Reduce heat, cover and simmer for 18 to 20 minutes or until rice is tender.
3. Sprinkle each serving with 1 tbsp (15 mL) Parmesan cheese.

Makes 4 servings

Shopping List

Italian sausage
boneless skinless chicken breasts
celery
carrots
frozen corn (optional)
canned tomatoes
Parmesan cheese

Substitute 3½ cups (875 mL) chopped fresh tomatoes for the canned tomatoes.

FREEZER TIP

This meal can be frozen for up to 3 months.

IS ALL RICE CREATED EQUAL?

Dietary fibre per 1 cup (250 mL) of rice	
Parboiled long grain white rice	0.8 g dietary fibre
Brown rice	3.3 g dietary fibre
Ready-to-serve instant white rice	1.3 g dietary fibre
Perfect Microwave Rice	1.7 g dietary fibre

Per serving

Calories	445
Protein	29g
Fat	18g
Carbohydrate	42g
Dietary fibre	3g

Excellent source of vitamin A, niacin, vitamin B6, vitamin B12

Good source of vitamin C, thiamine, calcium, iron, zinc

Moderate source of dietary fibre

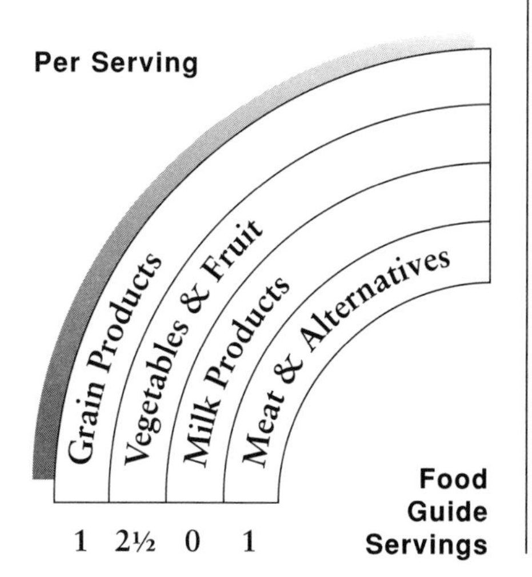

Filling in the Rainbow

Complete this meal with a glass of milk.

Creamy Macaroni and Cheese

Shopping List
medium Cheddar cheese
kiwifruit
oranges
bananas

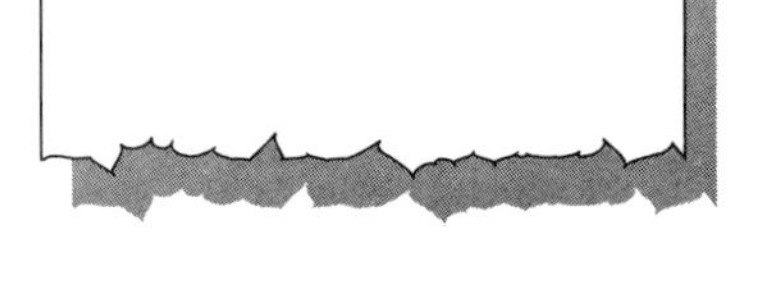

Bev's kids call this Mom's homemade macaroni and cheese. She has been making this for them since they were babies. Serving a fruit plate with the Macaroni and Cheese increases the vitamin C content of this meal from 0% to 90% of the Recommended Daily Intake for adults and increases the amount of dietary fibre from 1 to 4 grams per serving.

1½ cups	macaroni or small shell pasta	375 mL
3 cups	Cheese Sauce (recipe below)	750 mL

1. In saucepan of boiling water, cook pasta according to package directions; drain.
2. Stir in cheese sauce.

Makes 6 servings (1 cup/250 mL) each

Creamy Macaroni and Cheese can be stored in the refrigerator for up to 2 days. If necessary, thin with a little extra milk when reheating.

BABY-FRIENDLY TIP
Omit mustard. Use whole milk and mild or medium cheese. Divide prepared Creamy Macaroni and Cheese into ¼- to ½-cup (50 to 125 mL) portions and store in the freezer for up to 1 month.

Cheese Sauce

¼ cup	soft margarine	50 mL
¼ cup	all-purpose flour	50 mL
1 tsp	dry mustard	5 mL
3½ cups	2% milk	875 mL
¾ lb	shredded medium Cheddar cheese (about 4 cups/1 L)	375 g

1. In large saucepan, melt margarine over medium heat; remove from heat. Add flour and mustard; stir until blended.
2. Whisk in milk and bring to boil over medium heat, stirring constantly. Reduce heat and simmer for 5 to 7 minutes, stirring occasionally, or until thickened.
3. Remove from heat. Stir in cheese until blended.

Makes about 5 cups (1.25 L)

FREEZER TIP
Keep a supply of cheese sauce in airtight containers in the freezer for up to 1 month. Portion into ½-cup (125 mL) servings to use as a sauce over broccoli or cauliflower. If necessary, thin with a little extra milk when reheating.

Microwave Method for Cheese Sauce

1. In 8-cup (2 L) microwaveable measuring cup, melt margarine on High for 45 seconds. Add flour and mustard; stir until blended.
2. Add milk; whisk until blended. Microwave on High for 12 to 14 minutes, whisking at 2-minute intervals, or until thickened. Watch closely after the first 10 minutes as mixture may boil over.
3. Stir in cheese.

Fruit Plate

3	kiwifruit, cut in half (scoop out with spoon)	3
2	oranges, cut into sections	2
1	medium banana, sliced	1

Makes 6 servings

Supper includes Creamy Macaroni and Cheese and Fruit Plate

Per serving of supper

Calories	391
Protein	16g
Fat	18g
Carbohydrate	42g
Dietary fibre	3g

Excellent source of vitamin C, riboflavin, calcium

Good source of vitamin A, thiamine, niacin, folic acid, vitamin B12, zinc

Moderate source of dietary fibre

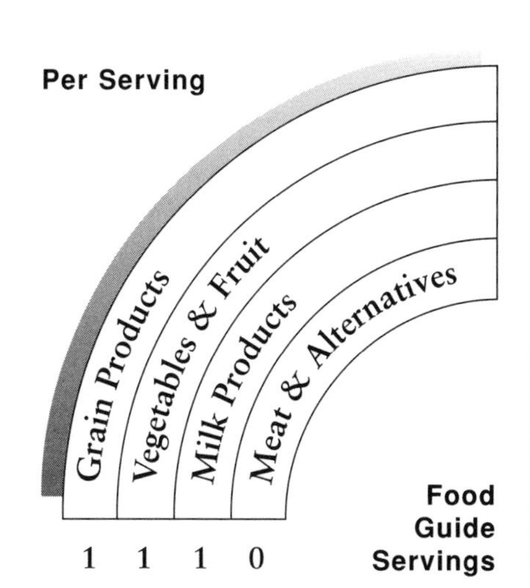

Filling in the Rainbow

This supper meal does not contain a serving from the Meat & Alternatives group. Plan to get the 2 to 3 servings from this food group at other meals and snacks throughout the day. For example, peanut butter and toast at breakfast and a meat or fish sandwich at lunch count as 2 servings from the Meat & Alternatives group.

Curried Beef in a Pita

This recipe is an adaptation of one produced by The Beef Information Centre. It is a fabulous Meal To Go and is particularly popular with teenagers. Hand them a container of milk or yogurt as they breeze through the kitchen. This will give them a complete meal.

Shopping List
inside round steak
broccoli
green and red peppers
whole wheat pita breads

Prepare vegetables while meat is marinating.

For a variation substitute 8 (8-inch/20 cm) flour tortillas for pita pockets and roll up; or serve with 4 cups (1 L) Perfect Microwave Rice (page 45) instead of pita pockets.

FOOD SAFETY TIP
Any marinade that has contained raw meat must be thoroughly cooked before it is eaten. See Step 3 of recipe.

NUTRITION TIP
Use whole wheat pita bread to boost fibre: One small whole wheat pita has 4.4 grams of fibre, while the same size of white pita provides only 0.3 grams of fibre.

Marinade

¼ cup	sodium-reduced soy sauce	50 mL
1 tbsp	packed brown sugar	15 mL
1 tbsp	lemon juice	15 mL
1	clove garlic, minced	1
1 to 2 tsp	curry powder	5 to 10 mL
½ tsp	ground ginger	2 mL
¾ lb	inside round or sirloin steak, cut into 3- x ½-inch (8 x 1 cm) strips	375 g

Stir-Fry

2 tsp	vegetable oil	10 mL
1	small onion, chopped	1
2 cups	coarsely chopped broccoli	500 mL
1	medium sweet red pepper, sliced	1
1	medium sweet green or sweet yellow pepper, sliced	1
1	stalk celery, sliced (optional)	1
4	whole wheat pita breads (60 g each)	4

1. In 4-cup (1 L) measuring cup, combine soy sauce, sugar, lemon juice, garlic, curry powder and ginger; stir in steak. Marinate for 10 to 15 minutes.
2. In large nonstick skillet, heat oil over medium-high heat. Using slotted spoon, add steak to skillet, reserving marinade. Stir-fry for 3 minutes or until no longer pink. Remove steak and set aside.

3. Add onion, broccoli and peppers to pan; stir-fry for 2 to 3 minutes. Add reserved marinade and bring to boil; reduce heat and simmer for 2 minutes or until vegetables are tender-crisp. Return steak to pan and heat through.
4. Warm pita breads. Cut each in half; open to form pocket. Fill with steak mixture.

Makes 4 servings, 2 pita pocket halves each

Per serving

Calories	345
Protein	29g
Fat	6g
Carbohydrate	46g
Dietary fibre	7g

Excellent source of vitamin C, niacin, vitamin B6, vitamin B12, iron, zinc

Good source of vitamin A, riboflavin, folic acid

Very high source of dietary fibre

To warm 4 pita breads, microwave on Low for 1 to 2 minutes.

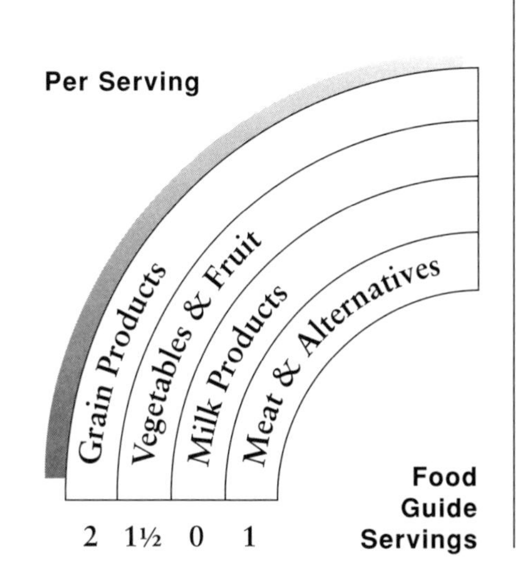

Filling in the Rainbow

Complete this meal with a serving from the Milk Products group.

Greek Pasta Salad

Shopping List
feta cheese
cucumber
tomatoes
black olives
green onions
green pepper
fresh mint

This great summer salad is adapted from one produced by the Dairy Farmers of Canada. Fresh mint makes this salad special, but if you don't have any, add 1 tbsp (15 mL) of dried mint leaves directly to the dressing. Crusty bread or rolls are a nice addition to this meal. One large crusty roll will give you 2 more servings from the Grain Products group.

4 oz	penne pasta (about 1½ cups/375 mL)	125 g
1 cup	crumbled feta cheese	250 mL
1 cup	diced cucumber	250 mL
2	large tomatoes, diced	2
⅓ cup	sliced black olives	75 mL
2	green onions, chopped	2
½	medium sweet green pepper, sliced	½
¼ cup	finely chopped fresh mint	50 mL

Dressing

2 tbsp	olive oil	25 mL
1	clove garlic, minced	1
2 tbsp	cider vinegar	25 mL
1 tsp	each granulated sugar and lemon juice	5 mL
½ tsp	dried oregano leaves	2 mL
¼ tsp	pepper	1 mL

1. In large pot of boiling water, cook pasta according to package directions; drain and rinse under cold water. Drain again.
2. In large bowl, combine pasta, feta cheese, cucumber, tomatoes, olives, green onions, green pepper and mint.

3. Dressing: In small bowl, blend together oil, garlic, vinegar, sugar, lemon juice, oregano and pepper; pour over salad and toss gently.

Makes 4 servings (1 ½ cups/375 mL each)

Per serving

Calories	300
Protein	10g
Fat	15g
Carbohydrate	33g
Dietary fibre	3g

Excellent source of vitamin C, riboflavin, vitamin B12

Good source of vitamin A, thiamine, niacin, vitamin B6, folic acid, calcium, iron, zinc

Moderate source of dietary fibre

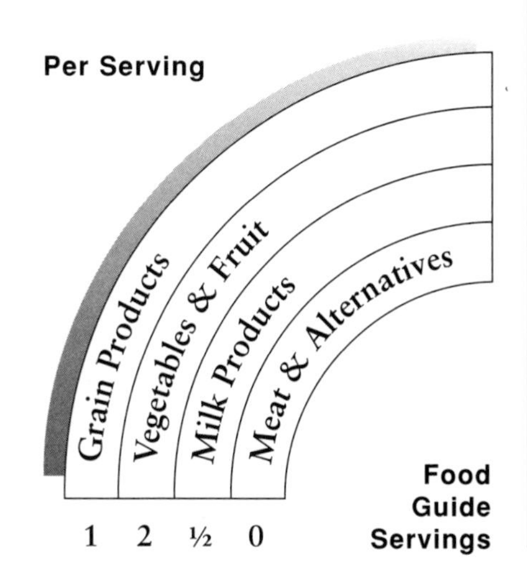

Filling in the Rainbow

It is not necessary to have a serving from the Meat & Alternatives group at every supper meal. It is easy to get 2 to 3 servings from this food group at other meals and snacks throughout the day. For example, French Toast with Peaches and Syrup (page 140) for breakfast and a meat or fish sandwich at lunch count as 2 servings from the Meat & Alternatives group.

Pork Souvlaki in a Pita

Since the dressing for this recipe is the same as the Greek Pasta Salad, why not make double the dressing and have Greek Pasta Salad one night for supper and Pork Souvlaki in a Pita the next night? If you don't have fresh mint, add 1 tbsp (15 mL) of dried mint leaves directly to the dressing.

Shopping List
boneless pork loin centre-cut chops
cucumber
tomatoes
fresh mint
whole wheat pita breads
low-fat plain yogurt (optional)

To warm 4 pita breads, microwave on Low for 1 to 2 minutes.

When you buy meat or poultry, consider the price per serving. Boneless cuts can be a better buy as there is little or no waste.

Dressing

2 tbsp	olive oil	25 mL
1	clove garlic, minced	1
2 tbsp	cider vinegar	25 mL
1 tsp	each granulated sugar and lemon juice	5 mL
½ tsp	dried oregano leaves	2 mL
¼ tsp	pepper	1 mL

Filling

1 lb	boneless pork loin centre-cut chops, trimmed of fat and cut into 1-inch (2.5 cm) cubes	500 g
1 cup	diced cucumber	250 mL
2	large tomatoes, diced (about 1 lb/500 g)	2
¼ cup	finely chopped fresh mint	50 mL
4	whole wheat pita breads (60 g each)	4
½ cup	low-fat plain yogurt (optional)	125 mL

1. Dressing: In small bowl, combine oil, garlic, vinegar, sugar, lemon juice, oregano and pepper; remove 2 tbsp (25 mL) to separate bowl to marinate pork. Set remaining dressing aside.
2. Add pork cubes to bowl containing 2 tbsp (25 mL) of dressing; marinate for 10 to 15 minutes.
3. In large nonstick skillet, cook pork with marinade over medium heat for 5 to 6 minutes or until no longer pink inside.

4. Transfer pork to large bowl. Add cucumber, tomatoes, mint and reserved dressing; toss to coat well.
5. Warm pita breads. Cut each in half; open to form pocket. Fill with pork mixture.
6. Divide yogurt (if using) evenly over filling.

Makes 4 servings, 2 pita pocket halves each

Choose leaner cuts of pork

Based on a 3-oz (90 g) serving of cooked, lean pork:

5 g of fat

- pork tenderloin
- pork leg, inside round, roast, steaks or cutlets
- baked ham
- deli ham

6 to 10 g of fat

- pork loin, centre-cut or tenderloin end, roast or chops
- pork shoulder butt, roast or chops
- back bacon
- picnic shoulder roast

Per serving

Calories	402
Protein	29g
Fat	14g
Carbohydrate	41g
Dietary fibre	6g

Excellent source of thiamine, niacin, vitamin B6, zinc

Good source of vitamin C, riboflavin, vitamin B12, iron

Very high source of dietary fibre

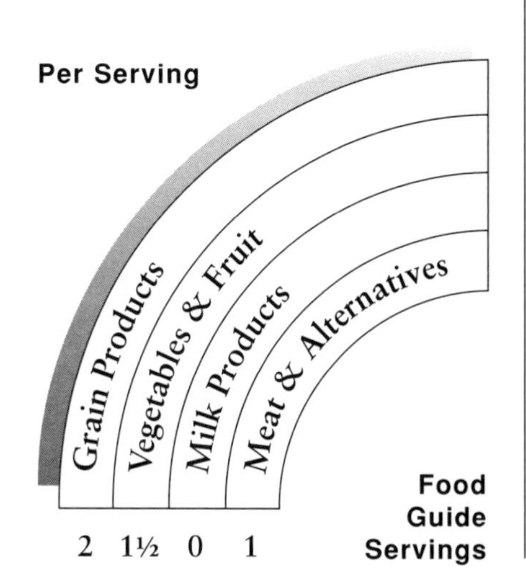

Filling in the Rainbow

Choose a serving from the Milk Products group, if necessary.

Spanish Rice with Lentils

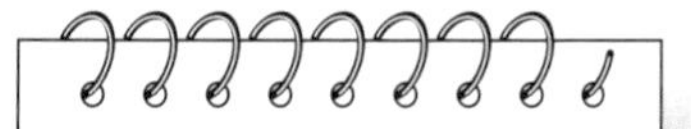

Shopping List
canned tomatoes
canned lentils
green pepper

Substitute 3½ cups (875 mL) of chopped fresh tomatoes for the canned tomatoes.

Meals containing beans and grains are an ideal high-fibre, lower-fat alternative to meat meals. In addition, this meal supplies 92 percent of an adult's Recommended Daily Intake for folic acid. It's a great choice for women who are considering pregnancy or women in their first trimester of pregnancy.

1 tbsp	vegetable oil	15 mL
1	clove garlic, minced	1
1	medium onion, chopped	1
1	can (28 oz/796 mL) tomatoes, broken up	1
1	can (19 oz/540 mL) lentils, drained and rinsed	1
1 cup	long grain rice	250 mL
1 cup	water	250 mL
½ tsp	each paprika, ground cumin and chili powder	2 mL
¼ tsp	red pepper flakes	1 mL
1	medium sweet green pepper, diced	1

1. In large saucepan or Dutch oven, heat oil over medium heat; add garlic and onion. Sauté for 3 to 5 minutes until onion is softened.
2. Add tomatoes, lentils, rice, water, paprika, cumin, chili powder and red pepper flakes. Bring to boil; reduce heat, cover and simmer for 20 minutes.
3. Add green pepper; simmer, uncovered, for 3 minutes or until rice is tender.

Makes 4 servings (2 cups/500 mL each)

Other bean, pea and lentil meals in* Suppertime Survival*:

- Three-Bean Chili with Couscous (page 122)
- Lentil and Pasta Soup (page 118)
- Bail-Out Bean Burritos (page 134)
- Black Bean, Corn and Couscous Salad (page 136)
- Sweet Beans and Toast (page 142)

Per serving

Calories	376
Protein	15g
Fat	5g
Carbohydrate	70g
Dietary fibre	8g

Excellent source of vitamin C, niacin, vitamin B6, folic acid, iron, zinc

Good source of vitamin A, thiamine

Very high source of dietary fibre

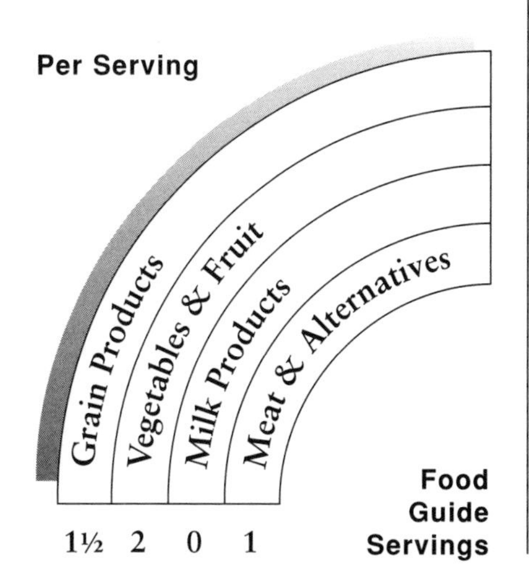

Filling in the Rainbow

Complete this meal with a serving from the Milk Products group.

Speedy Vegetable and Chicken Stir-Fry with Rice

This recipe is an ideal example of speed-scratch cooking. With a bag of frozen mixed vegetables handy in your freezer, this delicious stir-fry will be on the table before the family asks "What's for supper?"

Shopping List
boneless skinless chicken breasts
500 g bag frozen carrots, cauliflower and broccoli mixture
bean sprouts (optional)
hoisin sauce (optional)

Glaze

1 cup	water	250 mL
1	chicken or vegetable bouillon cube or sachet	1
1	clove garlic, minced, or ¼ tsp (1 mL) garlic powder	1
¼ cup	sodium-reduced soy sauce	50 mL
1 tbsp	each packed brown sugar and cornstarch	15 mL
1 tbsp	hoisin sauce (optional)	15 mL
½-1 tsp	ground ginger	2-5 mL

Stir-Fry

2 tbsp	vegetable oil	25 mL
¾ lb	boneless skinless chicken breasts, cut into 3- x ½-inch (8 x 1 cm) strips	375 g
1	small onion, sliced	1
1	package (500 g) frozen mixed vegetables (carrots, cauliflower, broccoli) (about 4 cups/1 L)	1
1 cup	bean sprouts (optional)	250 mL
4 cups	Perfect Microwave Rice	1 L

1. Glaze: In 2-cup (500 mL) measuring cup, combine water, bouillon cube, garlic, soy sauce, sugar, cornstarch, hoisin sauce (if using) and ginger. Set aside.
2. Stir-fry: In wok or large skillet, heat 1 tbsp (15 mL) of oil over medium-high heat. Add chicken and stir-fry for 4 to 5 minutes until no longer pink inside. Remove from skillet and set aside.

Extra rice can be refrigerated in airtight containers for up to 5 days, or frozen for up to 4 months. To reheat 2 cups (500 mL) of frozen rice: Place rice in microwaveable dish, cover and microwave on High for 3 to 4 minutes, stirring once, until hot.

Instead of using rice, serve with 4 cups (1 L) Quicky Couscous (page 77).

KID-FRIENDLY TIP
If children don't like their foods mixed together, cook extra chicken and serve it with the rice and some cut-up raw vegetables.

3. Add remaining oil to pan. Add onion; stir-fry for 1 minute. Add frozen vegetables; stir-fry for 5 to 7 minutes or until tender-crisp.
4. Add reserved chicken, glaze, and bean sprouts (if using). Stir-fry for 2 minutes until heated through and sauce has thickened. Serve with Perfect Microwave Rice.

Makes 4 servings

Variations

1. Substitute any 1-lb (500 g) bag of frozen mixed vegetables for the frozen carrots, cauliflower and broccoli.
2. Speedy Vegetable Stir-Fry: Omit chicken. Decrease vegetable oil to 1 tbsp (15 mL). Skip Step 2 of method.

Perfect Microwave Rice

1 cup	brown rice	250 mL
1½ cups	long grain rice	375 mL
4 cups	hot water	1 L

1. In 8-cup (2 L) microwaveable measuring cup or 12-cup (3 L) casserole dish, combine brown rice, long grain rice and water.
2. Cover and microwave on High for 24 to 26 minutes or until water is mostly absorbed.
3. Let stand for 10 minutes; fluff with fork.

Makes 8 cups (2 L)

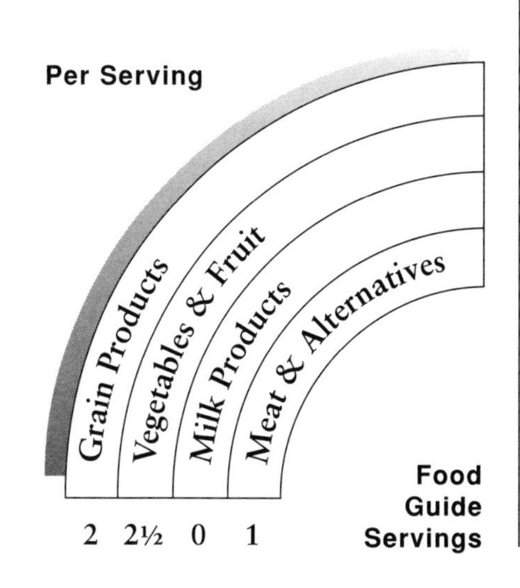

Per serving

Calories	448
Protein	29g
Fat	9g
Carbohydrate	62g
Dietary fibre	5g

Excellent source of vitamin A, vitamin C, niacin, vitamin B6, folic acid

Good source of thiamine, iron, zinc

High source of dietary fibre

Frozen vegetables are perfectly acceptable to use and contain more nutrients than vegetables that have been stored in your fridge all week. Use them in stir-fries, soups and casseroles.

Filling in the Rainbow

Complete this meal with a serving from the Milk Products group if necessary to balance the rest of the day.

Sweet and Sour Pork with Vermicelli

This is sure to become a family favourite. Kids like everything about this meal, especially the fact that there are no onions! Substitute 4 cups (1 L) of Perfect Microwave Rice (page 45) for the vermicelli noodles if you wish. The nutrients may change but the Rainbow Balance Chart will remain the same. Serve the extra pineapple tidbits for a quick snack.

Glaze

Half	can (14 oz/398 mL) pineapple tidbits, packed in unsweetened pineapple juice	Half
3 tbsp	sodium-reduced soy sauce	50 mL
1 tbsp	each cider vinegar and packed brown sugar	15 mL
2 tsp	cornstarch	10 mL
½ tsp	ground ginger	2 mL
	Pepper	
2 tsp	vegetable oil	10 mL
¾ lb	boneless pork loin centre-cut chops, trimmed of fat and cut into 3- x ½-inch (8 x 1 cm) strips	375 g
8 oz	vermicelli or spaghettini noodles	250 g
3	medium carrots, sliced	3
1	medium sweet green pepper, sliced or 1½ cups (375 mL) snow peas, trimmed	1

1. Glaze: Reserving pineapple, drain pineapple juice into 2-cup (500 mL) measuring cup; add enough water to equal ¾ cup (175 mL). Add soy sauce, vinegar, brown sugar, cornstarch, ginger and pepper. Set aside.

Shopping List
canned pineapple tidbits
boneless pork loin centre-cut chops
vermicelli noodles
carrots
green pepper

VARIATION

Sweet and Sour Chicken with Vermicelli: Substitute boneless skinless chicken strips for the pork.

Buy 1½ lb (750 g) of boneless pork loin centre-cut chops and cut into strips. Divide into two portions and freeze one for up to 4 months.

If you bake or barbecue foods, you don't need to add extra fat. Use small amounts of fat in stir-fries (2 tsp/10 mL) and use a measuring spoon for accuracy. Use a cooking oil that is high in poly or monounsaturated fat (corn, canola or safflower).

2. In large nonstick skillet, heat oil over medium-high heat. Add pork strips; stir-fry for 3 to 4 minutes or until no longer pink. Remove and set aside.
3. In large pot of boiling water, cook vermicelli according to package directions; drain.
4. Meanwhile, add carrots to skillet and stir-fry for 2 minutes; add green pepper and stir-fry for 2 minutes. Add pork, reserved pineapple and glaze to pan; reduce heat and simmer for 1 to 2 minutes or until thickened. Serve over noodles.

Makes 4 servings

Per serving

Calories	436
Protein	25g
Fat	8g
Carbohydrate	66g
Dietary fibre	5g

Excellent source of vitamin A, vitamin C, thiamine, riboflavin, niacin, vitamin B6, iron, zinc

Good source of folic acid, vitamin B12

High source of dietary fibre

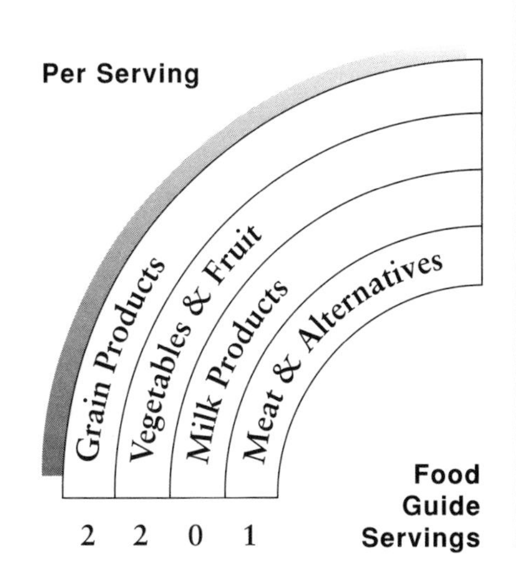

Filling in the Rainbow

Complete this meal with a serving from the Milk Products group

Shopping List
inside round steak
snow peas
canned baby corn
canned mandarin oranges

TIMESAVER
Buy 1½ lb (750 g) of inside round steak and cut into strips. Divide into two portions and freeze one for up to 4 months.

NUTRITION TIP
Iron intake is often low in diets that are low in calories. Red meats such as beef can give you an iron boost.

VARIATION
Substitute 1 medium sweet green pepper, sliced, for the snow peas.

Szechuan Beef and Mandarin Orange Stir-Fry with Rice

This quick and tasty stir-fry appeals to all ages. Kids love the baby corn and mandarin oranges. If it is too spicy for the small fry, decrease or eliminate the red pepper flakes.

Glaze

⅓ cup	orange juice	75 mL
3 tbsp	sodium-reduced soy sauce	50 mL
1	clove garlic, minced	1
1 tbsp	each cider vinegar and packed brown sugar	15 mL
2 tsp	cornstarch	10 mL
½ tsp	ground ginger	2 mL
¼ tsp	red pepper flakes	1 mL

Stir-Fry

2 tsp	vegetable oil	10 mL
¾ lb	inside round or sirloin steak, cut into 3- x ½-inch (8 x 1 cm) strips	375 g
2 cups	snow peas, trimmed	500 mL
1	can (14 oz/398 mL) baby corn, drained	1
1	can (10 oz/284 mL) mandarin oranges, drained	1
4 cups	Perfect Microwave Rice	1 L

1. Glaze: In bowl, combine orange juice, soy sauce, garlic, vinegar, brown sugar, cornstarch, ginger and red pepper flakes. Set aside.
2. Stir-Fry: In large nonstick skillet, heat oil over medium-high heat; add steak and stir-fry for 1 to 2 minutes or until browned.

3. Add snow peas and stir-fry for 2 minutes; add corn and orange juice mixture. Reduce heat and simmer for 2 minutes or until thickened. Gently stir in oranges and heat through. Serve with Perfect Microwave Rice.

Makes 4 servings

Perfect Microwave Rice

1 cup	brown rice	250 mL
1½ cups	long grain rice	375 mL
4 cups	hot water	1 L

1. Combine all ingredients in large 8-cup (2 L) glass measuring cup or 3 L casserole dish.
2. Cover and microwave on High for 24 to 26 minutes or until water is mostly absorbed.
3. Let stand for 10 minutes; fluff with fork.

Makes 8 cups (2 L)

LEAN BEEF CUTS

Very Lean (under 5% fat)	Lean (5-10% fat)
inside round steak	outside round steak/roast
sirloin steak	sirloin tip/inside round roast
rump roast	eye of round steak
eye of round roast	strip loin steak
	tenderloin; T-bone

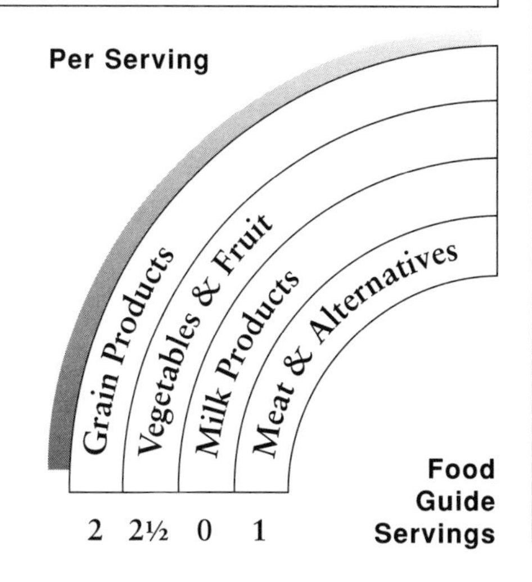

Per serving

Calories	432
Protein	28g
Fat	5g
Carbohydrate	67g
Dietary fibre	4g

Excellent source of vitamin C, niacin, vitamin B6, vitamin B12, iron, zinc

Good source of thiamine, riboflavin

High source of dietary fibre

DID YOU KNOW?

Beef today is 50 percent leaner and 34 percent lower in calories than it was 15 years ago.

Filling in the Rainbow

Complete this meal with a serving from the Milk Products group if daily requirements have not already been met earlier in the day.

Zucchini and Red Pepper Frittata

It is very important to use a nonstick skillet when making this frittata. It allows you to use less oil, and the finished frittata just slips out of the pan onto the serving plate. Wrap the handle of the frying pan with foil to prevent it from burning when you place the frittata under the broiler.

6	eggs	6
3 tbsp	water	50 mL
2 tsp	vegetable oil	10 mL
1	small onion, chopped	1
1	medium sweet red pepper, chopped	1
1	medium zucchini, diced (about ½ lb/250 g)	1
	Pepper	
1 cup	shredded part-skim mozzarella cheese	250 mL
3 tbsp	grated Parmesan cheese	50 mL

1. Preheat broiler.
2. In medium bowl whisk eggs with water; set aside.
3. In large nonstick skillet, heat oil over medium heat; add onion, red pepper and zucchini and sauté for 3 to 5 minutes until softened.
4. Pour eggs on top of vegetables. Sprinkle pepper, mozzarella and Parmesan cheeses on top of eggs; reduce heat to low and cook for 3 to 4 minutes or until bottom is lightly browned yet centre is still not set.
5. Broil for 1 to 3 minutes or until puffed and golden, watching closely as top will brown quickly.

Makes 4 servings

Shopping List

eggs
sweet red pepper
zucchini
part-skim mozzarella cheese
Parmesan cheese
whole grain bread/rolls

Use eggs to create all kinds of quick supper meals. For example, scrambled eggs, toast, fruit and milk make a complete supper meal.

If you are a frittata lover, try Asparagus Frittata (page 26) and Bacon and Potato Frittata (page 131).

Buy Canada Grade "A" eggs with clean, uncracked shells and store them in their carton in the main part of the refrigerator to maximize freshness.

Prepared foods that contain eggs, such as stratas and frittatas, should not be kept out of the refrigerator for more than 2 hours.

Other egg meals in Suppertime Survival

Asparagus Frittata (page 26)
Bacon and Potato Frittata (page 131)
Basil Zucchini Strata (page 120)
French Toast with Peaches and Syrup (page 140)
Spinach Frittata Fingers (page 70)

Per serving

Calories	254
Protein	20g
Fat	16g
Carbohydrate	7g
Dietary fibre	1g

Excellent source of vitamin A, vitamin C, riboflavin, vitamin B12, calcium

Good source of niacin, folic acid, zinc

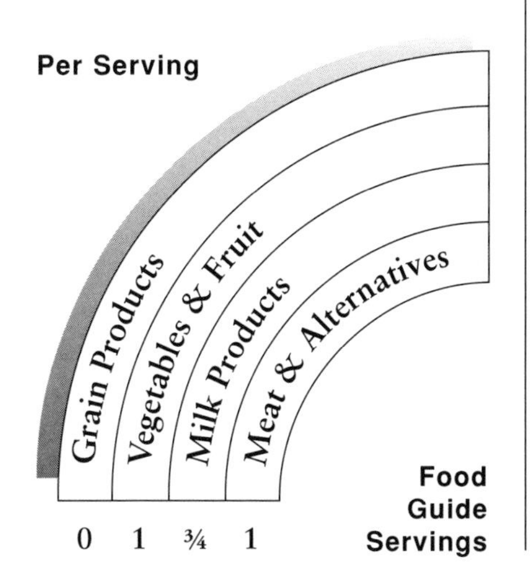

Filling in the Rainbow

Serve with whole grain bread/toast or rolls.

Blair's Rice Pudding

This baked rice pudding was created by Lynn's husband Blair. It's a perfect way to use up any leftover rice that has been prepared with water. If you like creamy rice pudding, use 1 cup (250 mL) of rice. For a thicker rice pudding, use up to 2 cups (500 mL) of rice. Make it after dinner and enjoy it as a warm bedtime snack or heat it up in the microwave for breakfast.

2 cups	2% or whole milk	500 mL
2	eggs	2
1 to 2 cups	cooked white rice	250 to 500 mL
½ cup	packed brown sugar	125 mL
½ cup	raisins	125 mL
Pinch	nutmeg (optional)	Pinch

1. Preheat oven to 325°F (160°C).
2. In medium-size ovenproof bowl or 8-cup (2 L) casserole dish, beat milk and eggs; stir in rice, brown sugar and raisins.
3. Sprinkle with nutmeg (if using). Place bowl in pan of hot water.
4. Bake uncovered for 75 minutes or until top is set, stirring once after the first 30 minutes.

Makes 6 servings

FOR A SIMPLE, ELEGANT LOW-FAT DESSERT TRY FRESH BERRIES WITH VANILLA YOGURT TOPPING

Divide 3 cups (750 mL) of assorted fresh berries among 6 serving dishes. In small bowl, combine ¾ cup (175 mL) low-fat plain yogurt, 2 tbsp (25 mL) packed brown sugar and ½ tsp (2 mL) vanilla. Serve over berries. Top with a sprinkle of cinnamon if desired. Each serving provides one Vegetables & Fruit serving. Makes 6 servings

Make and Bakes

These meals take about 20 minutes to prepare and 15 to 75 minutes to bake. They give you time to relax before supper, play with the kids, work in the garden, sneak in a run or enjoy other activities.

These recipes make between four and eight servings which, depending on the size of your family or the size of their appetites, should give you some "left-over" meals for another day.

Remember to promptly refrigerate (or freeze, if applicable) all leftovers and use them up within three days.

Desserts:

Baked Fish with Oven-Fried Potato Cubes

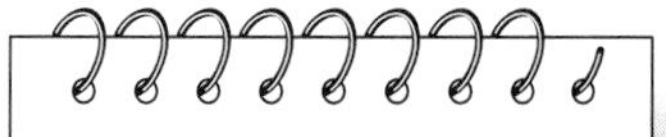

Shopping List
potatoes
dry bread crumbs
1 package (400 g) individually frozen fish fillets
frozen green peas
lemons

If you are out of peas, substitute any other fresh or frozen vegetable. The nutrients will change but the Rainbow Balance chart will stay the same.

1 medium sweet potato is about the same size (8 oz/250 g) as a large regular potato.

KID-FRIENDLY TIP
When serving fish to children, always check for bones that might cause them to choke.

We discovered during recipe testing that dipping the fish in an egg-and-water mixture resulted in the crispiest coating (according to our kids!)

This meal is always popular at our houses and can easily be doubled to serve 8. The oven-fried potato cubes are a big hit with the kids. Try the Oven-Fried Sweet Potatoes for a change (or a mixture of sweet potatoes and regular potatoes), because sweet potatoes are an excellent source of vitamin A and beta-carotene. Serve with frozen green peas and lemon wedges. Offer tartar sauce on the side.

Oven-Fried Potato Cubes

3	large potatoes, peeled or unpeeled (about 1½ lb/750 g), cut into 1-inch (2.5 cm) cubes	3
4 tsp	vegetable oil	20 mL
Pinch	each garlic powder and pepper	Pinch

Baked Fish

1	egg	1
1 tbsp	water	15 mL
⅓ cup	dry bread crumbs	75 mL
1 tbsp	unprocessed wheat bran	15 mL
½ tsp	dried thyme leaves	2 mL
Pinch	pepper	Pinch
1	package (400 g) individually frozen fish fillets, defrosted	1

1. Preheat oven to 400°F (200°C). Lightly grease 2 cookie sheets or spray with nonstick cooking spray.
2. Oven-Fried Potato Cubes: Toss potatoes with oil, garlic powder and pepper; place on cookie sheet. Bake for 25 minutes or until potatoes are tender and golden. Put potatoes in the oven 10 minutes before fish.
3. Baked Fish: Meanwhile, in bowl, lightly beat egg with water; set aside. In heavy plastic bag, combine bread crumbs, bran, thyme and pepper.

4. Dip fish fillets in egg mixture; place fillets, one at a time, in bag and shake gently to coat. Place on second cookie sheet.
5. Bake for 10 to 15 minutes or until fish is opaque and flakes easily with fork.

Makes 4 servings

Oven-Fried Sweet Potato Cubes

3	medium sweet potatoes (about 1½ lb/750 g), peeled and cut in 1-inch (2.5 cm) cubes	3
4 tsp	vegetable oil	20 mL
Pinch	pepper	Pinch

1. Preheat oven to 400°F (200°C). Lightly grease cookie sheet or spray with nonstick cooking spray.
2. Toss potatoes with oil and pepper; place on cookie sheet.
3. Bake for 20 to 25 minutes or until tender and golden.

Makes 4 servings

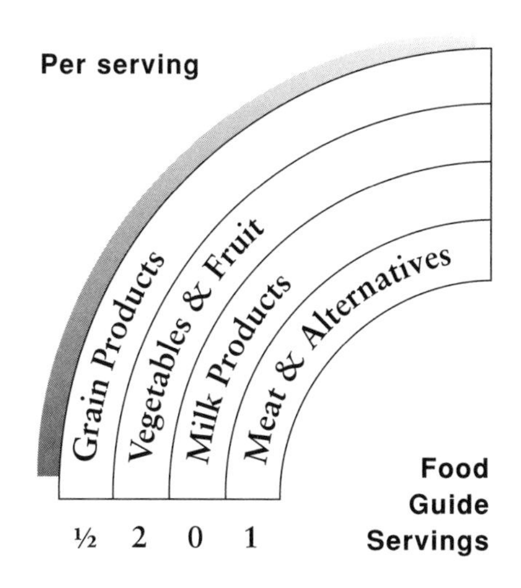

Supper includes Baked Fish with Oven-fried Potato Cubes and ½ cup (125 mL) frozen green peas

Per serving of supper

Calories	335
Protein	26g
Fat	7g
Carbohydrate	42g
Dietary fibre	6g

Excellent source of thiamine, niacin, vitamin B6, folic acid, vitamin B12

Good source of vitamin C, iron, zinc

Very high source of dietary fibre

TANGY TARTAR SAUCE

Combine ¼ cup (50 mL) sweet pickle relish or dill pickle relish, 2 tbsp (25 mL) light mayonnaise, ¼ tsp (1 mL) Dijon mustard in small bowl, until blended. Makes 6 tbsp (75 mL), about 5 g of fat per tbsp (15 mL).

Filling in the Rainbow

Serve with an extra serving from the Grain Products group and a glass of milk to round out this meal.

Broiled Minted Lamb Chops with Rosemary Potatoes

Serve these succulent lamb chops with rosemary potatoes, frozen green peas and extra mint sauce (if you wish). Make extra Rosemary Potatoes for Bacon and Potato Frittata (page 131), a Bail-Out Supper the next day. It is scrumptious!

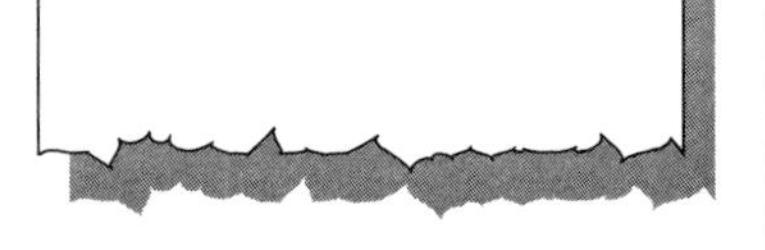

Shopping List
12 centre-cut loin lamb chops
prepared mint sauce
red or white potatoes
frozen green peas

NUTRITION TIP
This meal is based on 2 lamb chops per serving which provides about 5 grams of fat.

Substitute 12 small new red or white potatoes for the large potatoes.

3 tbsp	prepared mint sauce	50 mL
2 tsp	olive oil	10 mL
¼ tsp	pepper	1 mL
12	bone-in centre-cut loin lamb chops (about 2 lb/1 kg), trimmed of fat	12

Rosemary Potatoes

4	large red or white potatoes (about 2 lb/1 kg), unpeeled, scrubbed and cut in quarters	4
1 tbsp	olive oil	15 mL
1 tsp	crumbled dried rosemary	5 mL
	Pepper	

1. In shallow dish, combine mint sauce, oil and pepper; add lamb chops and turn to coat well. Marinate for 15 minutes or overnight in refrigerator.
2. In large saucepan of boiling water, cook potatoes for 20 to 25 minutes or until tender; drain; toss with oil, rosemary and pepper.
3. Meanwhile, preheat broiler. Broil chops, turning once for 8 to 10 minutes, or until desired doneness.

Makes 6 servings

Barbecued Minted Lamb Chops

Grill chops over medium heat, for 8 to 10 minutes, turning once or until desired doneness. Serve with Barbecued Potatoes (page 78) and any vegetable of your choice.

Supper includes Broiled Minted Lamb Chops, Rosemary Potatoes and frozen green peas (½ cup/ 125 mL each)

Per serving of supper

Calories	326
Protein	24g
Fat	9g
Carbohydrate	37g
Dietary fibre	5g

Excellent source of thiamine, niacin, vitamin B6, folic acid, vitamin B12, iron, zinc

Good source of vitamin C, riboflavin

High source of dietary fibre

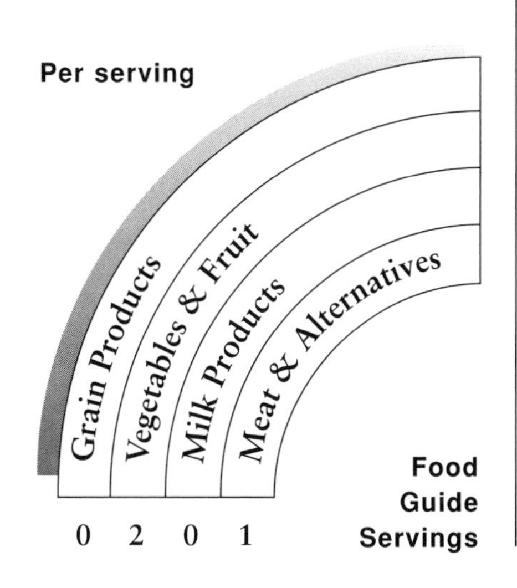

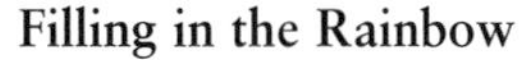

Filling in the Rainbow

Complete this meal with a serving each from the Grain Products group and Milk Products group.

Cabbage Roll Casserole

This remarkably simple casserole has all the flavour of traditional cabbage rolls without any of the fuss! It is an adaptation of a recipe first given to us by Mary Gauntlett. Substitute a slice of whole wheat bread for the Perfect Microwave Rice if you don't feel like making extra rice. If you like margarine or butter on your bread, keep in mind that every teaspoon (5 mL) adds 4 grams of fat to the meal. Make some Baked Apples (page 84) for dessert since the oven is already hot.

6 cups	shredded green cabbage (about half medium head)	1.5 L
1 lb	lean ground beef	500 g
2	medium onions, chopped	2
⅓ cup	long grain rice	75 mL
1 tbsp	Worcestershire sauce	15 mL
1	can (10 oz/284 mL) condensed tomato soup	1
1	can (19 oz/540 mL) tomatoes	1
¼ tsp	pepper	1 mL
3 cups	Perfect Microwave Rice	750 mL

1. Preheat oven to 350°F (180°C). Lightly grease 9- x 13-inch (3 L) glass baking dish or spray with nonstick cooking spray.
2. Spread cabbage over bottom of dish. Set aside.
3. In large skillet over medium heat, brown meat with onions for 3 to 4 minutes or until meat is no longer pink. Remove from heat; drain fat.
4. Add rice, Worcestershire sauce, soup, tomatoes and pepper to skillet; stir until combined. Spoon on top of cabbage.
5. Cover and bake for 65 to 75 minutes, uncovering for last 10 to 15 minutes of baking time. Serve with Perfect Microwave Rice.

Makes 6 servings

Shopping List
cabbage
lean ground beef
condensed tomato soup
canned tomatoes

Substitute 2½ cups (625 mL) chopped fresh tomatoes for the canned tomatoes.

For an even quicker Cabbage Roll Casserole: Omit lean ground beef and onions and omit step 3. Add 3 cups (750 mL) Batch Ground Meat and Vegetables (page 88) at step 4. Proceed with rest of recipe.

MAKE AHEAD

Assemble casserole up to 24 hours ahead and refrigerate. Increase baking time by 5 to 10 minutes. Baked casserole can be frozen for up to 3 months.

Extra-Speedy Spaghetti Supper (page 92)

Perfect Microwave Rice

1 cup	brown rice	250 mL
1½ cups	long grain rice	375 mL
4 cups	hot water	1 L

1. Combine all ingredients in large 8-cup (2 L) glass measuring cup or 3 L casserole dish.
2. Cover and microwave on High for 24 to 26 minutes or until water is mostly absorbed.
3. Let stand for 10 minutes; fluff with a fork.

Makes 8 cups (2 L)

Supper includes Cabbage Roll Casserole plus Perfect Microwave Rice (½ cup/125 mL each)

Per serving of Supper

Calories	345
Protein	20g
Fat	9g
Carbohydrate	48g
Dietary fibre	4g

Excellent source of niacin, vitamin B6, vitamin B12, zinc

Good source of vitamin C, thiamine, riboflavin, folic acid, iron

High source of dietary fibre

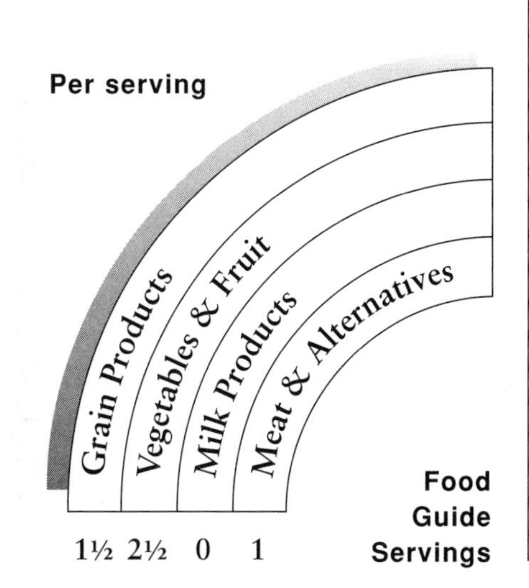

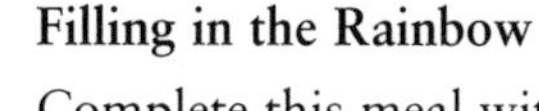

Filling in the Rainbow

Complete this meal with a serving from the Milk Products group.

Quick Barbecued Chicken with Pasta and Pepper Salad (page 74)

Photo courtesy of the Ontario Chicken Producers' Marketing Board

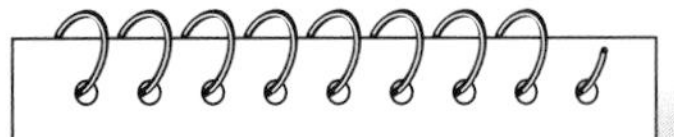

Shopping List
potatoes
boneless skinless chicken breasts
dry bread crumbs
broccoli

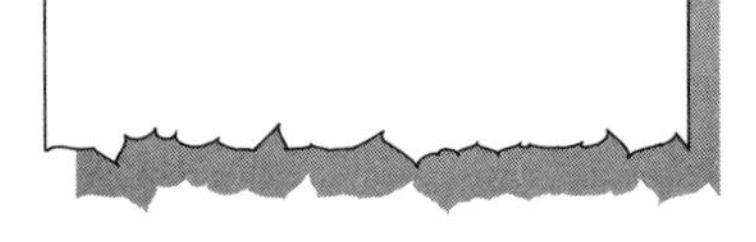

To prevent potatoes from going gray when cooked, toss with oil and spices as soon as possible after peeling.

As a general rule of thumb, 1 tbsp (15 mL) of oil will lightly coat 1 lb (500 g) of potatoes or sweet potatoes.

To increase your fibre intake, make your own whole wheat bread crumbs: Save whole wheat bread crusts in a open dish in your kitchen. Let bread dry out; process in a food processor or crush in a heavy plastic bag with a rolling pin until in fine crumbs. One slice of bread = ⅓ cup (75 mL) dry bread crumbs. Store in an air-tight container in a cool place or freeze.

Get a boost of vitamin A and beta-carotene by substituting Oven-Fried Sweet Potato Cubes (page 55) for the regular oven-fried potatoes.

Crispy Chicken Fingers with Oven-Fried Potato Cubes

This is a great meal to serve when your kids invite the neighbourhood to stay for supper! Serve with steamed broccoli or any vegetable that you have on hand. The nutrient analysis will change but the Rainbow Balance Chart will stay the same. Everyday Coleslaw (page 81) is a nice complement to this meal.

Oven-Fried Potato Cubes

6	large potatoes, peeled or unpeeled (about 3 lb/1.5 kg), cut into 1-inch (2.5 cm) cubes	6
3 tbsp	vegetable oil	50 mL
¼ tsp	each garlic powder and pepper	1 mL

Chicken Fingers

1	egg	1
1 tbsp	water or milk (2%)	15 mL
2 lb	boneless skinless chicken breasts cut into 3- x 1-inch (8 x 2.5 cm) strips	1 kg

Herbed Crumbs

¾ cup	dry bread crumbs	175 mL
¼ cup	unprocessed wheat bran	50 mL
1 tsp	dried thyme leaves	5 mL
¼ tsp	garlic powder (optional)	1 mL

1. Preheat oven to 400°F (200°C). Lightly grease 2 cookie sheets or spray with nonstick cooking spray.
2. Oven-Fried Potato Cubes: Toss potatoes with oil, garlic powder and pepper; place on cookie sheet. Bake for 25 minutes or until potatoes are tender and golden. Put potatoes in oven 5 to 10 minutes before chicken fingers.
3. Meanwhile, in bowl lightly beat egg with water; set aside.

4. Herbed Crumbs: In heavy plastic bag, combine bread crumbs, bran, thyme and garlic powder (if using).
5. Dip chicken strips in egg mixture; place 3 or 4 strips at a time in bag and shake gently to coat. Place on second cookie sheet.
6. Bake for 15 to 20 minutes or until juices run clear when chicken is pierced with fork. Serve with steamed broccoli.

Makes 8 servings

Serve with canned cranberry sauce or cranberry sauce (recipe page 108, margin), prepared plum sauce or prepared peanut sauce.

Herbed Crumb Variations

Italian

⅔ cup	dry bread crumbs	150 mL
⅓ cup	grated Parmesan cheese	75 mL
1 tsp	Italian seasoning or ½ tsp (2 mL) each dried basil and oregano leaves	5 mL

Mexican

1 cup	dry bread crumbs	250 mL
1 tsp	chili powder	5 mL
1 tsp	each ground cumin and coriander	5 mL
¼ tsp	each salt and cayenne pepper	1 mL

Serve with prepared salsa.

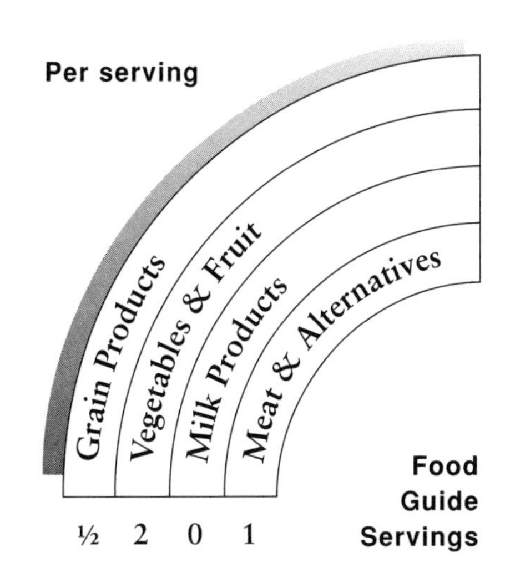

Supper includes Crispy Chicken Fingers with Oven-Fried Potato Cubes and steamed broccoli (½ cup /125 mL)

Per serving of Supper

Calories	333
Protein	31g
Fat	8g
Carbohydrate	34g
Dietary fibre	3g

Excellent source of niacin, vitamin B6

Good source of vitamin C, thiamine, folic acid, vitamin B12, iron, zinc

Moderate source of dietary fibre

Make a double batch of Crispy Chicken Fingers. Freeze cooked chicken fingers for up to 3 months. Defrost overnight in the refrigerator and reheat in a 350°F (180°C) oven or toaster oven for 5 to 8 minutes or until heated through.

Filling in the Rainbow

Complete this meal with a serving from the Milk Products and Grain Products group.

Family Tuna Noodle Casserole

This meal is an excellent source of calcium, iron and folic acid. It's perfect for the whole family and is a great comfort food. A can of cream of mushroom or cream of celery soup can be substituted for the cream of broccoli soup. If the kids don't like their foods mixed together, prepare the casserole without the broccoli. Just before serving, steam the broccoli and serve it on the side.

½ lb	small pasta shells or macaroni (about 2 cups/500 mL)	250 g
1	small bunch broccoli, chopped (about 3 cups/750 mL)	1
2	cans (each 6.5 oz /184 g) water-packed tuna, drained	2
1	can (10 oz/284 mL) condensed cream of broccoli soup	1
1 cup	2% milk	250 mL
1½ cups	shredded Cheddar cheese	375 mL
	Pepper	
¾ cup	crushed cornflakes	175 mL
2 tbsp	grated Parmesan cheese	25 mL

1. Preheat oven to 350°F (180°C). Lightly grease 9- x 13-inch (3 L) glass baking dish or spray with nonstick cooking spray.
2. In saucepan of boiling water, cook pasta according to package directions, adding broccoli for the last 2 minutes of cooking. Drain and place in baking dish.
3. In same saucepan, blend together tuna, soup, milk, Cheddar cheese and pepper; pour over pasta mixture and gently combine.
4. Sprinkle with crushed cornflakes and Parmesan cheese.
5. Bake for 25 to 30 minutes or until bubbling.

Makes 6 servings

Shopping List
broccoli
canned water-packed tuna
condensed cream of broccoli soup
Cheddar cheese
cornflake crumbs
Parmesan cheese

Making cornflake crumbs is a great kid-pleasing activity—if you can stand the crumbs on the floor! Place cornflakes in a plastic bag and crush with a rolling pin. Three cups (750 mL) of cornflakes makes about ¾ cup (175 mL) cornflake crumbs.

Casserole can be assembled up to 24 hours in advance and refrigerated until needed. Reheat at 350°F (180°C) for 35 to 40 minutes or until bubbling.

Substitute 1 can of broccoli-and-cheese soup for the cream of broccoli soup if you don't have time to grate cheese or if you don't have enough cheese.

Festive Turkey Noodle Casserole

Omit broccoli, tuna and broccoli soup. Substitute 2 cups (500 mL) cubed cooked turkey, 1 medium sweet red pepper chopped and sautéed in 1 tsp (5 mL) vegetable oil, 1 cup (250 mL) frozen peas and 1 can (10 oz/284 mL) condensed cream of chicken soup. Serve as part of a Christmas holiday buffet with Spinach Salad with Honey Orange Dressing (page 113) and assorted rolls. For dessert have raspberry or lime sherbet.

Per serving

Calories	460
Protein	32g
Fat	14g
Carbohydrate	50g
Dietary fibre	4g

Excellent source of vitamin C, thiamine, riboflavin, niacin, folic acid, vitamin B12, calcium, iron

Good source of vitamin A, vitamin B6, zinc

High source of dietary fibre

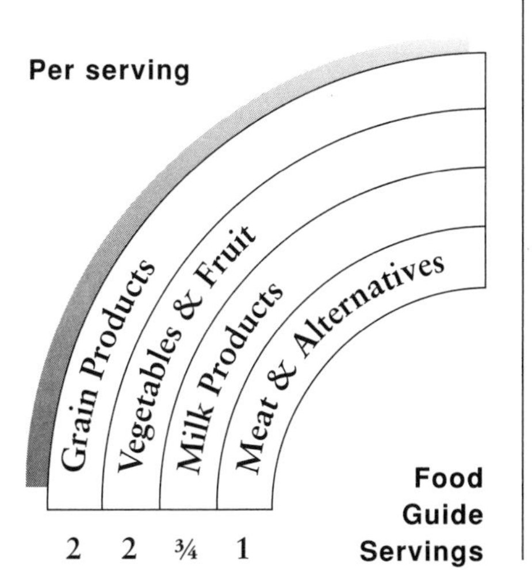

Filling in the Rainbow

This is a complete supper meal.

Flake and Bake Chicken

Serve this succulent chicken with baked potatoes that you cook in the same oven as the chicken. Frozen mixed vegetables, quickly cooked on the stovetop or in the microwave, complete the meal.

8	medium baking potatoes	8
1	egg	1
1 tbsp	water	15 mL
¾ to 1 cup	crushed cornflakes	175 to 250 mL
¼ cup	grated Parmesan cheese	50 mL
2 tsp	Italian herb seasoning	10 mL
¼ tsp	pepper	1 mL
4 lb	chicken breasts and legs (8 pieces), skinned	1.8 kg
1 cup	light sour cream (5% M.F.)	250 mL

1. Preheat oven to 375°F (190°C). Line cookie sheet with foil; lightly grease foil or spray with nonstick cooking spray.
2. Wash potatoes; bake for 45 to 50 minutes or until tender.
3. Meanwhile in bowl, lightly beat egg with water; set aside.
4. In heavy plastic bag, combine crushed cornflakes, Parmesan cheese, Italian seasoning and pepper.
5. Dip chicken in egg mixture; place, one piece at a time, in bag and shake to coat. Place on cookie sheet.
6. Bake for 45 to 50 minutes or until juices run clear when chicken is pierced with fork.
7. Serve each baked potato topped with 2 tbsp/25 mL light sour cream.

Makes 8 servings

Shopping List
cornflake crumbs
chicken breasts and legs
Parmesan cheese
baking potatoes
light sour cream
frozen mixed vegetables

To make cornflake crumbs, place cornflakes in plastic bag and crush with a rolling pin. Add remaining ingredients directly to bag. Four cups (1 L) of cornflakes will give you about 1 cup (250 mL) cornflake crumbs.

Substitute 1 tsp (5 mL) dried basil, ½ tsp (2 mL) dried oregano and ½ tsp (2 mL) dried rosemary for the Italian seasoning.

Cooked chicken can be frozen for up to 3 months. Defrost in refrigerator overnight and reheat in a 350°F (180°C) oven for 10 to 15 minutes.

Have a picnic

Flake and Bake Chicken is delicious served cold. Take it on a picnic with Easy Everyday Coleslaw (page 81), whole grain rolls and fresh assorted berries.

Be sure to have a safe picnic! Pack the chicken and coleslaw in separate containers. Keep these foods cold (40°F/4°C or below) by keeping them in an insulated carrying case with an ice pack. Try to eat your picnic lunch within 2 hours of leaving the house.

Supper includes Flake and Bake Chicken, one medium baked potato with 2 tbsp (25 mL) light sour cream and frozen mixed vegetables (½ cup/125 mL).

Per serving of supper

Calories	527
Protein	39g
Fat	6g
Carbohydrate	79g
Dietary fibre	9g

Excellent source of vitamin A, vitamin C, thiamine, riboflavin, niacin, vitamin B6, folic acid, iron, zinc

Good source of vitamin B12

Very high source of dietary fibre

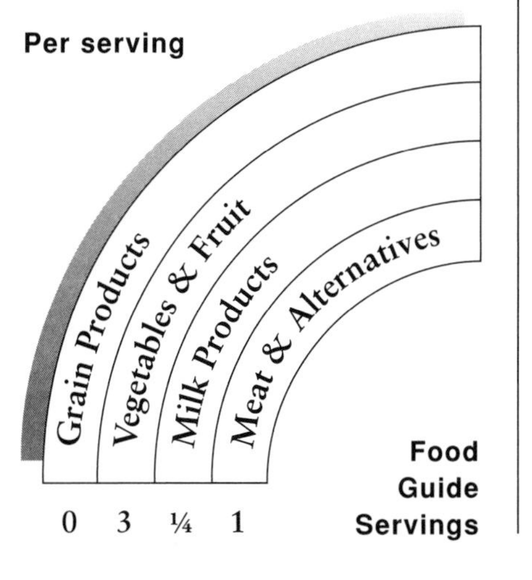

Filling in the Rainbow

Complete this meal with whole grain bread or rolls and a serving from the Milk Products group, if necessary, to balance the rest of the day.

Harvest Vegetables with Chicken and Penne

Shopping List
boneless skinless chicken breasts
green and red peppers
zucchini
tomato-based pasta sauce
Parmesan cheese

Begin cooking penne when you uncover the Harvest Vegetables and Chicken.

Take advantage of our autumn harvest and enjoy this meal when fall vegetables are at their peak. This great family meal is perfect for weeknight entertaining. Serve Pear Crisp (page 86) with light vanilla ice cream for dessert. It bakes in the same oven as the Harvest Vegetables with Chicken and Penne.

4 tsp	vegetable oil	20 mL
6	boneless skinless chicken breasts (about 1½ lb/750 g)	6
1	clove garlic, minced	1
1	medium onion, chopped	1
1	medium sweet green pepper, sliced	1
1	medium sweet red pepper, sliced	1
1	medium zucchini (about 8 oz/250 g), sliced	1
1	jar (750 mL) tomato-based pasta sauce	1
12 oz	penne pasta (about 4 cups/1 L)	375 g
⅓ cup	grated Parmesan cheese	75 mL

1. Preheat oven to 350°F (180°C). Lightly grease 9- x 13-inch (3 L) glass baking dish or spray with nonstick cooking spray.
2. In large nonstick skillet, heat 2 tsp (10 mL) of the oil over medium-high heat; sear chicken on both sides. Remove chicken and place in dish.
3. Add remaining oil to skillet; add garlic, onion, peppers and zucchini; sauté for 3 to 5 minutes or until softened. Spoon over chicken. Pour pasta sauce over top.
4. Cover and bake for 20 minutes. Uncover and bake for 10 to 20 minutes longer or until chicken is tender and no longer pink inside.

5. Meanwhile, in saucepan of boiling water, cook penne according to package directions. Drain.
6. Serve chicken mixture over penne. Sprinkle with Parmesan cheese.

Makes 6 servings

Per serving

Calories	540
Protein	40g
Fat	11g
Carbohydrate	69g
Dietary fibre	7g

Excellent source of vitamin A, vitamin C, thiamine, riboflavin, niacin, vitamin B6, iron, zinc

Good source of folic acid, vitamin B12

Very high source of dietary fibre

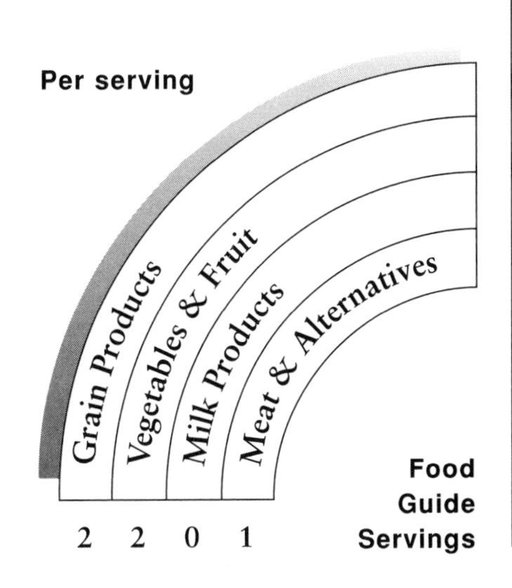

Filling in the Rainbow

Choose a serving from the Milk Products group to complete this meal.

Pork Tenderloin with Roasted Sweet Potatoes

Of all the meals we sent out to different families for testing, this one was the clear favourite! We served this meal with green beans and unsweetened applesauce and nobody missed the gravy!

2	pork tenderloins (each about ¾ lb/375 g)	2
2 tbsp	honey mustard	25 mL
2 tsp	sodium-reduced soy sauce	10 mL
4	medium sweet potatoes (about 2 lb/1 kg), peeled and cut into sixths	4
2 tbsp	vegetable oil	25 mL
¼ tsp	pepper	1 mL

1. Preheat oven to 375°F (190°C). Line cookie sheet with foil; lightly grease or spray with nonstick cooking spray.
2. Pat pork tenderloins dry; place in centre of cookie sheet. Combine mustard and soy sauce; brush over top and sides of pork.
3. Pat potatoes dry; toss with oil and pepper. Place around pork.
4. Bake for 40 to 45 minutes or until temperature on meat thermometer registers 160°F (70°C) and potatoes are golden. To serve, slice pork into ½-inch (1 cm) thick slices.

Makes 6 servings

Shopping List
2 pork tenderloins
sweet potatoes
green beans
unsweetened applesauce
whole grain bread/rolls

To avoid black discoloration on cooked potatoes, toss potatoes in oil as soon as possible after peeling.

Dark orange vegetables such as sweet potatoes are high in beta-carotene (the plant form of vitamin A). This meal provides 242% of the Recommended Daily Intake of vitamin A for adults!

Have light vanilla ice cream with chocolate syrup for dessert. It's a nice finish to a great meal.

Food Safety

Trichinosis is virtually non-existent in Canada. If present, it is destroyed by cooking pork to an internal temperature of 137°F (58°C). Roast pork should now be cooked to an internal temperature of 160°F (70°C) with a hint of pink remaining.

Remember that all ground pork and sausages should be cooked thoroughly until no pink remains.

When using a meat thermometer, always insert it into the centre of roasts and meat, making sure not to touch any bones.

Supper includes Pork Tenderloin with Roasted Sweet Potatoes, green beans (½ cup/125 mL) and unsweetened applesauce (¼ cup/50 mL)

Per serving of supper

Calories	357
Protein	27g
Fat	10g
Carbohydrate	41g
Dietary fibre	6g

Excellent source of vitamin A, vitamin C, thiamine, riboflavin, niacin, vitamin B6, zinc

Good source of folic acid, vitamin B12, iron

Very high source of dietary fibre

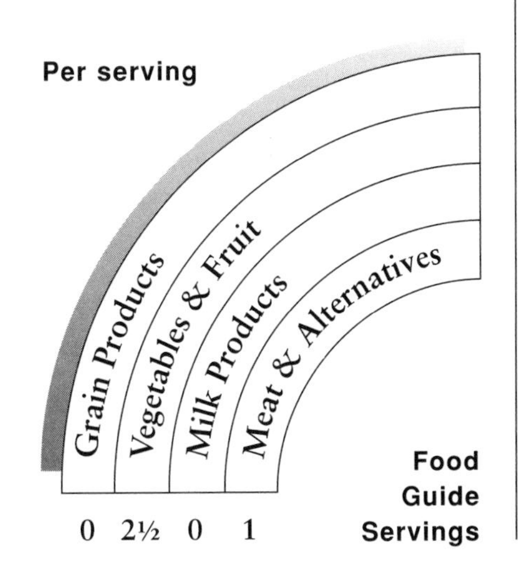

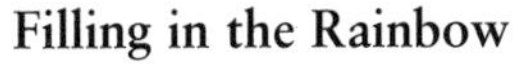

Filling in the Rainbow

Complete this meal with whole grain bread or rolls and a glass of milk.

Spinach Frittata Fingers

This recipe is an adaptation of one created by The Egg Producers of Ontario. Many women have difficulty getting enough calcium, iron and folic acid into their diets. This meatless meal is an excellent source of all three. We have served this supper meal with a small bagel (2 servings of Grain Products) plus 1 tsp (5 mL) of soft margarine and a fresh pear (1 serving of Vegetables & Fruit). You can substitute any other food choices from these 2 Food Groups to make your own complete meal. The nutrients will change but the Rainbow Balance Chart will remain the same.

1 tsp	vegetable oil	5 mL
1	small onion, chopped	1
Half	medium sweet red pepper, chopped	Half
6	eggs	6
1	package (300 g) frozen chopped spinach, thawed and squeezed dry	1
1 cup	small curd cottage cheese (2% M.F.)	250 mL
1 cup	shredded old Cheddar cheese	250 mL
2 tbsp	all-purpose flour	25 mL
½ tsp	baking powder	2 mL
½ tsp	dried basil	2 mL
¼ tsp	each ground nutmeg and pepper	1 mL

1. Preheat oven to 350°F (180°C). Lightly grease 8-inch (2 L) square glass baking dish or spray with nonstick cooking spray.
2. In large nonstick skillet, heat oil over medium-high heat; sauté onion and red pepper for 3 to 5 minutes or until softened. Set aside.

Shopping List

red pepper
eggs
frozen spinach
small curd cottage cheese
old Cheddar cheese
pears
bagels

Frittata Fingers do not freeze well but they can be prepared up to 2 days ahead. To reheat, microwave on a microwave-safe plate, on Medium for 1 to 2 minutes for each finger or until heated through.

DID YOU KNOW?

Two cups (500 mL) of cottage cheese equal 1 serving from the Milk Products group.

3. In large bowl, beat eggs. Blend in spinach, cottage and Cheddar cheeses, flour, baking powder, basil, nutmeg and pepper. Add onion mixture. Pour into prepared dish.
4. Bake for 30 to 40 minutes or until firm. Cool for 15 minutes. Cut into 6 fingers. Serve warm or at room temperature.

Makes 6 servings

Supper includes 1 Spinach Frittata Finger, 1 small bagel with 1 tsp (5 mL) margarine and 1 medium pear.

Per serving of supper

Calories	526
Protein	24g
Fat	18g
Carbohydrate	68g
Dietary fibre	7g

Excellent source of vitamin A, riboflavin, niacin, folic acid, vitamin B12, calcium, iron, zinc

Good source of vitamin C, thiamine, vitamin B6

Very high source of dietary fibre

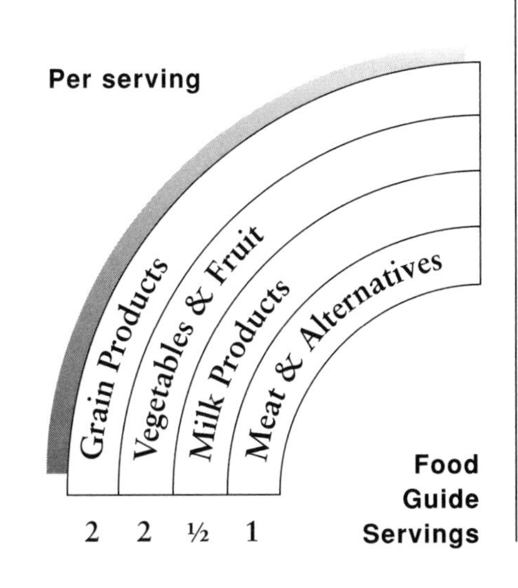

Filling in the Rainbow

Every food group is covered in this meal.

Tangy Barbecue Chicken with Rice

This meal is a real kid-pleaser. Have plenty of serviettes available for sticky hands because everyone will want to pick up the chicken with their fingers. Use any flavour of barbecue sauce—try sweet and sour. Serve with corn on the cob or frozen or canned corn niblets when corn on the cob is out of season.

4 lb	chicken breasts and legs (8 pieces), skinned	1.8 kg

Barbecue Sauce

1 cup	bottled barbecue sauce	250 mL
½ cup	ketchup	125 mL
¼ cup	packed brown sugar	50 mL
2 tbsp	white vinegar or lemon juice	25 mL
1 tbsp	prepared mustard	15 mL

8 cups	Perfect Microwave Rice	2 L

1. Preheat oven to 350°F (180°C). Lightly grease 9- x 13-inch (3 L) glass baking dish or spray with nonstick cooking stray.
2. Place chicken in single layer in dish.
3. In large measuring cup, combine barbecue sauce, ketchup, brown sugar, vinegar and mustard; pour over chicken.
4. Bake, uncovered, for 45 to 50 minutes or until juices run clear when chicken is pierced with fork. Serve with Perfect Microwave Rice.

Makes 8 servings

Shopping List
chicken breasts and legs (8 pieces)
bottled barbecue sauce
corn on the cob

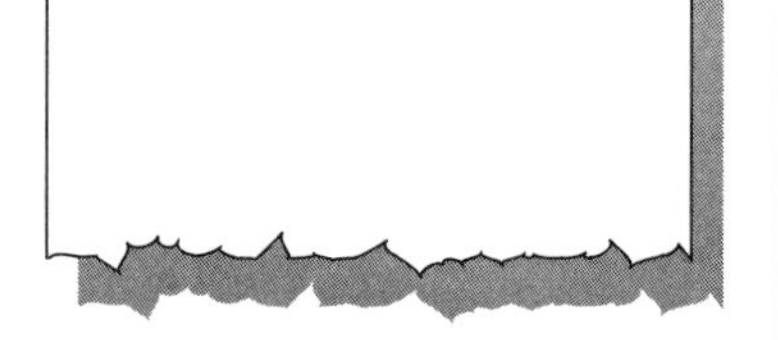

Compare the fat content of these two meals, which are the same except for the meat: Tangy Barbecue Chicken has 10 grams of fat; Tangy Barbecue Ribs have 22 grams of fat. Barbecue ribs are tasty and delicious once in a while but they are a higher-fat choice and should be eaten less often.

Tangy Barbecue Chicken with Rice and Tangy Barbecue Ribs with Rice are great planned left-over meals. Refrigerate for up to 3 days and serve with a different vegetable. Try Easy Everyday Coleslaw (page 81).

Perfect Microwave Rice

1 cup	brown rice	250 mL
1½ cups	long grain rice	375 mL
4 cups	hot water	1 L

1. Combine all ingredients in large 8-cup (2 L) glass measuring cup or 3 L casserole dish.
2. Cover and microwave on High for 24 to 26 minutes or until water is mostly absorbed.
3. Let stand for 10 minutes; fluff with a fork.

Makes 8 cups (2 L)

Tangy Barbecue Ribs with Rice

In large Dutch oven, combine 3 lb (1.5 kg) pork back ribs (cut into portions), 1 onion, sliced, 2 stalks celery, chopped, and 1 bay leaf. Barely cover with water and bring to boil; reduce heat and simmer for 25 to 30 minutes or until tender. Drain, discarding vegetables. Follow recipe for Tangy Barbecue Chicken with Rice but reduce baking time to 20 to 25 minutes.

To barbecue ribs, brush ribs with half the sauce before barbecuing; simmer remaining sauce in a small saucepan for 3 to 4 minutes and serve separately with ribs and rice.

Makes 8 servings

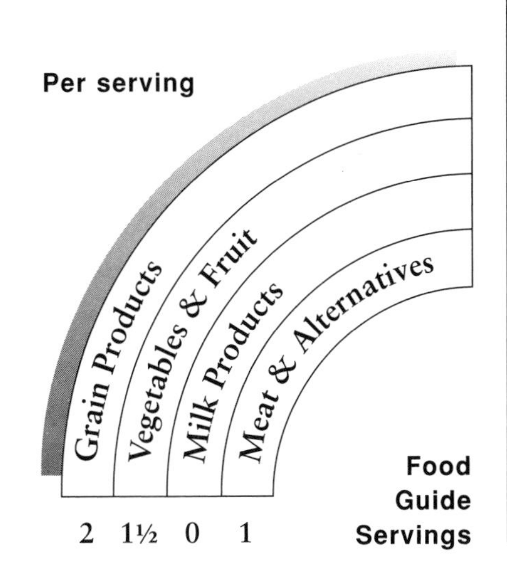

Supper includes Tangy Barbecue Chicken with Rice and 1 corn on the cob with 1 tsp (5 mL) butter

Per serving of supper

Calories	582
Protein	36g
Fat	10g
Carbohydrate	90g
Dietary fibre	8g

Excellent source of thiamine, niacin, vitamin B6, folic acid, zinc

Good source of riboflavin, vitamin B12, iron

Very high source of dietary fibre

Filling in the Rainbow

Complete this meal with a serving from the Milk Products group.

Shopping List
skinless bone-in chicken breasts
bottled calorie-reduced Catalina salad dressing
green and red peppers
tomato, (optional)

Quick Barbecued Chicken with Pasta and Pepper Salad

This speedy barbecue chicken supper was adapted from a recipe given to us by the Ontario Chicken Producers' Marketing Board. This is one of our lowest-fat supper meals. Enjoy Chocolate Angel Food Cake (page 85) for dessert.

½ cup	bottled calorie-reduced Catalina or Italian-style salad dressing	125 mL
4	skinless bone-in chicken breasts	4

1. Pour ¼ cup (50 mL) of the salad dressing into shallow microwaveable dish.
2. Add chicken, turning to coat; cover and marinate in refrigerator for 30 minutes or overnight, turning occasionally.
3. Microwave chicken in marinade on High for 5 minutes.
4. Meanwhile, preheat greased barbecue grill.
5. Discarding marinade, place chicken on grill, over medium-high heat; cook for 15 to 20 minutes, basting with remaining salad dressing, turning once, until juices run clear when chicken is pierced with fork.

Makes 4 servings

Pasta and Pepper Salad

This is one of the easiest pasta salads you will ever make! Choose a salad dressing that is labelled calorie-reduced or fat-free and contains 3 grams or less of fat per 1 tbsp (15 mL) serving. Instead of a whole red pepper, try half a red pepper and half a yellow pepper for a rainbow of colour.

6 oz	fusilli pasta (about 2 cups/500 mL)	175 g
1	medium sweet green pepper, sliced	1
1	medium sweet red pepper, sliced	1
1	large tomato, diced (about 8 oz/250 g, optional)	1
½ cup	bottled calorie-reduced vinaigrette-type salad dressing	125 mL

1. In saucepan of boiling water, cook fusilli according to package directions; drain and rinse under cold water. Drain again. Place in large bowl.
2. Add peppers and tomato (if using). Add salad dressing; toss to coat well.

Makes 4 servings

Supper includes Quick Marinated Barbecued Chicken with Pasta and Pepper Salad

Per serving of supper

Calories	352
Protein	33g
Fat	4g
Carbohydrate	45g
Dietary fibre	3g

Excellent source of vitamin C, thiamine, riboflavin, niacin, vitamin B6

Good source of vitamin A, folic acid, vitamin B12, iron, zinc

Moderate source of dietary fibre

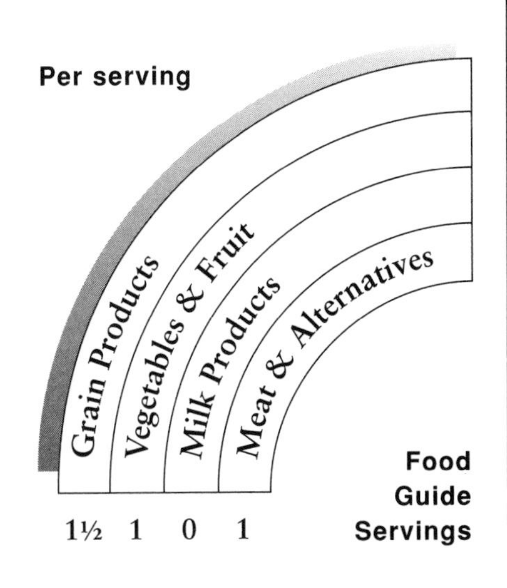

Filling in the Rainbow

A serving from the Milk Products group will complete this meal.

Barbecued Salmon Supper

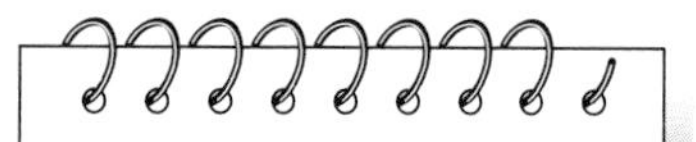

Shopping List
fresh salmon tail or 4 fillets
lemon
couscous
asparagus

To trim asparagus, gently bend the stalk until the woody end snaps off.

Salmon can also be cooked, covered, over medium-high heat in a nonstick skillet for 10 minutes per inch (2.5 cm) of thickness.

If you use a barbecue fish basket, turn salmon once halfway through cooking.

KID-FRIENDLY TIP
When serving children fish, always check for bones that might cause them to choke.

This tasty early summer barbecue is ideal for weeknight entertaining. We like our salmon plain and simple with a squeeze of lemon and a touch of olive oil. Feel free to add some chopped fresh herbs such as thyme, dill and tarragon, to the marinade. Serve with couscous and Asparagus with Honey-Orange Dressing. When asparagus is out of season, substitute the Spinach Salad with Honey-Orange Dressing (page 113).

1 tbsp	fresh lemon juice	15 mL
1 tsp	olive oil	5 mL
	Pepper	
1	salmon tail (about 1 lb/500 g) or 4 salmon fillets (each about 4 oz/125 g)	1

1. Combine lemon juice, olive oil, and pepper to taste; brush over salmon. Let marinate for 10 to 15 minutes.
2. Meanwhile, preheat greased barbecue grill.
3. Place salmon, skin side down, on grill; close lid and cook over medium-high heat for 10 minutes per inch (2.5 cm) of thickness or until opaque and flakes easily when tested with fork.

Makes 4 servings

Asparagus with Honey-Orange Dressing

1 to 1½ lb	asparagus, trimmed	500 to 750 g
2 tbsp	rice vinegar or cider vinegar	25 mL
2 tbsp	orange juice	25 mL
1 tbsp	olive oil	15 mL
1 tbsp	liquid honey	15 mL
¼-½ tsp	dried tarragon	1-2 mL
Pinch	each salt and pepper	Pinch

1. In small measuring cup, combine vinegar, orange juice, olive oil, honey, tarragon, salt and pepper.
2. Meanwhile, steam asparagus for 2 to 3 minutes or until tender-crisp. Serve with Honey-Orange Dressing.

Makes 4 servings

Quicky Couscous

2 cups	water	500 mL
2 tsp	olive oil	10 mL
1½ cups	quick-cooking couscous	375 mL
	Salt and pepper	

1. In medium saucepan, bring water and olive oil to boil. Stir in couscous.
2. Cover and remove from heat; let stand for 5 minutes. Fluff with fork. Add salt and pepper to taste.

Makes 4 cups (1 L)

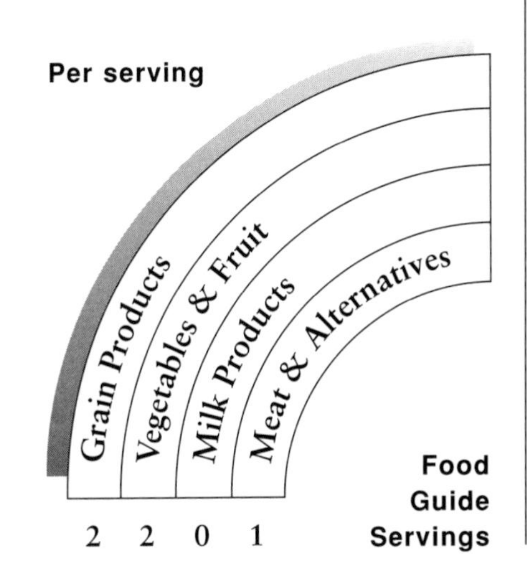

Supper includes Barbecued Salmon Supper, couscous (1 cup/250 mL) and Asparagus with Honey-Orange Dressing

Per serving of supper

Calories	514
Protein	32g
Fat	14g
Carbohydrate	64g
Dietary fibre	5g

Excellent source of thiamine, riboflavin, niacin, vitamin B6, folic acid, vitamin B12

Good source of iron, zinc

When purchasing salmon, try to choose fillets that have been cut closest to the tail of the salmon (or buy a l lb/500 g salmon tail), because the end of the salmon is naturally boneless.

Filling in the Rainbow

A choice from the Milk Products group will complete this supper meal.

Barbecued Steak Supper

Shopping List
balsamic vinegar
boneless sirloin steak
new red or white potatoes
broccoli

This makes a great last-minute supper on a hot day. Let the steak marinate while you get the potatoes prepared and on the grill. Serve with Barb's Balsamic Broccoli or any other vegetable of your choice. The nutrients will change but the Rainbow Balance Chart will remain the same.

2 tbsp	balsamic vinegar or red wine vinegar	25 mL
2 tbsp	Dijon mustard	25 mL
1	clove garlic, minced	1
	Pepper	
1½ lb	boneless sirloin steak (1 to 1½ inches/2.5 to 4 cm thick), trimmed of fat	750 g

Barbecued Potatoes

12	small new red or white potatoes (about 2 lb/1 kg)	12
2 tbsp	vegetable oil	25 mL
¼ tsp	pepper	1 mL

1. In shallow dish, combine vinegar, mustard, garlic, and pepper to taste. Add steak, turning to coat well; cover and marinate for at least 10 minutes or refrigerate overnight.
2. Barbecued Potatoes: Scrub potatoes but do not peel; cut into quarters. Place in centre of large piece of heavy-duty foil. Sprinkle with oil and pepper. Fold foil up around potatoes and seal to form a rectangular package.
3. Lightly grease half of barbecue grill (for steak). Preheat barbecue.
4. Place potatoes on ungreased half of grill; cook over medium heat for 20 minutes, turning once after 10 minutes through cooking. Reduce heat to low; cook for 10 to15 minutes longer or until tender.
5. Meanwhile, place steak on greased half of grill; cook over medium-high heat until desired doneness (see chart opposite).

6. Slice steak on the diagonal into ¼ inch (5 mm) thick slices.

Makes 6 servings

Barb's Balsamic Broccoli

Our friend Barb McHughan shared this recipe with us. It's perfect with the steak and potatoes. Green vegetables change colour from bright green to dark green when they are tossed with vinegar or lemon juice so toss broccoli with balsamic vinegar just before serving.

1	small bunch broccoli, cut lengthwise into stalks	1
1 tbsp	balsamic vinegar	15 mL
1 tsp	olive oil	5 mL
¼ tsp	pepper	1 mL
1 tbsp	sesame seeds (optional)	15 mL

1. Steam broccoli for 3 to 4 minutes or until tender-crisp.
2. Toss with balsamic vinegar, olive oil, pepper, and sesame seeds (if using).

Makes 6 servings

STEAK COOKING TIMES (minutes per side)

Thickness	Rare	Medium	Well
1 inch (2.5 cm)	5-7	7-9	9-11
1½ inches (4 cm)	7-9	9-11	15-18

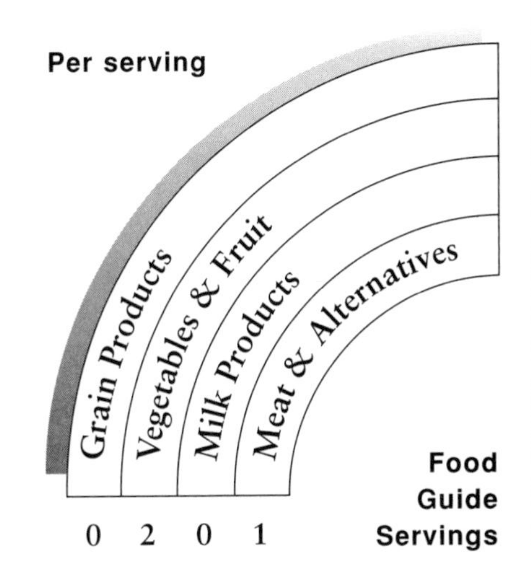

Supper includes Barbecued Steak, Barbecued Potatoes and Barb's Balsamic Broccoli

Per serving of supper

Calories	383
Protein	26g
Fat	13g
Carbohydrate	41g
Dietary fibre	5g

Excellent source of vitamin C, niacin, vitamin B6, vitamin B12, iron, zinc

Good source of thiamine, riboflavin, folic acid

High source of dietary fibre

This steak is best cooked to rare, medium-rare or medium.

Filling in the Rainbow

Complete this meal with a serving from the Grain Products group and Milk Products group to balance the rest of the day, if necessary.

Grilled Lemon Chicken on a Bun

Shopping List
boneless, skinless chicken breasts
part-skim mozzarella cheese slices
whole wheat buns
tomatoes
cabbage
carrots
red pepper

This is a combination Make and Bake and Make Ahead Supper. Up to two hours before serving time, or the night before, begin marinating the chicken and make the coleslaw. This great meal-to-go is also delicious served cold. Substitute other low-fat cheeses for the part-skim mozzarella. For variety, serve Veggies and Dip (page 91) instead of the coleslaw.

Marinade:

3 tbsp	lemon juice	50 mL
1 tbsp	each olive oil and Dijon mustard	15 mL
1 tsp	dried basil leaves or dried dillweed	5 mL
¼ tsp	pepper	1 mL
5	boneless skinless chicken breasts (about 1¼ lb/625 g)	5
1	200 g package sliced part-skim mozzarella cheese	1
5	large whole wheat or kaiser buns	5
3 tbsp	honey mustard	50 mL
2	large tomatoes, thickly sliced	2
	Lettuce (optional)	

1. In shallow dish combine lemon juice, olive oil, Dijon mustard, basil and pepper; add chicken turning to coat well. Marinate for at least 15 minutes or overnight in the refrigerator.
2. Preheat greased barbecue grill. Grill chicken breasts for 12 to 15 minutes, turning once, or until juices run clear when pierced with a fork. Top chicken with mozzarella cheese during last 1 to 2 minutes of grilling.
3. Meanwhile, slice and warm buns; spread with honey mustard. Top with grilled chicken and melted cheese, tomatoes and lettuce, if using. Serve with Easy Everyday Coleslaw.

Makes 5 servings

Easy Everyday Coleslaw

A food processor is not necessary to prepare this coleslaw! Use a large knife to cut the cabbage into ¼-inch (5 mm) slices. Prepare and store coleslaw in the same bowl to make clean-up a breeze! Refrigerate any leftover coleslaw for up to three days.

8 cups	shredded cabbage (about half a large head)	2 L
2	large carrots, grated (about 1 cup/250 mL)	2
Half	medium sweet red pepper, diced	Half
	Dressing	
⅓ cup	cider vinegar	75 mL
¼ cup	vegetable oil	50 mL
1 tbsp	each granulated sugar and Dijon mustard	15 mL
½ tsp	salt	2 mL
½ tsp	celery seed (optional)	2 mL
¼ tsp	pepper	1 mL

1. In large bowl combine cabbage, carrots and red pepper.
2. In 1-cup (250 mL) measuring cup, blend together vinegar, oil, sugar, mustard, salt, celery seed (if using) and pepper; pour over cabbage. Toss together.
3. Refrigerate for at least 2 hours or overnight to blend flavours.

Makes 7 cups (1.75 L) 1 serving = ½ cup (125 mL)

Supper includes Grilled Lemon Chicken on a Bun and Easy Everyday Coleslaw (½ cup/125 mL)

Per serving of supper

Calories	573
Protein	47g
Fat	18g
Carbohydrate	60g
Dietary fibre	8g

Excellent source of vitamin A, vitamin C, thiamine, riboflavin, niacin, vitamin B6, folic acid, vitamin B12, calcium, iron, zinc

Very high source of dietary fibre

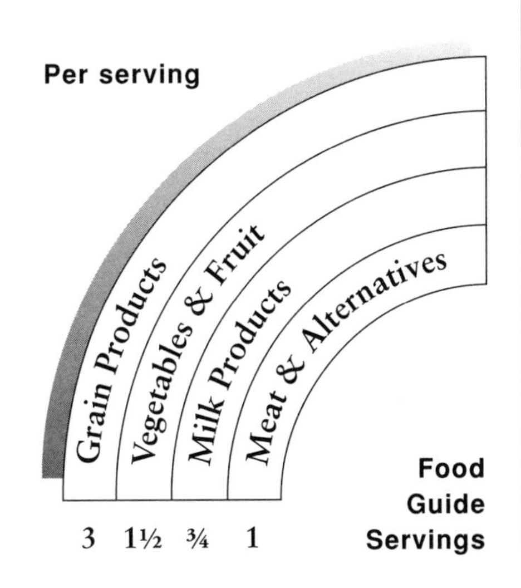

Filling in the Rainbow

This meal contains something from all four food groups.

Marinated Beef and Vegetable Kabobs

Shopping List
balsamic vinegar
sirloin steak
Spanish onion
red, green, yellow peppers
zucchini
corn on the cob

Extra rice can be frozen for up to 4 months. To reheat 2 cups (500 mL) of rice: Place rice in a microwaveable dish, cover and microwave on High for 3 to 4 minutes, stirring once.

Cooking rice in the microwave isn't any faster than making it on top of the stove but it is always perfectly cooked (if you measure accurately) and if you happen to forget about it you won't have a scorched pot to clean!

If using wooden skewers, soak for 30 minutes in water before using to prevent them from burning.

Get a jump start on supper by marinating and assembling the kabobs ahead of time. Serve with Perfect Microwave Rice and corn on the cob or frozen or canned corn niblets when corn on the cob is out of season. Refrigerate or freeze any extra Perfect Microwave Rice for another meal.

Marinade

2 tbsp	balsamic vinegar or red wine vinegar	25 mL
2 tbsp	sodium-reduced soy sauce	25 mL
½ tsp	dried thyme	2 mL
1	clove garlic, minced	1
¼ tsp	pepper	1 mL
1 lb	sirloin steak (about 1½ inches/ 4 cm thick), cut into 16 cubes	500 g
Quarter	medium sweet Spanish or red onion, cut into chunks	Quarter
Half	each medium sweet red, green and yellow pepper, each cut into 8 chunks	Half
1	medium zucchini (about 8 oz/ 250 g), cut into 16 chunks	1
4 cups	Perfect Microwave Rice	1 L

1. Marinade: In medium bowl, combine vinegar, soy sauce, thyme, garlic and pepper.
2. Add steak cubes, tossing to coat. Marinate for at least 15 minutes or cover and refrigerate overnight.
3. Alternately thread beef, onions, peppers and zucchini onto four 12-inch (30 cm) long skewers. Brush with any extra marinade.
4. Preheat greased barbecue grill. Cook kabobs over medium-high heat for 10 to 15 minutes, turning once, or until desired doneness.

Makes 4 servings

Perfect Microwave Rice

1 cup	brown rice	250 mL
1½ cups	long grain rice	375 mL
4 cups	hot water	1 L

1. Combine all ingredients in a large 8-cup (2 L) glass measuring cup or 3 L casserole dish.
2. Cover and microwave on High for 24 to 26 minutes or until water is mostly absorbed.
3. Let stand for 10 minutes; fluff with a fork.

Makes 8 cups (2 L)

Supper includes Marinated Beef and Vegetable Kabobs with Rice and 1 medium corn on the cob with 1 tsp/5 mL butter

Per serving of supper

Calories	564
Protein	37g
Fat	11g
Carbohydrate	82g
Dietary fibre	8g

Excellent source of vitamin C, thiamine, riboflavin, niacin, vitamin B6, folic acid, vitamin B12, iron, zinc

Good source of vitamin A

Very high source of dietary fibre

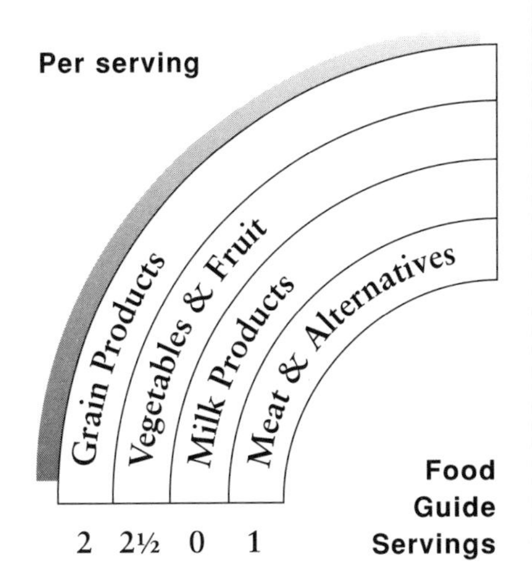

Filling in the Rainbow

Complete this meal with a serving from the Milk Products group.

Baked Apples

These make a delicious syrup when they are baking. Serve them warm with a small scoop of light vanilla ice cream and spoon the syrup on top.

6	medium McIntosh apples (unpeeled)	6
⅓ cup	packed brown sugar	75 mL
½ tsp	cinnamon	2 mL
1 tbsp	soft margarine	15 mL

If you prefer a firmer baked apple, substitute Cortland or Golden Delicious apples.

1. Lightly grease 10-inch (25 cm) glass pie plate or spray with nonstick cooking spray.
2. Core apples; score around middle with sharp knife. Place in pie plate.
3. In small bowl, combine brown sugar and cinnamon; spoon into centre of each apple. Top each apple with ½ tsp (2 mL) margarine. Add ¼ cup (50 mL) of water to pie plate.
4. Bake, uncovered, at 350°F (180°C) for 45 to 55 minutes or until apples are tender.

Makes 6 servings (3 g of fat per serving)

Chocolate Angel Food Cake

This light and delicious cake is a great example of how a little whipping cream can go a long way. Serve this cake with fresh berries on the side and you have an elegant dessert for any special occasion.

1	300 g store-bought angel food cake	1

Icing

1 cup	whipping cream	250 mL
¼ cup	chocolate syrup	50 mL

1. Place cake on serving plate. Set aside.
2. In bowl, whip cream with chocolate syrup on high speed until soft peaks form. Spread on top and sides of cake. Serve immediately or refrigerate for up to 6 hours.

Makes 8 servings (10 g of fat per serving)

Chocolate syrup has only 0.2 grams of fat per 2 tbsp (25 mL). Do not confuse this thin type of chocolate syrup (the kind used to mix with milk to make chocolate milk) with the higher-fat fudge-type chocolate syrup and sauces, which have 6 or more grams of fat per 2 tbsp (25 mL) serving.

Pear Crisp

We love fruit crisps, but don't like peeling and cutting up all of the fruit. This recipe solves the problem and takes less than 10 minutes to prepare. Bev's daughter, Sarah, loves to eat leftover Pear Crisp for breakfast with yogurt or a glass of milk!

2	cans (each 28 oz/796 mL) juice-packed sliced pears	2
¼ cup	packed brown sugar	50 mL
2 tbsp	lemon juice	25 mL
1 tbsp	all-purpose flour	15 mL
¼ to ½ tsp	ground ginger	1 to 2 mL

Topping

1 cup	quick-cooking rolled oats	250 mL
½ cup	packed brown sugar	125 mL
⅓ cup	whole wheat flour	75 mL
1 tsp	cinnamon	5 mL
¼ cup	unprocessed bran	50 mL
¼ cup	soft margarine	50 mL

1. Preheat oven to 350°F (180°C). Lightly grease 10-cup (2.5 L) casserole dish or spray with nonstick cooking spray.
2. Drain pears, reserving ¾ cup (175 mL) juice. In dish, stir together pears, reserved juice, brown sugar, lemon juice, flour and ginger.
3. Topping: In separate bowl, combine oats, sugar, flour, cinnamon and bran; cut in margarine with pastry blender or 2 knives (Bev uses her hands). Sprinkle over pears.
4. Bake for 35 to 45 minutes or until bubbly.

Makes 8 servings

VARIATION

For Rhubarb Crisp: Omit pears, brown sugar, lemon juice and ginger. Substitute 6 cups (1.5 L) chopped fresh rhubarb (1-inch/2.5 cm pieces) or frozen rhubarb (defrosted and drained), 1¼ cups (300 mL) granulated sugar and increase flour to 2 tbsp (25 mL). Use the same topping and proceed the same as for Pear Crisp.

Make-Ahead Meals

These meals take 30 minutes or more to prepare, but the time invested is worth it. Most of them can be prepared completely ahead of time and kept in the fridge for two or three days or stored in the freezer and pulled out when you just don't have time to cook.

If you prepare one recipe a week from this section, you will always have a steady supply of different meals that can be pulled from the freezer on those extra-busy days.

Batch Ground Meat and Vegetables

Shopping List
4 lb (1.8 kg) lean ground beef
onions
carrots
celery (optional)
garlic

BABY-FRIENDLY TIP

Omit garlic. Divide mixture into 2-tbsp (25 mL) portions. Two to 2½ cups (500-625 mL) of Batch Ground Meat and Vegetables fills one standard ice cube tray and makes 16 cubes of Batch Ground Meat and Vegetables. Freeze cubes in an airtight container for up to 3 months.

If you mince or grate the vegetables, the kids won't even know they are there!

When cooking up large batches of ground meat, it is important to keep stirring the meat and make sure that no pink, or uncooked, meat remains.

MAXIMUM FAT CONTENT OF GROUND BEEF

extra lean	10%
lean	17%
medium	23%
regular	30%

This recipe is the foundation for many different supper meals. You might want to prepare the whole recipe and freeze it in 2-cup (500 mL) portions for use in Extra-Speedy Spaghetti Supper or you might like to make and freeze a couple of lasagnas for Friday night when the gang is coming for supper. If you are not into large batch cooking, halve the recipe or make the recipe for 2 cups (500 mL) as directed. Batch Ground Meat and Vegetables was inspired by Lynn and is now a staple in each of our freezers!

4 lb	lean ground beef	1.8 kg
4	medium cooking onions, chopped or minced	4
8	medium carrots, chopped or minced	8
4	stalks celery, chopped or minced (optional)	4
4	cloves garlic, minced or 1 tsp (5 mL) garlic powder	4

1. In Dutch oven, cook meat over medium-high heat, breaking up with back of spoon, for 8 to 10 minutes or until no longer pink; drain fat.
2. Add onions, carrots, celery (if using) and garlic; simmer, uncovered, for 12 to 15 minutes or until vegetables are tender.
3. Cool mixture and divide into 1-cup (250 mL), 2-cup (500 mL), 3-cup (750 mL) or 4-cup (1 L) portions. Refrigerate for up to 2 days or freeze for up to 3 months.

Makes 10 to 12 cups (2.5 to 3 L)

To make 2 cups (500 mL) of Batch Ground Meat and Vegetables

¾ lb	lean ground beef	375 g
1	medium onion, chopped or minced	1

1	medium carrot, chopped or minced	1
1	stalk celery, chopped or minced (optional)	1
1	clove garlic, minced, or ¼ tsp (1 mL) garlic powder	1

1. In large nonstick skillet, cook meat over medium-high heat, breaking up with back of spoon, for 4 to 5 minutes or until no longer pink; drain fat.
2. Add onion, carrot, celery (if using) and garlic; simmer, uncovered, for 5 to 6 minutes. Use immediately or cool and refrigerate for up to 2 days or freeze for up to 3 months.

Makes 2 cups (500 mL)

Recipes using 4 cups (1 L) Batch Ground Meat and Vegetables:

Homemade Spaghetti Sauce
Shepherd's Pie
Chili and Cornbread

Recipe using 3 cups (750 mL) Batch Ground Meat and Vegetables:

Cabbage Roll Cassarole (Variation)

Recipes using 2 cups (500 mL) Batch Ground Meat and Vegetables:

Extra-Speedy Spaghetti Supper

Easy On Ya Lasagna

Ground Beef Stroganoff

Bail-Out Bean Burritos (Variation)

Recipe using 1 cup (250 mL) of Batch Ground Meat and Vegetables:

Warm Taco Salad

If you are planning to make and freeze any of the recipes requiring Batch Ground Meat and Vegetables, always use Batch Ground Meat and Vegetables that have not been previously frozen.

Choose lean ground beef and be sure to drain all fat after cooking.

Homemade Spaghetti Supper

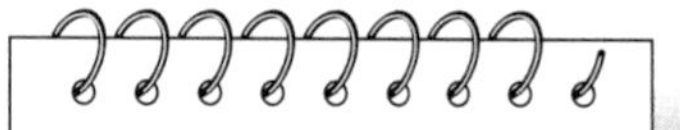

Shopping List
canned tomatoes
tomato paste
mushrooms (optional)
carrots
green pepper
cucumber
low-fat plain yogurt
Parmesan cheese

If you don't have Italian herb seasoning, substitute 1 tsp (5 mL) each dried oregano, basil and rosemary for every tablespoon (15 mL) of Italian herb seasoning.

Refrigerate Homemade Spaghetti Sauce for up to 3 days or freeze for up to 3 months. Do not refreeze Homemade Spaghetti Sauce if previously frozen Batch Ground Meat and Vegetables was used.

There's nothing like a homemade spaghetti supper to satisfy a hungry family. Make the Homemade Spaghetti Sauce ahead and freeze in portion sizes suitable to your family's needs. Serve Veggies and Dip for everyone to munch on while the sauce is defrosting and the noodles are cooking.

¾ lb	spaghetti	375 g
4 cups	Homemade Spaghetti Sauce	1 L
4 tbsp	grated Parmesan cheese	60 mL

1. In large pot of boiling water, cook spaghetti according to package directions; drain.
2. In large microwaveable dish, microwave spaghetti sauce on High for 6 to 8 minutes or until hot. Serve over spaghetti.
3. Sprinkle each serving with Parmesan cheese.

Makes 6 servings

Homemade Spaghetti Sauce

4 cups	Batch Ground Meat and Vegetables (page 88)	1 L
3	cans (each 28 oz/796 mL) tomatoes (undrained)	3
2	cans (each 5½ oz/156 mL) tomato paste	2
1 tbsp	each granulated sugar and dried basil	15 mL
2 tbsp	dried Italian herb seasoning	25 mL
1 lb	mushrooms, sliced (about 6 cups/1.5 L, optional)	500 g
½ tsp	pepper	2 mL

1. In large pot or Dutch oven, combine Batch Ground

Meat and Vegetables, tomatoes, tomato paste, sugar, basil, Italian seasoning and mushrooms (if using) and pepper.

2. Simmer, uncovered, stirring occasionally, for 1 hour or until thickened. (If mushrooms are used, sauce may need to simmer for 15 to 20 minutes longer.)

Makes 12 cups (3 L)

Veggies and Dip

3	medium carrots, cut into sticks	3
1½	medium sweet green peppers, cut into strips	1½
one-third	English cucumber, sliced	one-third
	Dip	
½ cup	low-fat plain yogurt	125 mL
3 tbsp	light mayonnaise	50 mL
1 tbsp	packaged dip seasoning mix	15 mL

1. Dip: Combine yogurt, mayonnaise and seasoning mix, blending well.
2. Serve surrounded with carrots, green pepper and cucumber.

Makes 6 servings

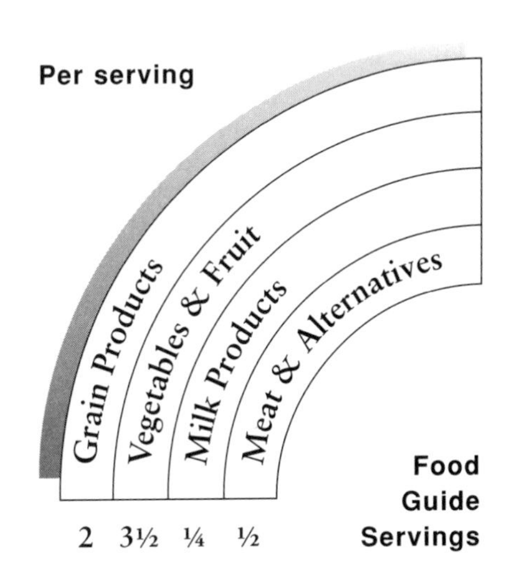

Supper includes Homemade Spaghetti Supper and Veggies and Dip

Per serving of supper

Calories	408
Protein	20g
Fat	10g
Carbohydrate	62g
Dietary fibre	7g

Excellent source of vitamin A, vitamin C, thiamine, riboflavin, niacin, vitamin B6, vitamin B12, iron, zinc

Good source of folic acid, calcium

Very high source of dietary fibre

Feel free to substitute other vegetables for the Veggies and Dip. (Check the Food Guide for amounts.) The nutrients may change, but the Rainbow Balance Chart will remain the same.

Filling in the Rainbow

Add a serving from the Milk Products group to complete the meal, if necessary to balance the rest of the day.

Extra-Speedy Spaghetti Supper

Here's one recipe that older kids and caregivers can pull together in a flash! Even Mom or Dad has been known to come up with this one during desperate times! We've added a fruit plate to round out the meal and make it very high in fibre. Go ahead and substitute a variety of different fruits for the fruit plate. The nutrients may change but the Rainbow Balance Chart will remain the same.

Shopping List
tomato-based pasta sauce
apples
kiwifruit
grapes
cantaloupe
Parmesan cheese

1 lb	spaghetti (about half 900 g package)	500 g
2 cups	Batch Ground Meat and Vegetables (page 88)	500 mL
1	jar (750 mL) tomato-based pasta sauce	1
⅓ cup	water (use to rinse jar of pasta sauce)	75 mL
6 tbsp	grated Parmesan cheese	90 mL

1. In large pot of boiling water, cook spaghetti according to package directions; drain.
2. Meanwhile, in saucepan, simmer Batch Ground Meat and Vegetables, pasta sauce and water for 3 to 5 minutes or until heated through. Serve over spaghetti.
3. Sprinkle each serving with Parmesan cheese.

Makes 8 servings

Try not to put the container of Parmesan cheese on the table. Not only is it expensive, but each tablespoon (15 mL) adds 2 grams of fat.

Refrigerate any leftover Extra-Speedy Spaghetti Sauce for up to 3 days.

Fruit Plate

2	medium apples, cored and sectioned	2
2	kiwifruit, cut in half	2
¼ lb	grapes	125 g
Half	medium cantaloupe, peeled and cut in wedges	Half

1. Arrange apples, kiwifruit, grapes and cantaloupe on serving plate.

Makes 8 servings

Cooking perfect pasta!

1. Use a large pot.
2. Use plenty of boiling water, about 16 cups (4 L) per pound (500 g) of dry pasta. It is not necessary to add salt to the water.
3. Cook pasta, uncovered and stirring occasionally. This will keep the pasta from sticking together. There is no need to add oil to the water to keep pasta from sticking if you use lots of boiling water and stir pasta occasionally.

Supper includes Extra-Speedy Spaghetti Supper and Fruit Plate

Per serving of supper

Calories	483
Protein	19g
Fat	10g
Carbohydrate	82g
Dietary fibre	7g

Excellent source of vitamin A, vitamin C, thiamine, riboflavin, niacin, vitamin B6, vitamin B12, iron, zinc

Good source of folic acid

Very high source of dietary fibre

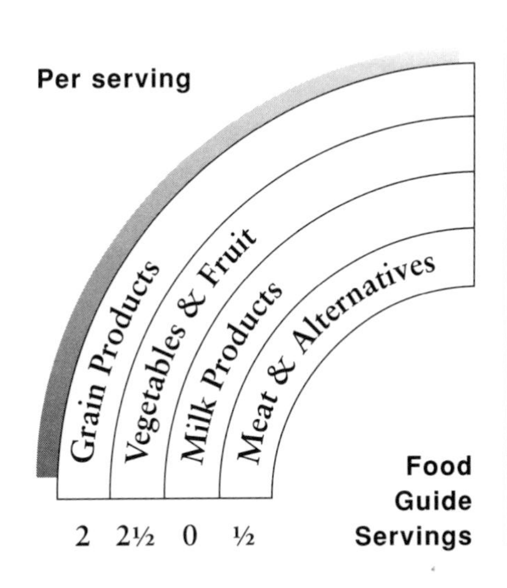

Filling in the Rainbow

Complete this meal with a serving from the Milk Products group.

Ground Beef Stroganoff with Noodles

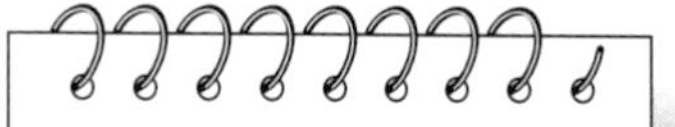

Shopping List
mushrooms
condensed golden mushroom soup
broad egg noodles
light sour cream
parsley (optional)

Do not boil stroganoff once sour cream has been added because it will curdle.

This speedier version of Beef Stroganoff uses Batch Ground Meat and Vegetables. If you have Batch Ground Meat and Vegetables in the freezer, this supper can be on the table in 20 minutes.

1 tbsp	vegetable oil	15 mL
¾ lb	mushrooms, sliced (about 4 cups/1 L)	375 g
2 cups	Batch Ground Meat and Vegetables	500 mL
2 tbsp	sherry	25 mL
1	can (10 oz/ 284 mL) condensed golden mushroom soup	1
½ cup	water	125 mL
¼ tsp	pepper	1 mL
1	package (375 g) broad egg noodles	1
1 cup	light sour cream (5% M.F.)	250 mL
2 tbsp	chopped fresh parsley (optional)	25 mL

1. In large nonstick skillet, heat oil over medium-high heat; add mushrooms and sauté for 6 to 8 minutes until golden and moisture has evaporated.
2. Add Batch Ground Meat and Vegetables, sherry, soup, water and pepper; reduce heat and simmer, uncovered, for 2 minutes.
3. Meanwhile, in large pot of boiling water, cook noodles according to package directions; drain.
4. Remove sauce from heat; stir in sour cream, and parsley (if using). Serve over noodles.

Makes 6 servings

To make 2 cups (500 mL) of Batch Ground Meat and Vegetables

¾ lb	lean ground beef	375 g
1	medium onion, chopped or minced	1
1	medium carrot, chopped or minced	1
1	stalk celery, chopped or minced (optional)	1
1	clove garlic, minced, or ¼ tsp (1 mL) garlic powder	1

1. In large nonstick skillet, cook meat over medium-high heat, breaking up with back of spoon, for 4 to 5 minutes or until no longer pink; drain fat.
2. Add onion, carrot, celery (if using) and garlic; simmer, uncovered, for 5 to 6 minutes. Use immediately or cool and refrigerate for up to 2 days or freeze for up to 3 months.

Makes 2 cups (500 mL)

Calories	453
Protein	24g
Fat	14g
Carbohydrate	57g
Dietary fibre	5g

Excellent source of vitamin A, thiamine, riboflavin, niacin, vitamin B12, iron, zinc

Good source of vitamin B6

High source of dietary fibre

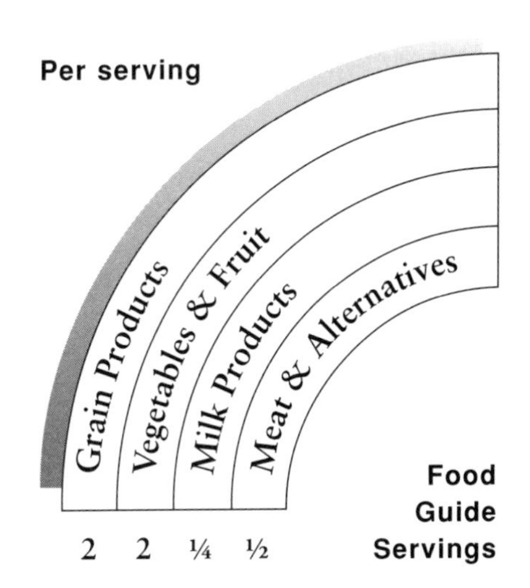

Filling in the Rainbow

This meal provides a ¼ serving from the Milk Products group and a ½ serving from the Meat & Alternatives group. This may be enough to balance the rest of your day. If not, choose additional servings from these two food groups as required.

Chili and Cornbread

This hearty meal is a great crowd-pleaser after a day at the hockey rink or on the slopes.

4 cups	Batch Ground Meat and Vegetables (page 88)	1 L
2	cans (each 28 oz/796 mL) tomatoes, 1 drained and 1 undrained	2
1	can (10 oz/284 mL) condensed tomato soup	1
2	cans (each 19 oz/540 mL) red kidney beans, drained but not rinsed	2
1	large purple onion, chopped	1
1	medium sweet green pepper, chopped	1
2 tbsp	chili powder	25 mL
½ tsp	Tabasco sauce (optional)	2 mL

1. In large pot or Dutch oven, combine Batch Ground Meat and Vegetables, tomatoes, tomato soup, kidney beans, onion, green pepper, chili powder and Tabasco sauce, if using.
2. Simmer, stirring occasionally, for 45 to 60 minutes or until thickened. Serve with Cornbread.

Makes 12 servings, 1 cup (250 mL) each

Refrigerate extra chili to use:

- as baked potato topping with grated cheese
- as Sloppy Joes
- in Warm Taco Salad (page 102)
- in Bail-Out Bean Burritos (Variation) (page 134)

Shopping List

canned tomatoes
condensed tomato soup
canned red kidney beans
large purple onion
green pepper
cornmeal
low-fat plain yogurt

Refrigerate chili for up to 3 days or freeze in 1-cup (250 mL), 2-cup (500 mL) or 4-cup (1 L) portions for up to 3 months. Do not refreeze chili if Batch Ground Meat and Vegetables was previously frozen.

Instead of Cornbread, which provides 2 servings from the Grain Products group, you can substitute 1 cup (250 mL) Perfect Microwave Rice (page 45), 1 cup (250 mL) Quicky Couscous (page 77) or simply serve with 2 slices of whole wheat toast.

Cornbread can also be made in greased or paper-lined muffin tins. Bake for 15 to 18 minutes or until tester inserted in centre comes out clean. Makes 24 small muffins (1 Grain Products serving, and 4 g fat and 146 calories per muffin).

Cornbread

2¾ cups	all-purpose flour	675 mL
1½ cups	cornmeal	375 mL
½ cup	granulated sugar	125 mL
1 tbsp	baking powder	15 mL
1 tsp	baking soda	5 mL
½ tsp	salt	2 mL
2 cups	low-fat plain yogurt (1 to 2% M.F.)	500 mL
⅓ cup	vegetable oil	75 mL
2	eggs	2

1. Preheat oven to 375°F (190°C). Lightly grease 9- x 13-inch (3 L) baking dish or spray with nonstick cooking spray.
2. In large bowl, combine flour, cornmeal, sugar, baking powder, baking soda and salt.
3. In separate bowl, whisk together yogurt, oil and eggs; add to dry ingredients, stirring gently until just blended. Spread in baking dish.
4. Bake for 25 to 30 minutes or until tester inserted in centre comes out clean.

Makes 12 servings

Per serving

Calories	527
Protein	25g
Fat	14g
Carbohydrate	75g
Dietary fibre	10g

Excellent source of vitamin A, thiamine, riboflavin, niacin, folic acid, vitamin B12, iron, zinc

Good source of vitamin C, vitamin B6, calcium

Very high source of dietary fibre

Cornbread can be frozen whole or in individual servings for up to 3 months.

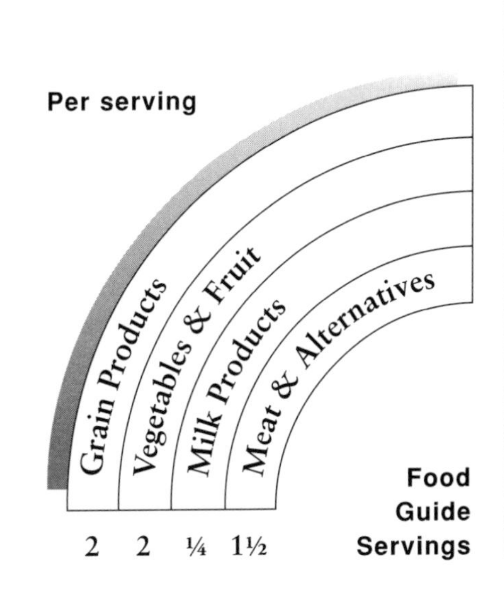

Filling in the Rainbow

Complete this meal with a serving of Milk Products, if necessary to balance the rest of the day.

Shopping List

tomato-based pasta sauce
cottage cheese
part-skim mozzarella cheese
oven-ready lasagna noodles
carrots
green pepper
cucumber
low-fat plain yogurt

Use a 200 gram package of shredded part-skim mozzarella cheese to speed up preparation time.

Easy On Ya Lasagna

We first started testing this recipe using regular noodles. After trying it, Bev's friend Anna Dawson suggested using oven-ready lasagna noodles as they were so much faster and easier to work with. We gave them a try and were completely convinced! We have included the Veggies and Dip as part of the complete supper meal. Serve them before supper while the lasagna is cooking.

2 cups	Batch Ground Meat and Vegetables (page 88)	500 mL
1	jar (750 mL) tomato-based pasta sauce	1
1 cup	hot water	250 mL
1	egg	1
1	package (300 g) frozen chopped spinach, thawed and squeezed dry (optional)	1
1	container (500 g) cottage cheese (2% M.F.)	1
8 oz	part-skim mozzarella cheese, shredded	250 g
12 to 15	oven-ready lasagna noodles	12 to 15
¼ cup	grated Parmesan cheese	50 mL

1. Preheat oven to 350°F (180°C). Lightly grease 9- x 13-inch (3 L) glass baking dish or spray with nonstick cooking spray.
2. In 8-cup (2 L) measuring cup, combine Batch Ground Meat and Vegetables, pasta sauce and hot water to make 6 cups (1.5 L). Set aside.
3. In medium bowl, lightly beat egg; stir in spinach (if using), cottage cheese and mozzarella cheese, reserving ½ cup (125 mL) of mozzarella cheese to sprinkle on top of the lasagna.

4. Cover bottom of prepared dish with about 1 cup (250 mL) sauce. Top with 4 or 5 noodles, trimming to fit. Spread half of the cheese mixture over top. Top with about 1½ cups (375 mL) of the sauce. Arrange 4 or 5 more noodles over top, trimming to fit. Spread with remaining cheese mixture. Repeat sauce and noodle layers once. Top with remaining 2 cups (500 mL) sauce. Sprinkle with Parmesan and reserved mozzarella cheese.
5. Bake, uncovered, for 40 to 45 minutes or until bubbling. Let stand for 10 minutes. Serve with Veggies and Dip.

Makes 8 servings

Veggies and Dip

4	medium carrots, cut into sticks	4
2	medium sweet green peppers, cut into strips	2
½	English cucumber, sliced	½

Dip

⅔ cup	low-fat plain yogurt (1-2% M.F.)	150 mL
¼ cup	light mayonnaise	50 mL
4 tsp	packaged dip seasoning mix	20 mL

1. Combine yogurt, mayonnaise and seasoning mix, blending well.
2. Serve surrounded with carrots, green pepper and cucumber.

Makes 8 servings

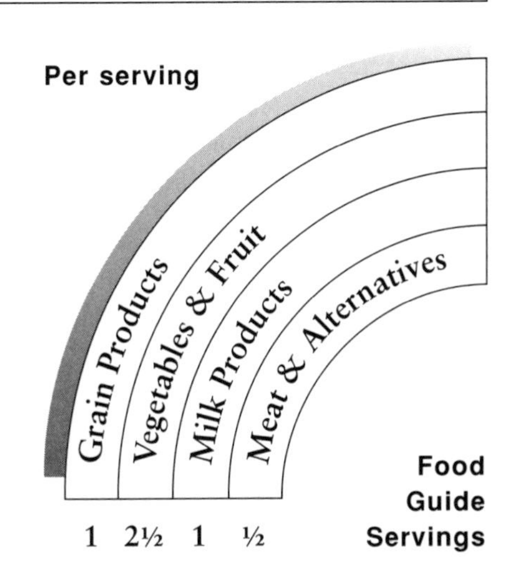

Supper includes Easy on Ya Lasagna and Veggies and Dip

Per serving of supper

Calories	498
Protein	34g
Fat	18g
Carbohydrate	52g
Dietary fibre	5g

Excellent source of vitamin A, vitamin C, thiamine, riboflavin, niacin, vitamin B6, folic acid, vitamin B12, calcium, iron, zinc

High source of dietary fibre

Cooked lasagna can be frozen in individual portions. To reheat, cover and microwave frozen portion on microwaveable dish on Medium-Low for 7 to 10 minutes or until heated through.

If you use Batch Ground Meat and Vegetables that have been previously frozen, do not freeze lasagna.

Filling in the Rainbow

This meal provides a ½ serving from the Meat & Alternatives group, which may be all that is needed to balance the rest of the day.

Shepherd's Pie

This is a warm family favourite. It can be made up very quickly if you have a supply of Batch Ground Meat and Vegetables stored in the freezer. Cook the potatoes while you are preparing the filling. If the kids don't like their veggies all mixed up with the Shepherd's Pie, make it without the frozen vegetables and serve them on the side. Substitute a can of tomato soup for the Italian-style tomato soup, if you wish.

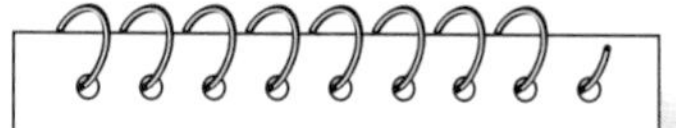

Shopping List

potatoes
Italian-style tomato soup
frozen mixed vegetables

Shepherd's Pie can also be made in two 10-inch (25 cm) pie plates.

Shepherd's Pie does not freeze well.

Shepherd's Pie can be completely assembled up to one day ahead and refrigerated; increase cooking time by 10 to 15 minutes.

Use a soft margarine made from canola, corn, safflower or olive oil. Make sure your margarine has a high amount of polyunsaturated and monounsaturated fat (6 grams or more per 10 gram serving).

Mashed Potatoes

3 lb	potatoes (about 6 large), peeled and quartered	1.5 kg
½ cup	2% milk or buttermilk	125 mL
2 tbsp	soft margarine	25 mL
	Salt and pepper	
½ tsp	paprika	2 mL

Filling

4 cups	Batch Ground Meat and Vegetables (page 88)	1 L
1	can (10 oz/284 mL) Italian-style tomato soup	1
2 cups	frozen mixed vegetables (peas, carrots, corn)	500 mL
1 tbsp	Worcestershire sauce	15 mL

1. In large pot, cover potatoes with water; bring to boil. Reduce heat, cover and simmer for 20 to 25 minutes or until tender; drain. Add milk, margarine, salt and pepper; mash until smooth. Set aside.
2. Meanwhile, preheat oven to 350°F (180°C). Lightly grease 9- x 13-inch (3 L) glass baking dish or spray with nonstick cooking spray.

3. Combine Batch Ground Meat and Vegetables, soup, frozen vegetables and Worcestershire sauce. Spread in prepared dish.
4. Top with mashed potatoes; sprinkle with paprika.
5. Bake for 30 to 40 minutes or until bubbling.

Makes 8 servings

Per serving

Calories	346
Protein	20g
Fat	11g
Carbohydrate	42g
Dietary fibre	4g

Excellent source of vitamin A, niacin, vitamin B6, vitamin B12, zinc

Good source of thiamine, riboflavin, folic acid, iron

High source of dietary fibre

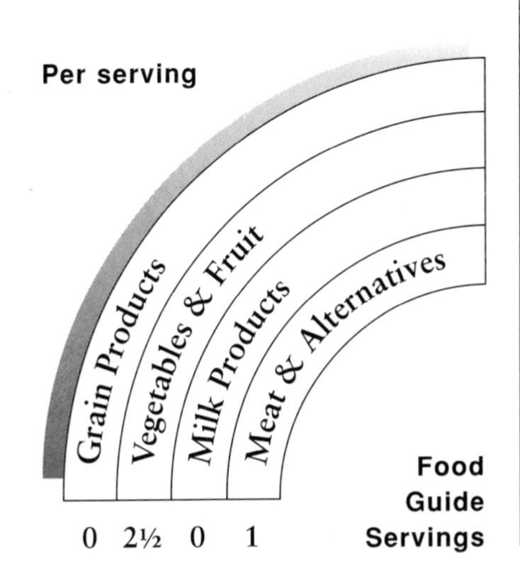

Filling in the Rainbow

Complete this meal with a serving each from the Grain Products and the Milk Products group, if necessary, to balance the rest of the day.

Shopping List
lettuce
tortilla chips
tomato
green pepper
low-fat plain yogurt
prepared salsa
part-skim mozzarella cheese

When shopping for greens, choose dark, leafy ones to get more nutrients. Spinach, romaine and green leafy lettuce are good choices.

Warm Taco Salad

This speedy salad can be enjoyed year round. Substitute 1 cup (250 mL) of leftover Chili (page 96) or Vegetarian Pasta Sauce (page 124) for the Batch Ground Meat and Vegetables, spices, cornstarch and water. This meal contains 20 grams of fat per serving, so balance the rest of your day with lower-fat choices at other meals and snacks.

1 cup	Batch Ground Meat and Vegetables (page 88)	250 mL
½ tsp	each ground coriander, cumin and chili powder	2 mL
½ tsp	cornstarch	2 mL
¼ cup	water	50 mL
6 cups	torn lettuce	1.5 L
4 cups	tortilla chips or broken taco shells	1 L
1	large tomato, chopped (about 8 oz/250 g)	1
1	medium sweet green or yellow pepper, sliced	1
½ cup	low-fat plain yogurt (1 to 2% M.F.)	125 mL
½ cup	prepared salsa	125 mL
1 cup	shredded part-skim mozzarella cheese	250 mL

1. In large nonstick skillet over medium heat, cook Batch Ground Meat and Vegetables, coriander, cumin and chili powder for 1 to 2 minutes or until fragrant.
2. In small bowl, blend cornstarch with water; add to pan and cook, stirring, for 2 to 3 minutes or until thickened.

3. Place 1½ cups (375 mL) lettuce on each of 4 dinner plates. Arrange tortilla chips on top of lettuce around edge.
4. Sprinkle ¼ cup (50 mL) meat mixture on top of lettuce and chips. Top with tomato, pepper, yogurt and salsa. Sprinkle with cheese.

Makes 4 servings

Per serving

Calories	418
Protein	22g
Fat	20g
Carbohydrate	40g
Dietary fibre	6g

Excellent source of vitamin A, vitamin C, riboflavin, niacin, folic acid, vitamin B12, calcium, zinc

Good source of thiamine, vitamin B6, iron

Very high source of dietary fibre

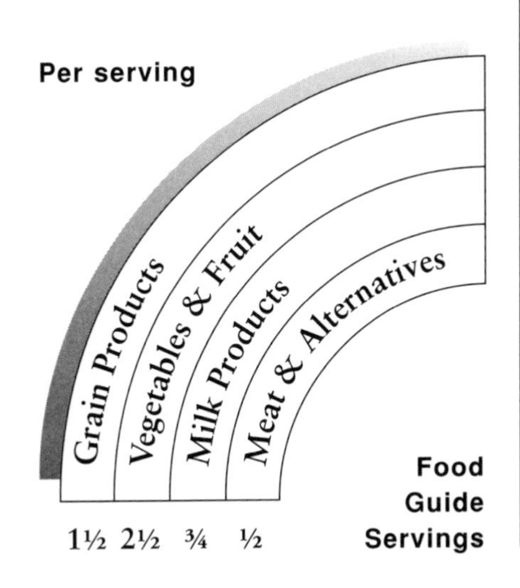

Filling in the Rainbow

This meal includes something from all four food groups. It provides ½ serving from the Meat & Alternatives group, which may be all that is needed if choices from this group are made earlier in the day.

Perfect Pizza Dough

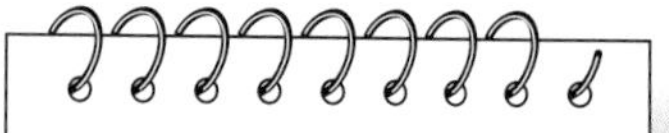

Shopping List
part-skim mozzarella cheese
prepared pizza sauce
pepperoni

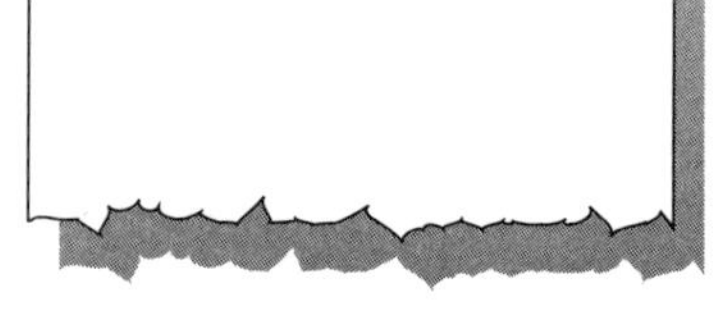

This recipe can also be made using 2½ cups (625 mL) of all-purpose flour.

After Step 3, pizza dough can be refrigerated, wrapped in oiled plastic wrap, for up to 2 days or frozen for up to 4 months. Defrost dough overnight in the refrigerator. Let dough come to room temperature before shaping. (Microwave on Low for 1-2 minutes.)

Make up a batch or two of Perfect Pizza Dough ahead of time and keep it handy in the fridge or freezer for quick suppers on those extra-busy days. Bags of prepared pizza dough can be purchased at the grocery store. One bag usually makes two 12-inch (30 cm) pizza rounds.

2 cups	all-purpose flour (approx)	500 mL
½ cup	whole wheat flour	125 mL
1 tbsp	quick-rising instant yeast	15 mL
1 tsp	granulated sugar	5 mL
½ tsp	salt	2 mL
1 cup	warm water	250 mL
1 tbsp	olive oil	15 mL

1. In large bowl, combine all-purpose and whole wheat flours, yeast, sugar and salt. Stir in water and oil until blended.
2. Turn dough onto lightly floured surface; knead for 8 to 10 minutes or until smooth and elastic, adding more flour as required to prevent dough from sticking. Cover and let rest for 10 minutes.
3. Divide dough into 2 balls; flatten into 2 disks.

Makes enough for two 12-inch (30 cm) pizza rounds or 8 pizza pockets

Food Processor Method

In food processor combine flours, yeast, sugar and salt; process for 5 to 10 seconds until combined. In small measuring cup, combine water and oil. With machine running, pour through feed tube, processing for 60 to 90 seconds. Turn dough onto floured work surface; knead in more flour, if necessary, to form smooth ball. Cover and let rest for 10 minutes before shaping into 2 disks.

Pizza Pockets

These freeze well, so double the recipe as they disappear fast! Our kids ask for these all the time. Once the dough is made, kids can make their own pizza pockets with a little help.

1 tbsp	cornmeal	15 mL
2 cups	shredded part-skim mozzarella cheese	500 mL
1 cup	prepared pizza sauce	250 mL
1 cup	thinly sliced pepperoni rounds (about 4 oz/125 g)	250 mL
1 recipe	Perfect Pizza Dough (opposite)	1 recipe

1. Preheat oven to 450°F (230°C). Lightly grease cookie sheet or spray with nonstick cooking spray; dust with cornmeal.
2. In bowl, combine mozzarella cheese, pizza sauce and pepperoni. Set aside.
3. Divide Perfect Pizza Dough into 8 equal balls; flatten each into 6- to 8-inch (15 to 20 cm) round disk. Top each with ⅛ of the sauce mixture.
4. Lightly wet dough around edges; fold in half over filling and seal edges by pressing together well with back of fork. Place on prepared cookie sheet.
5. Bake in bottom half of oven for 12 to 15 minutes or until golden brown.

Makes 8 servings

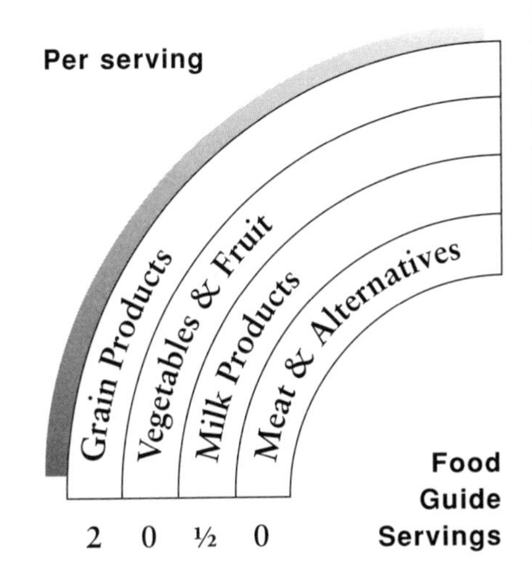

Per serving

Calories	341
Protein	16g
Fat	15g
Carbohydrate	35g
Dietary fibre	2g

Excellent source of niacin, folic acid, vitamin B12

Good source of thiamine, riboflavin, calcium, iron, zinc

Moderate source of dietary fibre

MEAL TO GO

Wrap heated Pizza Pocket in paper towel and then in foil. Pizza Pocket will stay hot for up to 1 hour.

Filling in the Rainbow

The amount of tomato sauce and pepperoni in each Pizza Pocket is not enough to equal half a serving from the Vegetables & Fruit and Meat & Alternatives groups. A serving of Veggies and Dip (page 91) or a piece of fruit will round out this meal. Have 2 to 3 servings from the Meat & Alternatives group throughout the day.

Shopping List

flatbread round (if using)
part-skim mozzarella cheese
large tomato
feta cheese
black olives (optional)
sweet onion (optional)

Canada's Food Guide to Healthy Eating tells us to eat 5 to 10 servings of vegetables and fruit each day. Most grocery stores in Canada have more than 200 different vegetables and fruits to choose from. So go ahead and try something new!

Mediterranean Pizza

This pizza is a nice change from the usual variety. It's also good cold and makes a great meal to go. Try fresh basil if you have it available. It does make a difference! Serve with a salad or fresh fruit for dessert to top up your servings from the Vegetables & Fruit group.

1 tbsp	cornmeal	15 mL
1	12-inch (30 cm) Perfect Pizza Dough round or 1 flatbread round	1
1 tbsp	olive oil	15 mL
1 cup	shredded part-skim mozzarella cheese	250 mL
1	large tomato, sliced (8 oz/250 g)	1
¼ cup	crumbled feta cheese	50 mL
¼ cup	each sliced black olives and thinly sliced sweet onion (optional)	50 mL
1 tbsp	dried basil or ¼ cup (50 mL) chopped fresh basil	15 mL

1. Preheat oven to 450°F (230°C) if using Perfect Pizza Dough or 400°F (200°C) if using flatbread round. Lightly grease cookie sheet or 12-inch (30 cm) pizza pan or spray with nonstick cooking spray; dust with cornmeal.
2. Arrange Perfect Pizza Dough round on prepared pan. Brush with olive oil. Sprinkle with mozzarella.
3. Top with tomato, feta cheese, olives and onion (if using) and basil.
4. Bake in bottom half of oven for 10 to 15 minutes or until crust is golden and filling is bubbly. Cut into 6 slices.

Makes 3 servings, 2 slices each

For a Speedy Salad

Wash lettuce ahead of time, wrap in paper towels and store in a heavy plastic bag or ventilated container. Choose dark green leafy greens such as romaine or spinach because they are higher in nutrients. Toss with grated carrots and All-Purpose Vinaigrette (page 136) or a calorie-reduced or fat-free salad dressing for a quick salad. One cup (250 mL) of fresh green salad counts as 1 serving from the Vegetables & Fruit group.

Chunky No-Lettuce Salad

Washing salad greens always takes time. Instead, cut up 3 cups (750 mL) raw vegetables of your choice. Toss with 1/4 cup (50 mL) bottled calorie-reduced vinaigrette-type salad dressing. Makes 3 cups (750 mL). One serving of this salad counts as two servings from the Vegetables & Fruit group.

Per serving

Calories	417
Protein	19g
Fat	16g
Carbohydrate	49g
Dietary fibre	4g

Excellent source of riboflavin, niacin, folic acid, vitamin B12, calcium, zinc

Good source of vitamin A, thiamine, vitamin B6, iron

High source of dietary fibre

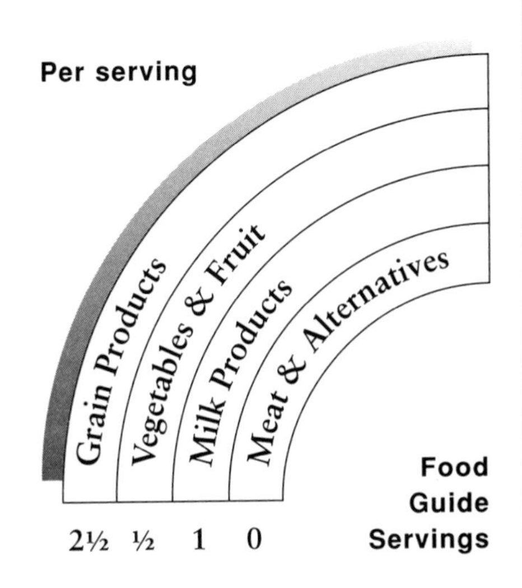

Filling in the Rainbow

This meal does not include a serving from the Meat & Alternatives group. Scrambled eggs for breakfast and a ham sandwich at lunch will meet your daily requirement of 2 to 3 servings from this group.

Roast Turkey Breast and Vegetable Supper

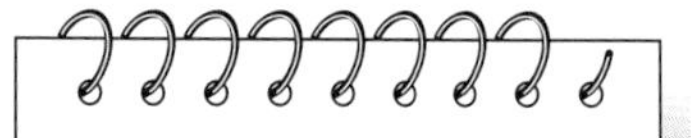

Shopping List
1 turkey breast (about 2 lb/1 kg)
potatoes
acorn squash
fresh or frozen cranberries
frozen peas

CRANBERRY SAUCE
In large saucepan, combine 1 package (12 oz/350 g) fresh cranberries, 1 cup (250 mL) each granulated sugar and water, grated rind of 1 small lemon (optional). Stir to dissolve sugar. Bring to boil over medium heat; reduce heat and simmer for 8 to 10 minutes until thickened. Makes 2½ cups (625 mL).

Why not cook two turkey breasts and use the extra one to make Turkey Pot Pie (page 112) or Curried Turkey Salad (page 110)? Leftover roast turkey can also be cubed and frozen in airtight containers for up to 3 months.

Here is a quick lower-fat alternative to the traditional turkey dinner. Now there is no excuse not to prepare a roast turkey supper more often.

1	large turkey breast, bone in with skin on (about 2 lb/1kg)	1
½ tsp	each dried thyme and savory leaves and dried rosemary	2 mL
¼ tsp	pepper	1 mL
1½ cups	water or 1 cup (250 mL) water plus ½ cup (125 mL) white wine	375 mL

Pan Gravy

4 tsp	all-purpose flour	20 mL
1 cup	reserved cooking liquid from mashed potatoes or water	250 mL
	Salt and pepper	

1. Preheat oven to 350°F (180°C).
2. Sprinkle thyme, savory, rosemary and pepper over top of turkey breast; place in small roasting pan. Pour in water.
3. Roast for 70 to 80 minutes or until juices run clear when turkey is pierced with fork and meat thermometer registers 170°F (77°C). Remove to large plate and keep warm.
4. Pan Gravy: Sprinkle flour over pan juices; whisk until blended. Whisk in reserved cooking liquid from mashed potatoes until combined. Bring to boil over medium heat; reduce heat and simmer for 3 to 5 minutes or until thickened. Season with salt and pepper to taste. Add water to thin gravy, if necessary.
5. Remove skin from turkey breast. Slice and serve with pan gravy, cranberry sauce, mashed potatoes, Sugar Baked Squash and frozen peas.

Makes 6 servings

Mashed Potatoes

2 lb	potatoes (about 4 large), peeled and quartered	1 kg
⅓ cup	2% milk or buttermilk	75 mL
1 tbsp	soft margarine or butter	15 mL
	Salt and pepper	

1. In large pot, cover potatoes with water; bring to boil. Reduce heat, cover and simmer for 20 to 25 minutes or until tender; drain and reserve 1 cup (250 mL) cooking liquid for Pan Gravy.
2. Add milk, margarine, salt and pepper; mash.

Makes 6 servings

Sugar-Baked Squash

1	medium acorn or hubbard squash (about 2 lb/1 kg), seeded and cut into 6 wedges	1
2 tsp	soft margarine or butter	10 mL
1 tbsp	packed brown sugar	15 mL
	Pepper	

1. Preheat oven to 350°F (180°C). Place squash, cut sides up, in 8-cup (2 L) casserole dish; spread each wedge with margarine and sugar. Sprinkle with pepper.
2. Pour ¼ cup (50 mL) water into dish. Cook, covered, for 1 hour, uncovering for last 15 minutes of cooking.

Makes 6 servings

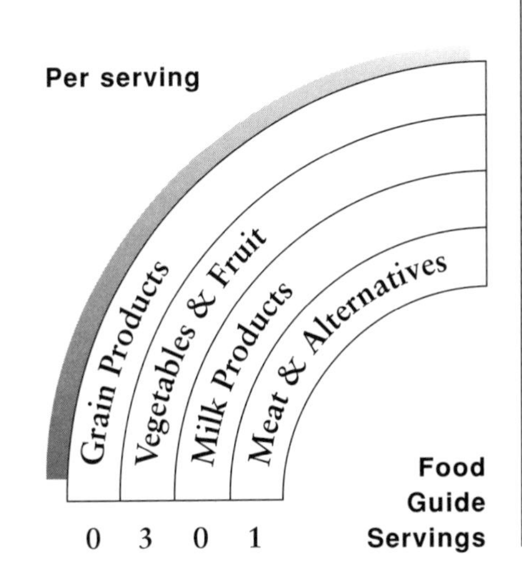

Supper includes Roast Turkey, Pan Gravy, Cranberry Sauce (2 tbsp/25 mL), Mashed Potatoes, Sugar-Baked Squash and frozen green peas (½ cup/125 mL.)

Per serving of supper

Calories	511
Protein	36g
Fat	14g
Carbohydrate	62g
Dietary fibre	9g

Excellent source of thiamine, niacin, vitamin B6, folic acid, iron, zinc

Good source of vitamin C, riboflavin, vitamin B12

Very high source of dietary fibre

For easier and safer cutting, pierce squash 3 or 4 times with knife; and microwave on High for 4 minutes.

Filling in the Rainbow

This meal is missing a serving from the Grain Products group and the Milk Products group. Make sure that the rest of the day includes 5 to 12 Grain Products and 2 to 4 Milk Product servings.

Curried Turkey Salad

This recipe is an adaptation of one produced by The Canadian Turkey Marketing Agency. This salad is best when it is prepared and served on the same day. Try it as a Meal to Go stuffed into a whole wheat pita bread.

1 lb	cubed cooked turkey breast (about 3 cups/750 mL)	500 g
2	stalks celery, sliced	2
2 cups	cantaloupe chunks	500 mL
1	can (14 oz/398 mL) pineapple chunks, drained, or 1 cup (250 mL) cubed fresh pineapple	1
1 cup	seedless red grapes, halved	250 mL
¼ cup	toasted slivered almonds (optional)	50 mL

Dressing

½ cup	light mayonnaise	125 mL
½ cup	low-fat plain yogurt (1-2% M.F.)	125 mL
2 tbsp	frozen orange juice concentrate	25 mL
½ to 1 tsp	curry powder	2 to 5 mL

1. In bowl, combine turkey, celery, cantaloupe, pineapple, grapes and almonds (if using).
2. Dressing: In small bowl, mix together mayonnaise, yogurt, orange juice concentrate and curry powder. Stir into turkey mixture. Chill.

Makes 6 servings

Shopping List
celery
cantaloupe
canned pineapple chunks
seedless red grapes
slivered almonds (optional)
light mayonnaise
low-fat plain yogurt

TARRAGON TURKEY SALAD
Substitute 2 tsp (10 mL) dried tarragon leaves for the curry powder.

BEAT THE HEAT:
Try barbecuing two 2-lb (1 kg) turkey breasts (bone-in, skin on): Sprinkle herbs over top of turkey breasts; close lid and barbecue over medium heat, skin side up, for 65 to 75 minutes or until juices run clear when turkey is pierced with fork and meat thermometer registers 170°F (77°C).

To toast almonds, bake in 350°F (180°C) oven for 3 to 6 minutes or until lightly brown, watching carefully as they burn easily. Alternatively, microwave on High for 3 to 5 minutes, stirring at 1-minute intervals.

Turkey is a lean meat that is an excellent source of protein and other essential nutrients. Here's the comparison between light and dark meat:

3 oz (90 g)	Light Meat	Dark Meat
Calories	141	168
Protein	27 g	26 g
Fat	3 g	6 g
Iron	1.2 mg	2.1 mg

Per serving

Calories	271
Protein	25g
Fat	9g
Carbohydrate	23g
Dietary fibre	1g

Excellent source of vitamin C, niacin, vitamin B6

Good source of vitamin A, folic acid, vitamin B12, zinc

MAKE-AHEAD

Refrigerate turkey mixture (without the almonds) and dressing separately for up to 1 day. Toss together just before serving. Sprinkle with almonds.

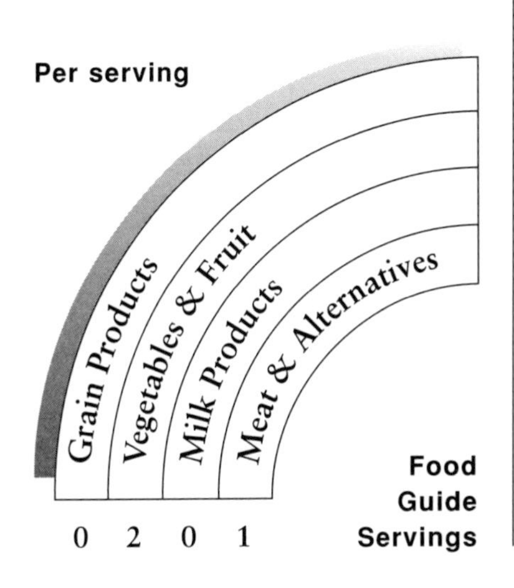

Filling in the Rainbow

Complete this meal with a serving from the Grain Products group and a serving from the Milk Products group. Since this meal is low in fibre, choose a low-fat bran muffin or a whole grain bread or roll to boost the fibre content.

Turkey Pot Pie

This incredibly simple Turkey Pot Pie is a delicious way to use up leftover cooked turkey. For mid-week entertaining serve with Spinach Salad with Honey-Orange Dressing (see opposite page) and assorted whole grain dinner rolls.

Shopping List
frozen baby carrots
frozen peas
9-inch (23 cm) unbaked frozen pie crust

MAKE-AHEAD
Turkey Pot Pie can be refrigerated for up to 1 day. Cool sauce before combining it with vegetables and cubed turkey. Add pie crust just before baking and increase cooking time at 350°F (180°C) by 5 to 10 minutes.

Since the pie crust is 1 inch (2.5 cm) smaller than the pie plate, it fits perfectly onto the top of the pot pie filling. There are no edges to crimp and no edges to burn!

1	9-inch (23 cm) unbaked frozen pie crust (175 g)	1
2 tbsp	soft margarine	25 mL
3 tbsp	all-purpose flour	50 mL
1	chicken bouillon cube or sachet	1
¾ cup	hot water	175 mL
1 cup	2% milk	250 mL
¼ tsp	ground thyme	1 mL
2 cups	cubed cooked turkey breast	500 mL
2 cups	frozen baby carrots	500 mL
1 cup	frozen peas	250 mL
	Pepper	

1. Preheat oven to 400°F (200°C). Lightly grease a 10-inch (20 cm) glass pie plate or spray with nonstick cooking spray. Defrost pie crust at room temperature for 20 to 30 minutes.
2. In large saucepan, melt margarine over medium heat; remove from heat. Add flour and stir until blended. Dissolve bouillon cube in hot water; whisk into pan along with milk and thyme. Bring to boil over medium heat; reduce heat and cook, stirring constantly, for 3 to 5 minutes until thickened. Remove from heat.
3. Stir in turkey, carrots, peas and pepper to taste; spoon into pie plate.
4. Gently fold pie crust in half and transfer to top of filling, unfolding to cover. Cut small vent hole in centre of pie crust.

5. Bake for 15 to 20 minutes; reduce oven temperature to 350°F (180°C) and continue baking for 20 to 25 minutes or until crust is golden and filling is bubbly.

Makes 4 servings

Per serving of Turkey Pot Pie

Calories	467
Protein	29g
Fat	23g
Carbohydrate	35g
Dietary fibre	4g

Excellent source of vitamin A, niacin, vitamin B6, zinc

Good source of thiamine, riboflavin, folic acid, vitamin B12, iron

High source of dietary fibre

Spinach Salad with Honey-Orange Dressing

1	package (10 oz/300 g) OR 1 bunch fresh spinach, washed well and spun dry	1
1	medium sweet yellow pepper, thinly sliced	1
1 cup	sliced mushrooms	250 mL
1	can (10 oz/284 mL) mandarin oranges, drained	1
	Honey-Orange Dressing:	
2 tbsp	rice vinegar or cider vinegar	25 mL
2 tbsp	orange juice	25 mL
1 tbsp	olive oil	15 mL
1 tbsp	liquid honey	15 mL
¼ tsp	dried tarragon	1 mL
Pinch	each salt and pepper	Pinch

1. Honey-Orange Dressing: In small measuring cup, combine vinegar, orange juice, oil, honey, tarragon, salt and pepper. Add the honey after the oil and the honey will "slip off" the measuring spoon.
2. Place spinach, pepper, mushrooms and oranges in large salad bowl; toss with dressing.

Makes 4 to 6 servings

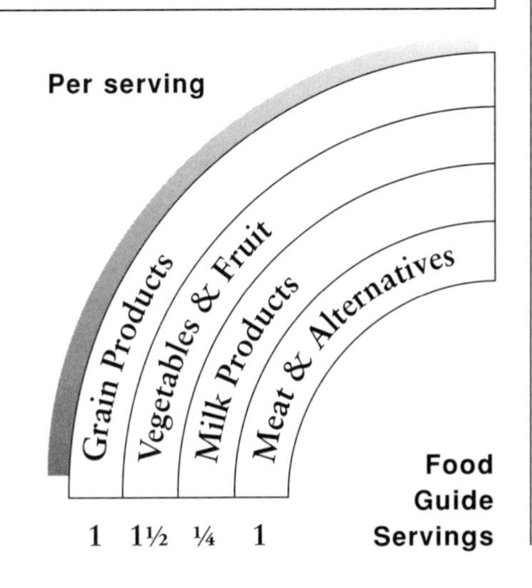

Filling in the Rainbow
This meal includes something from each of the four food groups. An additional serving from the Milk Products group may still be necessary for some family members to balance the rest of the day.

"Souper" Suppers

The nutrient-packed soups on the next four pages are great for supper. Team them up with a sandwich for a hearty meal. These soups take about 30 minutes or less to prepare and can all be made ahead of time. Store them in the fridge for up to 3 days or freezer for up to 3 months, with the exception of Spicy Garden Gazpacho which should not be frozen.

"Souper" Supper Suggestions

The soups that follow all provide at least one serving from the Vegetables & Fruit Group. What you need to balance your meal is something from the other three food groups. Try some of the combinations below or choose foods from the lists opposite to make your own complete "Souper" Supper meal.

1. Broccoli Soup (page 116); egg or tuna salad sandwich on whole wheat bread; chocolate pudding.
2. Carrot Ginger Soup (page 117); ham and cheese sandwich on a pumpernickel bagel; fresh fruit.
3. Spicy Garden Gazpacho (page 119), Hummus (opposite) and whole wheat pita bread triangles; frozen yogurt.
4. Lentil and Pasta Soup (page 118); peanut butter and crackers; glass of milk.
5. Carrot Ginger Soup (page 117); raisin bran muffin and chunk of Cheddar cheese.

Use reduced-fat salad dressing or light mayonnaise when making chicken, egg, tuna, turkey or salmon salad sandwiches.

Try lower-fat condiments in sandwiches such as mustard or salsa instead of mayonnaise, or use half mayonnaise and half of another condiment. Try spreading one slice of whole wheat bread with light mayonnaise and the other slice with cranberry sauce when making sliced turkey and chicken sandwiches.

Grain Products	Milk Products	Meat & Alternatives
2 servings • 2 slices whole grain or enriched bread (whole wheat, rye, pumpernickle, oatmeal, mixed grains); • 1 small bagel, roll, bun or muffin; • 8 crackers; • 1 small whole-wheat pita bread	**1 serving** • 1 cup (250 mL) skim, 1%, 2%, whole milk, or buttermilk; • 2 slices process cheese; • ¾ cup (175 mL) low-fat yogurt; • 50 g cheese (3" x 1" x 1") **½ serving** • ½ cup (125 mL) pudding; • 1 cup (250 mL) low-fat frozen yogurt; • ¾ cup (175 mL) light ice cream; • 1 cup (250 mL) low-fat cottage cheese (2% M.F.)	**1 serving** 50-100 g lean chicken, turkey or roast beef; • ⅓-⅔ can (6½ oz/184 g) tuna; • ⅓-⅔ can (7½/213 g) salmon; • 1-2 eggs; • 2 tbsp (25 mL) peanut butter; • ⅓-½ cup (75 mL-125 mL) Hummus

Don't double up the fat in sandwiches. Skip the butter or margarine on the bread when using sandwich fillings made with mayonnaise or salad dressing, such as egg, tuna, or chicken salad.

Add lettuce, sliced tomatoes, alfalfa sprouts, sliced cucumber and shredded carrot to sandwiches to increase your servings from the Vegetables & Fruit group.

Hummus (Chick-Pea Spread)

Serve with plain or toasted whole wheat pita bread triangles.

¼ cup	smooth peanut butter	50 mL
1 to 2	cloves garlic	1 to 2
3 tbsp	lemon juice	50 mL
½ tsp	ground cumin (optional)	2 mL
1	can (19 oz/540 mL) chick-peas, drained	1
¼ cup	water	50 mL

1. In food processor, blend peanut butter, garlic, lemon juice, and cumin (if using) until smooth.
2. Add chick-peas and water; blend until smooth. Add extra water, 1 tbsp (15 mL) at a time, to thin mixture if too thick.

Makes about 2 cups (500 mL)

Broccoli Soup

Per Serving of Broccoli Soup

Calories	106
Protein	5g
Fat	5g
Carbohydrate	12g
Dietary fibre	3g

Excellent source of vitamin A, vitamin C

Good source of folic acid

Moderate source of dietary fibre

One serving of Broccoli Soup provides 2 servings from the Vegetables & Fruit group. Use the "Souper" Supper Suggestions to complete your supper meal.

2 tbsp	soft margarine	25 mL
1	medium onion, chopped	1
1	large carrot, chopped	1
2 tbsp	all-purpose flour	25 mL
1	bunch fresh broccoli, chopped or 4 cups (1 L) frozen broccoli, thawed	1
3 cups	water	750 mL
2	vegetable or chicken bouillon cubes or sachets	2
1 cup	2% milk	250 mL
¼ tsp	pepper	1 mL
Dash	Tabasco sauce	Dash

1. In large saucepan, melt margarine over medium heat. Add onion and carrot; sauté for 5 minutes. Remove from heat; blend in flour.
2. Add broccoli, water and bouillon cubes; bring to boil over medium heat. Reduce heat and simmer, uncovered, for 5 to 7 minutes or until broccoli is tender. Keeping the lid off helps to keep the broccoli bright green.
3. In food processor or blender, purée soup, in batches, until smooth; return to saucepan.
4. Add milk, pepper and Tabasco; heat through but do not boil.

Makes 6 servings, 1 cup (250 mL) each

Carrot Ginger Soup

2 tbsp	soft margarine	25 mL
1	medium onion, chopped	1
5 cups	sliced carrots (about 1½ lb/750 g)	1.25 L
5 cups	water	1.25 L
3	vegetable or chicken bouillon cubes or sachets	3
1 cup	2% milk	250 mL
½ to ¾ tsp	ground ginger	2 to 4 mL
¼ tsp	pepper	1 mL
Pinch	ground nutmeg	Pinch

1. In large saucepan, melt margarine over medium heat; add onion and sauté for 3 minutes until softened.
2. Add carrots, water and bouillon cubes; bring to boil. Reduce heat, cover and simmer for 20 to 25 minutes or until carrots are tender.
3. In food processor or blender, purée soup, in batches, until smooth. Return to saucepan.
4. Add milk, ginger, pepper and nutmeg; heat through but do not boil.

Makes 8 servings, 1 cup (250 mL) each

Dark orange vegetables such as carrots and sweet potatoes are high in Beta-Carotene. High consumption of Beta-Carotene-rich vegetables and fruit is linked with a reduced risk of cancer. Currently there is no recommended nutrient intake for Beta-Carotene, however, eating 5 to 10 servings of vegetables and fruit per day with an emphasis on dark green or orange vegetables and fruit will satisfy your daily needs.

Per Serving of Carrot Ginger Soup

Calories	84
Protein	2g
Fat	4g
Carbohydrate	11g
Dietary fibre	2g

Excellent source of vitamin A

Moderate source of dietary fibre

If you like a creamy soup, decrease water to 4 cups (1 L) and increase milk to 2 cups (500 mL) Freeze soup without milk. Add milk to soup during reheating.

One serving of Carrot Ginger Soup provides 1½ servings from the Vegetables & Fruit group. Use the "Souper" Supper Suggestions to complete your supper meal.

Lentil and Pasta Soup

1 tbsp	vegetable oil	15 mL
2	medium onions, chopped	2
2	cloves garlic, minced	2
3	medium carrots, sliced	3
2 cups	sliced fennel (about 1 medium bulb) or celery	500 mL
1	can (19 oz/540 mL) lentils (undrained)	1
2	vegetable or chicken bouillon cubes or sachets	2
2	cans (each 28 oz/796 mL) tomatoes (undrained)	2
1½ cups	water	375 mL
2 tbsp	granulated sugar	25 mL
½ tsp	each dried savory and thyme	2 mL
¼ tsp	pepper	1 mL
½ cup	small pasta shells or macaroni	125 mL

1. In Dutch oven or large saucepan, heat oil over medium heat. Add onions and garlic; sauté for 3 to 5 minutes until onions are softened.
2. Add carrots, fennel, lentils, bouillon cubes, tomatoes, water, sugar, savory, thyme and pepper. Bring to boil; reduce heat and simmer for 25 to 30 minutes or until vegetables are tender, adding pasta for last 15 minutes of cooking. If soup is too thick, thin with water.

Makes 12 servings, 1 cup (250 mL) each

Shopping List
carrots
fennel bulb
canned lentils
canned tomatoes

Per serving of Lentil and Pasta Soup

Calories	122
Protein	6g
Fat	2g
Carbohydrate	23g
Dietary fibre	4g

Excellent source of vitamin A, folic acid

Good source of vitamin B6, iron

High source of dietary fibre

One serving of Lentil and Pasta soup provides 2 servings from the Vegetables & Fruit group. Use the "Souper" Supper Suggestions to complete your supper meal.

Spicy Garden Gazpacho

1	clove garlic	1
Quarter	medium sweet Spanish or Vidalia onion, cut in chunks	Quarter
1	medium sweet red pepper, cut in chunks	1
Half	medium cucumber, cut in chunks (about 1½ cups/375 mL)	Half
4	large tomatoes, cut in chunks (about 4 cups/1 L)	4
1	can (1½ cups/375 mL) vegetable juice cocktail	1
2 tbsp	olive oil	25 mL
2 tbsp	red wine vinegar	25 mL
¼ tsp	Tabasco sauce	1 mL
¼ tsp	pepper	1 mL

1. In food processor and with machine running, add garlic and onion; process for 1 minute or until minced.
2. Add red pepper, cucumber and tomatoes; process with on/off pulses until chopped, 45 to 90 seconds.
3. Transfer to large bowl; stir in vegetable juice, oil, vinegar, Tabasco and pepper.
4. Chill for 1 hour or overnight to allow flavours to blend.

Makes 12 servings, ⅔ cup (150 mL) each

Shopping List
Spanish onion
red pepper
cucumber
tomatoes
vegetable juice cocktail

Per Serving
Spicy Garden Gazpacho

Calories	47
Protein	1g
Fat	3g
Carbohydrate	6g
Dietary fibre	1g

Excellent source of vitamin C

Serve with a dollop (1 tbsp/ 15 mL) of light sour cream (5% M.F.). This will add 0.7 gram of fat per serving.

One serving of Spicy Garden Gazpacho provides 1 serving from the Vegetables & Fruit group. Use the "Souper" Supper Suggestions to complete your supper meal.

Basil Zucchini Strata

This recipe has been adapted from one produced by The Egg Producers of Ontario. It is an ideal late-summer or early fall make-ahead dish that can be served for supper, brunch or lunch. Dried basil can be substituted for the fresh, but the fresh basil really does make a difference. Serve with a simple Fresh Tomato Salad and you have a menu that will impress any guest!

6 cups	whole wheat bread cubes (about 8 slices), preferably stale	1.5 L
3 cups	finely diced zucchini (about 1 lb/500 g)	750 mL
1½ cups	shredded Swiss cheese	375 mL
6	eggs	6
2 cups	2% milk	500 mL
¼ cup	chopped fresh basil or 1 tbsp (15 mL) dried	50 mL
½ tsp	dry mustard	2 mL
¼ tsp	each ground nutmeg and pepper	1 mL

1. Lightly grease 10-cup (2.5 L) casserole dish or spray with nonstick cooking spray.
2. Spread half of the bread cubes in casserole dish; top with half of the zucchini and half of the cheese. Repeat layers.
3. In large bowl, beat eggs with milk, basil, mustard, nutmeg and pepper; pour over strata. Cover and refrigerate for at least 1 hour or overnight.
4. Preheat oven to 350°F (180°C).
5. Bake, uncovered, for 45 to 55 minutes or until golden and set in centre.

Makes 6 servings

Shopping List
whole wheat bread
zucchini
Swiss cheese
eggs
fresh basil
tomatoes
balsamic vinegar

Substitute old Cheddar cheese for the Swiss cheese.

MAKE-AHEAD
Tomatoes can be sliced and refrigerated for up to 2 hours ahead.

This meal contains 18 grams of fat, which is less than one-third of a woman's daily fat limit of 65 grams per day and one-fifth of a man's daily fat limit of 90 grams per day.

Basil Zucchini Strata is also tasty served with Spicy Garden Gazpacho (page 119).

Fresh Tomato Salad

There is nothing sweeter than garden-fresh tomatoes at the peak of the season. If you don't want to bother with the dressing, just slice the tomatoes and serve them with freshly ground pepper and a sprinkling of chopped fresh basil.

6	large tomatoes (about 3 lb/1.5 kg), sliced	6
2 tbsp	balsamic vinegar	25 mL
2 tsp	olive oil	10 mL
1 tsp	dried basil or 1 tbsp (15 mL) chopped fresh basil	5 mL
Pinch	pepper	Pinch

1. Arrange tomato slices on large plate.
2. Combine vinegar and oil; drizzle over tomatoes. Sprinkle with basil and pepper.

Makes 6 servings

Supper includes Basil Zucchini Strata and Fresh Tomato Salad

Per serving of supper

Calories	384
Protein	23g
Fat	18g
Carbohydrate	37g
Dietary fibre	6g

Excellent source of vitamin A, vitamin C, thiamine, riboflavin, niacin, folic acid, vitamin B12, calcium, zinc

Good source of vitamin B6, iron

Very high source of dietary fibre

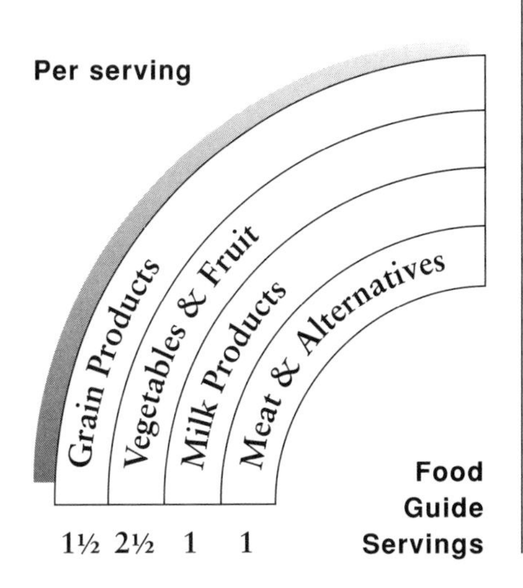

Filling in the Rainbow

This meal contains something from all 4 food groups.

Three-Bean Chili with Couscous

This meal contains only 5 grams of fat so why not finish the meal with ½ cup (125 mL) of light ice cream? This adds 5 grams of fat, or try ½ cup (125 mL) sherbet, which adds only 2 grams of fat. Defrost chili overnight in the refrigerator for a quick supper the next day. One serving of Cornbread (page 97) or 1 cup (250 mL) of Perfect Microwave Rice (page 45) are a nice change from the couscous and do not affect the Rainbow Balance Chart.

6 cups	Three Bean Chili (recipe opposite)	1.5 L
4 cups	Quicky Couscous (recipe below)	1 L

1. Heat chili. Serve with couscous.

Makes 4 servings

Quicky Couscous

2 cups	water	500 mL
2 tsp	olive oil	10 mL
1½ cups	quick-cooking couscous	375 mL
	Salt and pepper	

1. In medium saucepan, bring water and olive oil to boil. Stir in couscous.
2. Cover and remove from heat; let stand for 5 minutes. Fluff with fork. Add salt and pepper to taste.

Makes 4 cups (1 L)

Shopping List

red and green peppers
eggplant
canned red kidney beans
canned romano beans
canned black beans
canned tomatoes

It is more economical to use cooked dried beans than canned beans. Two cups (500 mL) of cooked dried beans can be substituted for one (19 oz/540 mL) can of drained beans. Freeze cooked dried beans in 2-cup (500 mL) amounts in airtight containers for up to 6 months. One lb (500 g), or 2 to 2½ cups (500 to 625 mL) of dried beans yields 5 to 6 cups (1.25 to 1.5 L) of cooked beans.

Beans, peas and lentils are high in fibre and low in fat. If you are following a vegetarian diet, choose beans, peas and lentils and grain foods such as rice, couscous, bread or pasta throughout the day to ensure an adequate protein intake. In addition, plan meals that also include foods that are high in iron, zinc and vitamin B12.

Baked Fish with Oven-Fried Potato Cubes (page 54)

Three-Bean Chili

1 tbsp	olive oil	15 mL
6	cloves garlic, minced	6
1	large sweet onion, chopped	1
1	each medium sweet red and green pepper, diced	1
1	small unpeeled eggplant, diced (about 1 lb/500 g)	1
1	can (19 oz/540 mL) red kidney beans, drained and rinsed	1
1	can (19 oz/540 mL) romano beans, drained and rinsed	1
1	can (19 oz/540 mL) black beans, drained and rinsed	1
3	cans (each 28 oz/796 mL) tomatoes, 2 tins drained, 1 tin undrained	3
2 tbsp	chili powder	25 mL
1 tbsp	each ground cumin, dried oregano and granulated sugar	15 mL
½ tsp	pepper	2 mL

1. In Dutch oven, heat oil over medium-high heat. Add garlic, onion, red and green peppers and eggplant; sauté for 8 to 10 minutes or until softened.
2. Add kidney, romano and black beans, tomatoes, chili powder, cumin, oregano, sugar and pepper; bring to boil. Reduce heat and simmer for 1 hour or until thickened.

Makes 18 cups (4.5 L)

Per serving

Calories	483
Protein	20g
Fat	5g
Carbohydrate	91g
Dietary fibre	13g

Excellent source of vitamin C, thiamine, niacin, folic acid, iron

Good source of vitamin A, riboflavin, vitamin B6, zinc

Very high source of dietary fibre

Three-Bean Chili can be frozen for up to 3 months. Store in 1-cup (250 mL), 2-cup (500 mL) or 4-cup (1 L) containers for speedy weeknight suppers.

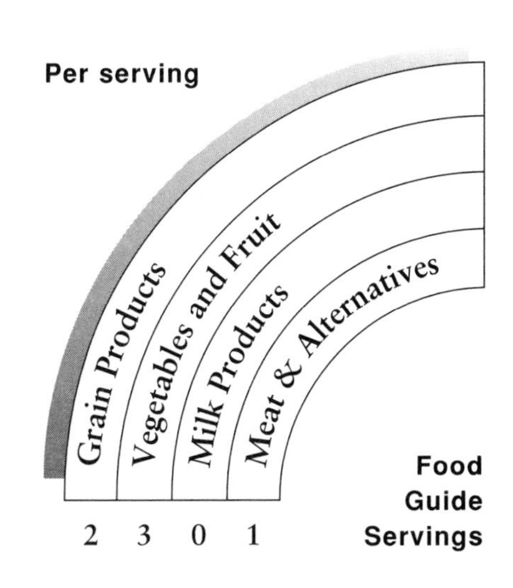

Filling in the Rainbow

Complete this meal with a serving from the Milk Products group.

Greek Pasta Salad (page 38)

Photo courtesy of Dairy Farmers of Canada

Fusilli with Vegetarian Pasta Sauce

Shopping List
eggplant
zucchini
mushrooms
Spanish onion
tomato-based pasta sauce
Parmesan cheese

Vegetarian Pasta Sauce can be frozen for up to 3 months. Freeze some in a 4-cup (1 L) portion to use in Vegetarian Lasagna (page 126).

This can be a bail-out meal in minutes if you keep Vegetarian Pasta Sauce in your freezer and defrost it overnight in the fridge. For a change, substitute penne or rotini pasta for the fusilli (see page 104).

8 oz	fusilli or penne pasta (about 3 cups/750 mL)	250 g
4 cups	Vegetarian Pasta Sauce (recipe opposite)	1 L
¼ cup	grated Parmesan cheese	50 mL

1. In large pot of boiling water, cook fusilli according to package directions; drain.
2. Meanwhile, in large bowl, microwave Vegetarian Pasta Sauce on High for 5 to 7 minutes or until heated through. Serve over fusilli.
3. Sprinkle each serving with Parmesan cheese.

Makes 4 servings

Purée Vegetarian Pasta Sauce in a food processor or blender and use it as a tasty alternative to prepared pizza sauce. Add ½ to 1 tsp (2 to 5 mL) dried Italian herb seasoning to 2 cups (500 mL) sauce if desired.

Substitute freshly shaved pieces of Parmesan cheese for the grated Parmesan cheese. It really makes the dish special!

Vegetarian Pasta Sauce

This makes a full pot. Everything will fit in!

2 tbsp	olive oil	25 mL
1	small eggplant, unpeeled (about 1 lb/500 g), coarsely chopped	1
3	medium zucchini, sliced (about 1½ lb/750 g)	3
1 lb	mushrooms, sliced (about 6 cups/1.5 L)	500 g
1	large Spanish or Vidalia onion, chopped	1
3	cloves garlic, minced	3
2	jars (each 750 mL) tomato-based pasta sauce	2

1. In Dutch oven, heat oil over medium heat; sauté eggplant, zucchini, mushrooms, onion and garlic for 30 to 40 minutes or until softened and moisture has evaporated.
2. Add pasta sauce; rinse each jar with ¼ cup (50 mL) water and add to pan.
3. Reduce heat and simmer for 5 to 10 minutes or until heated through.

Makes 10 to 12 cups (2.5 to 3 L)

Per serving

Calories	434
Protein	14g
Fat	10g
Carbohydrate	75g
Dietary fibre	8g

Excellent source of thiamine, riboflavin, niacin, vitamin B6, folic acid, iron

Good source of vitamin A, vitamin C, zinc

Very high source of dietary fibre

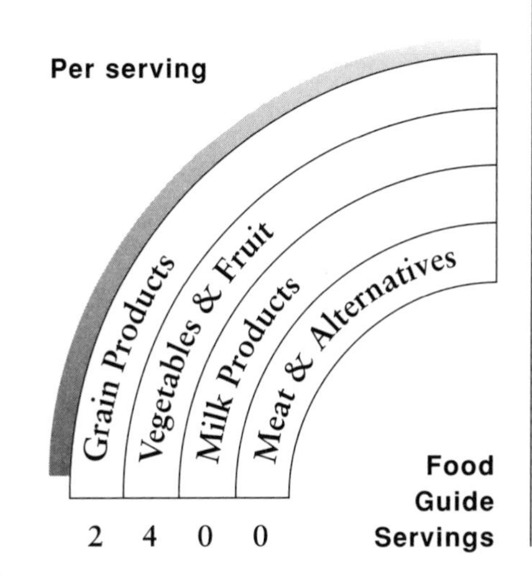

Filling in the Rainbow

Complete this meal with a serving from the Milk Products group. This meal does not contain a Meat & Alternatives serving. You can easily get a serving from this group earlier in the day. For example, a lean turkey sandwich at lunch and peanut butter on toast at breakfast will satisfy your daily needs.

Vegetarian Lasagna

This lasagna has a nice meaty texture due to the eggplant in the Vegetarian Pasta Sauce. Thanks to oven-ready lasagna noodles, it can be assembled in 20 minutes or less. Garlic Bread (opposite) is a tasty complement to this meal. One serving of Garlic Bread adds one serving of Grain Products and about 5 grams of extra fat.

Shopping List
light ricotta cheese
frozen chopped spinach
part-skim mozzarella cheese
oven-ready lasagna noodles
Parmesan cheese

4 cups	Vegetarian Pasta Sauce (page 125)	1 L
2 cups	hot water	500 mL
2	eggs	2
1	container (450 g) light ricotta cheese (5% M.F.)	1
1	package (300 g) frozen chopped spinach, thawed and squeezed dry	1
8 oz	shredded part-skim mozzarella cheese	250 g
12 to 15	oven-ready lasagna noodles	12 to 15
¼ cup	grated Parmesan cheese	50 mL

1. Preheat oven to 350°F (180°C). Lightly grease 9- x 13-inch (3 L) glass baking dish or spray with nonstick cooking spray.
2. In 8-cup (2 L) measuring cup, combine Vegetarian Pasta Sauce and hot water. Set aside. You should have 6 cups/1.5 L of sauce.
3. In separate bowl, beat eggs; blend in ricotta cheese, spinach and mozzarella.
4. Cover bottom of prepared dish with 2 cups (500 mL) sauce. Top with 4 or 5 noodles, trimming to fit. Spread half of the cheese mixture over top. Repeat layers once.
5. Top with about 1 cup (250 mL) sauce. Arrange remaining 4 to 5 noodles over sauce. Top with remaining sauce. Sprinkle with Parmesan cheese.
6. Bake, uncovered, for 45 to 55 minutes or until bubbling. Let stand for 10 minutes.

Makes 8 servings

Use a 200 gram package of shredded part-skim mozzarella cheese to speed up preparation time.

Unbaked Vegetarian Lasagna can be refrigerated for up to 1 day. Increase baking time by 5 to 10 minutes.

Cooked lasagna can be frozen for up to 3 months.

Microwave individual portions of frozen cooked lasagna on microwaveable plate, covered, on Medium-Low for 7 to 10 minutes or until heated through.

Garlic Bread

1	baguette or crusty bread 275 g (about 24 inches/ 60 cm long)	1
3 tbsp	soft margarine	50 mL
¼ tsp	garlic powder or 1 clove minced garlic	1 mL
2 tsp	chopped fresh herbs, (optional)	10 mL

1. Slice baguette into sixteen 1½-inch (4 cm) thick slices.
2. Blend margarine with garlic powder; divide mixture and spread on one side of each slice.
3. Wrap baguette in foil; heat at 350°F (180°C) for 5 minutes.

Makes 8 servings, 2 slices per serving

Per serving

Calories	385
Protein	24g
Fat	14g
Carbohydrate	43g
Dietary fibre	5g

Excellent source of vitamin A, riboflavin, niacin, folic acid, calcium, zinc

Good source of thiamine, vitamin B6, vitamin B12, iron

High source of dietary fibre

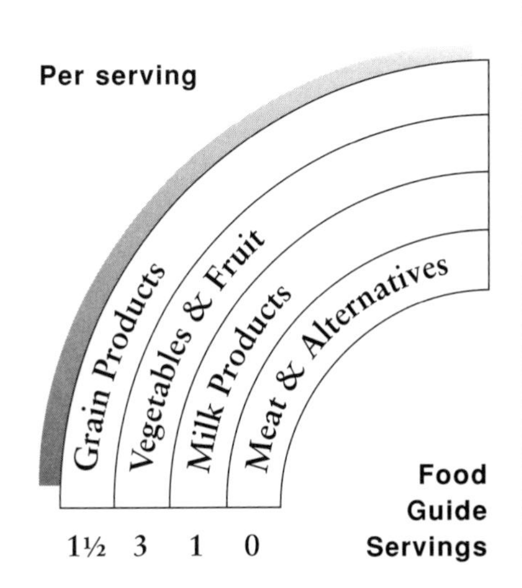

Filling in the Rainbow

This meal does not include a serving from the Meat & Alternatives group. An omelette for breakfast and Sweet Beans and Toast (page 142) at lunch will give you the necessary 2 to 3 servings from this food group to balance your day.

How Much Pasta Should I Cook?

One cup (250 mL) of cooked pasta according to Canada's Food Guide to Healthy Eating is 2 servings from the Grain Products group.

An average adult (or growing child) would eat about 1 cup (250 mL) of pasta (or more!) in a complete supper meal.

Preschoolers (age 2 to 5 years) would eat about ½ cup (125 mL) of cooked pasta, and babies and toddlers (age 9 months to 2 years) would eat ¼ cup to ½ cup (50 to 125 mL). These amounts represent one child-size serving according to Canada's Food Guide to Healthy Eating for Preschoolers (Health Canada – 1995). If your child is hungry on a particular day, he or she may ask for more. This is completely normal and extra servings should be offered (one at a time) if at all possible.

1 cup (250 mL) cooked pasta equals	½ cup (125 mL) uncooked macaroni or small shells
	½ inch (1 cm) diameter uncooked spaghetti, spaghettini, fettuccine, linguine or vermicelli (60 g)
	¾ cup (175 mL) uncooked fusilli or penne
	⅔ cup (150 mL) uncooked rotini

BAIL-OUT MEALS

These no-fuss meals can be made in 15 to 20 minutes. They don't require any advance preparation and use common pantry ingredients mostly from the Smart Kitchen Basic Shelf Ingredients list (page 12) and some pre-packaged frozen items.

These meals are great for days when you want to spend as little time as possible in the kitchen. Teens and caregivers can easily prepare these meals with a few simple instructions and a minimum of supervision.

Anytime Pizza

Most kids like their pizza plain with just sauce, cheese and pepperoni. This pizza fills the bill. It's also great for people who don't get home delivery or for those who prefer to make their own. To get half a Vegetables & Fruit serving for this meal, we have used ¾ cup/175 mL sauce per pizza. Because of the large amount of sauce, this pizza is best made with flatbread rounds because they absorb some of the pizza sauce. Extra pizza is great in lunch boxes, as a meal to go or a snack, anytime!

	Cornmeal	
2	12-inch (30 cm) round flatbreads	2
1½ cups	prepared pizza sauce	375 mL
8 oz	shredded part-skim mozzarella cheese	250 g
3 oz	thinly sliced pepperoni	100 g

1. Preheat oven to 400°F (200°C). Lightly grease 2 cookie sheets or two 12-inch (30 cm) round pizza pans; dust with cornmeal.
2. Place flatbreads on prepared pans; spread each with ¾ cup (175 mL) pizza sauce. Sprinkle evenly with cheese; top with pepperoni.
3. Bake in bottom half of oven for 10 to 12 minutes or until crust is golden and cheese is bubbly. Cut each pizza into 6 slices.

Makes 2 pizzas or 6 servings, 2 slices per serving

Shopping List
round flatbreads
prepared pizza sauce
part-skim mozzarella cheese
sliced pepperoni

NON-SLIP TIP
Sprinkle mozzarella on top of sauce before adding other ingredients. The cheese will keep the other ingredients from sliding off.

CONVENIENCE TIP
Pizza sauce comes in a variety of different sizes. We have used a 375 mL jar which provides 1½ cups of sauce.

Tips About Fat

You can add other toppings but watch how much extra fat you add. Here's the fat content of some popular pizza toppings (amount suitable for one 12-inch/30 cm pizza).

Pizza Toppings	Fat
Regular mozzarella cheese (170 g)	38g
Part-skim mozzarella cheese (170 g)	26g
Bacon (50 g)	23g
Pepperoni (50 g)	22g
Sausage (50 g)	17g
Olives (20 olives, 80 g)	12g
Feta cheese (50 g)	11g
Anchovies (50 g)	4g
Lean ham (50 g)	3g
Green, red, yellow pepper (1 medium)	trace
Mushrooms (½ cup/125 mL sliced)	trace
Pineapple (½ cup/125 mL sliced) 130 g	trace
Sliced tomatoes (1 medium)	trace
Hot peppers	trace

Per serving

Calories	579
Protein	28g
Fat	20g
Carbohydrate	70g
Dietary fibre	2g

Excellent source of vitamin B12, calcium, iron

Good source of niacin, zinc

Moderate source of dietary fibre

Per serving

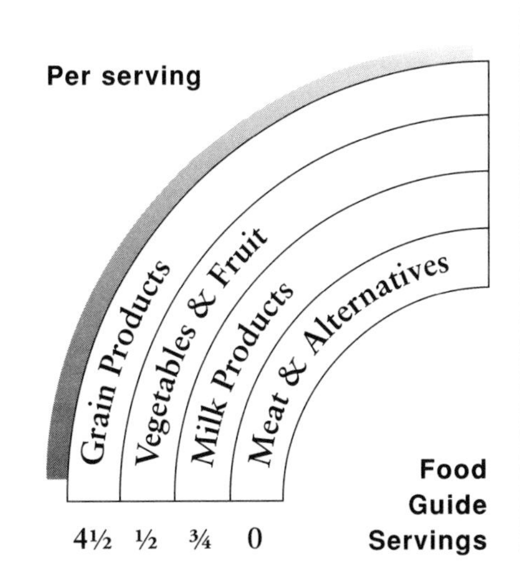

Filling in the Rainbow

Serve this meal with a fruit plate or cut-up raw vegetables to increase the number of Vegetables & Fruit servings. Choose high-nutrient fruits such as cantaloupe, oranges and berries. Have 2 to 3 servings of Meat & Alternatives at other meals and snacks throughout the day.

Bacon and Potato Frittata

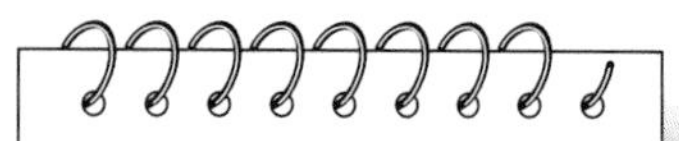

Shopping List

eggs
bacon
green onions
old Cheddar cheese
apples

Keep bacon handy in the freezer. Buy a 1-lb (500 g) package and divide it into 4 portions. Freeze each portion in airtight packages for up to 1 month. Defrost ¼ lb (125 g) of bacon in the microwave for 3 to 4 minutes.

Try Asparagus Frittata (page 26) and Zucchini and Red Pepper Frittata (page 50) if you are a frittata fan!

This meal shows how a little bit of bacon can go a long way in adding flavour to a dish without adding a lot of extra fat. Moderation is the key. This frittata has 21 grams of fat so balance the rest of your day accordingly. For a lower-fat alternative, substitute ¼ lb (125 g) of diced lean cooked ham for the bacon. Serve this frittata with crisp apple slices.

6	eggs	6
3 tbsp	water	50 mL
¼ lb	side bacon, diced	125 g
2	large potatoes (about 1 lb/500 g), peeled or unpeeled, cut into ½-inch (1 cm) cubes, or 2 cups (500 mL) cooked cubed potatoes	2
3	green onions, chopped	3
¼ tsp	pepper	1 mL
1 cup	shredded old Cheddar cheese	250 mL

1. Wrap handle of large nonstick skillet with foil, if necessary, to prevent it from burning when the frittata is placed under the broiler.
2. Preheat broiler.
3. In medium bowl whisk eggs with water; set aside.
4. In large nonstick skillet, fry bacon over medium heat until crisp; drain fat. Remove bacon and pat dry with paper towels; set aside.
5. Add potatoes to pan; sauté over medium heat for 8 to 10 minutes or until tender. (If using cooked potatoes, sauté for 2 to 3 minutes or until heated through.)
6. Add onions; sauté for 1 minute. Return bacon to pan.

7. Pour eggs over mixture; sprinkle with pepper and cheese. Reduce heat to low; cook for 3 to 4 minutes until bottom is lightly browned yet centre is still not set.
8. Broil for 1 to 3 minutes or until puffed and golden, watching closely as top will brown quickly.

Makes 4 servings

Supper includes Bacon and Potato Frittata and one medium apple

Per serving of supper

Calories	428
Protein	21g
Fat	21g
Carbohydrate	40g
Dietary fibre	4g

Excellent source of riboflavin, niacin, vitamin B12, zinc

Good source of vitamin A, thiamine, vitamin B6, folic acid, calcium, iron

High source of dietary fibre

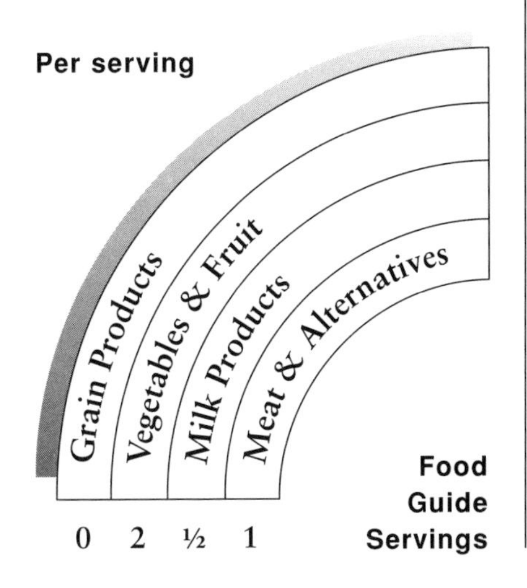

Filling in the Rainbow

Serve this meal with a whole grain bread or roll.

Bail-Out Bean Burritos

This great meal is a real crowd-pleaser and works well on camping trips. It is especially popular with teens. Keep the ingredients handy and they can fix you supper!

1	can (14 oz/398 mL) refried beans, lightly mashed	1
1 tsp	chili powder	5 mL
½ tsp	each ground cumin and dried oregano leaves	2 mL
¼ tsp	ground coriander	1 mL
10	8-inch (20 cm) flour tortillas (1 package)	10
1	large tomato, diced (about 8 oz/250 g)	1
2 cups	shredded part-skim mozzarella or Cheddar cheese	500 mL
1 cup	prepared salsa	250 mL
½ cup	low-fat plain yogurt (2% M.F.)	125 mL
	Shredded lettuce (optional)	

1. In microwaveable bowl, combine refried beans, chili powder, cumin, oregano and coriander; microwave on Medium for 2 to 3 minutes or until heated through. If mixture seems thick, add 1 to 2 tablespoons (15 to 25 mL) water. Place bowl on table. Place tortillas on plate on table.
2. Place tomato, cheese, salsa, yogurt, and lettuce (if using) in separate bowls on table.
3. Let people make their own burrito by placing ingredients in centre of tortilla then folding up bottom and sides.

Makes 5 servings, 2 burritos per serving

Shopping List
canned refried beans
flour tortillas
tomato
part-skim mozzarella cheese
low-fat plain yogurt
prepared salsa

Use packaged, shredded part-skim mozzarella cheese to speed up preparation time.

Rainbow sherbet is a refreshing finale to this meal.

Variations

1. Omit refried beans. In skillet over medium heat, cook 2 cups (500 mL) Batch Ground Meat and Vegetables with spices for 1 to 2 minutes. In small bowl, combine 1 tsp (5 mL) cornstarch and ½ cup (125 mL) water; add to meat mixture and simmer for 1 to 2 minutes until thickened and heated through.
2. Omit refried beans. Substitute 2 cups (500 mL) Chili (page 96), Three-Bean Chili (page 122) or Vegetarian Pasta Sauce (page 124).

Per serving

Calories	528
Protein	27g
Fat	14g
Carbohydrate	74g
Dietary fibre	8g

Excellent source of vitamin A, riboflavin, niacin, folic acid, vitamin B12, calcium, iron, zinc

Good source of vitamin C

Very high source of dietary fibre

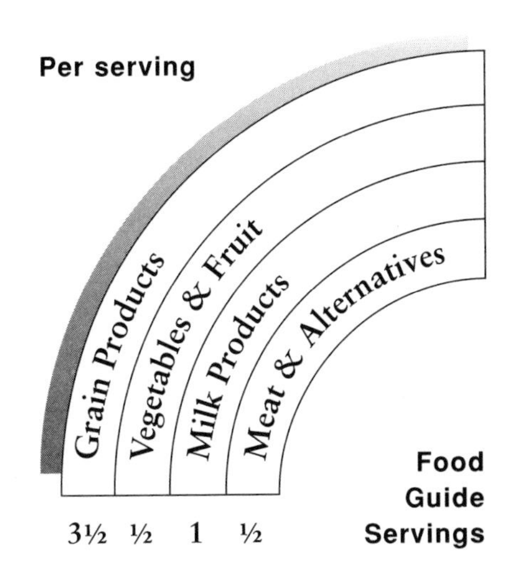

Filling in the Rainbow

This meal provides something from each of the four food groups. Serve this meal with a fruit plate or cut-up raw vegetables to increase the number of Vegetables & Fruit servings.

Black Bean, Corn and Couscous Salad

This is an ideal one-dish supper meal that keeps well for up to two days in the refrigerator. If you don't have fresh coriander available, add ¼ tsp (1 mL) of ground coriander to the All-Purpose Vinaigrette. If you don't like coriander, skip it completely. Serve with whole wheat rolls.

1	can (19 oz/540 mL) black beans, drained and rinsed	1
1½ cups	frozen corn kernels, rinsed	375 mL
1	medium sweet red pepper, diced	1
2	green onions, chopped	2
¼ cup	chopped fresh coriander (optional)	50 mL
2 cups	Quicky Couscous	500 mL

All-Purpose Vinaigrette

¼ cup	rice wine vinegar	50 mL
2 tbsp	olive oil	25 mL
1 tsp	Dijon mustard	5 mL
1 tsp	lemon or lime juice	5 mL
1	small clove garlic, minced or ¼ tsp (1 mL) garlic powder	1
¼ tsp	each salt and pepper	1 mL

1. All-Purpose Vinaigrette: In small bowl or measuring cup, blend together vinegar, oil, mustard, lemon juice, garlic, salt and pepper.
2. In large bowl, combine beans, corn, red pepper, green onions, coriander (if using) and Quicky Couscous; toss gently with vinaigrette.

Makes 4 servings, 1½ cups (375 mL) each

Shopping List
canned black beans
frozen corn
red pepper
green onions
fresh coriander (optional)
whole wheat rolls

COMPLETE SUMMER SUPPER

Serve 2 slices of cold meat, ¾ cup (175 mL) Black Bean, Corn and Couscous Salad, tomato slices, whole wheat bread and fruit yogurt.

If you don't have time to make a dressing, omit the All-Purpose Vinaigrette and substitute about a ½ cup (125 mL) calorie-reduced or fat-free vinaigrette-type salad dressing. Add ½ tsp (2 mL) ground cumin to bottled dressing for extra flavour if you like. A low-fat dressing must contain less than 3 grams of fat per 1 tbsp (15 mL).

If you need two salads for a crowd, make one recipe of Quicky Couscous. Divide it into two 2-cup (500 mL) portions. Make one recipe of Black Bean, Corn and Couscous Salad and one recipe of Chick-Pea and Couscous Salad.

Chick-Pea and Couscous Salad:

Omit black beans, corn and coriander. Substitute 1 can (19 oz/540 mL) chick-peas, drained and rinsed, and 2 diced medium carrots. Add ½ tsp (2 mL) ground cumin to All-Purpose Vinaigrette.

Black Bean, Corn and Rice Salad

Omit couscous. Substitute 2 cups (500 mL) Perfect Microwave Rice (page 45).

Quicky Couscous

One cup (250 mL) of couscous equals 2 servings of Grain Products.

2 cups	water	500 mL
2 tsp	olive oil	10 mL
1½ cups	quick-cooking couscous	375 mL
	Salt and pepper	

1. In medium saucepan, bring water and olive oil to boil. Stir in couscous.
2. Cover and remove from heat; let stand for 5 minutes. Fluff with fork. Add salt and pepper to taste.

Makes 4 cups (1 L)

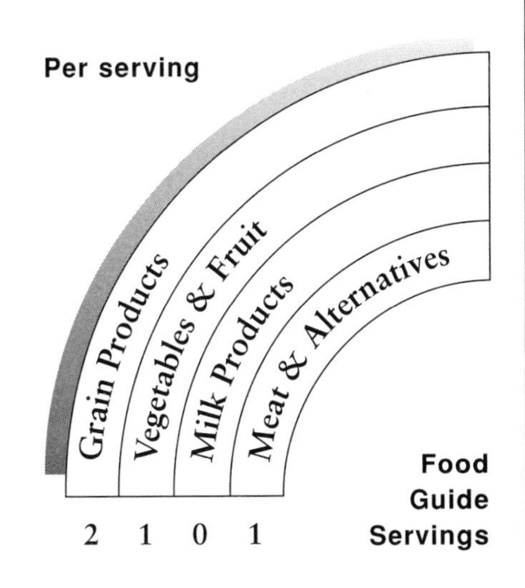

Supper includes Black Bean, Corn and Couscous Salad, one whole wheat roll and 1 tsp (5 mL) soft margarine

Per serving of supper

Calories	489
Protein	19g
Fat	11g
Carbohydrate	84g
Dietary fibre	11g

Excellent source of vitamin C, thiamine, niacin, folic acid, iron, zinc

Good source of vitamin A, vitamin B6

Very high source of dietary fibre

Rice vinegar is a very mild vinegar, an ideal choice for salad dressings because much less oil is needed to contrast the sharp vinegar flavour.

Filling in the Rainbow

This meal could use a serving from the Milk Products group. Have a low-fat fruit yogurt for dessert.

Fast Fish in the Microwave

Shopping List
1 lb fish fillets
fresh herbs (optional)
green pepper
zucchini
prepared salsa

SEASONAL SERVING SUGGESTIONS

Spring: serve with small boiled new potatoes and fresh asparagus.

Summer: serve with Perfect Microwave Rice (page 45) and fresh green beans.

Winter: serve with Perfect Microwave Rice (page 45) or couscous and steamed broccoli with Cheese Sauce (page 34).

KID-FRIENDLY TIP

When serving fish to children, remember to always check for bones that may cause them to choke.

With frozen fish in the freezer and couscous in your cupboard, this meal can be quickly pulled together when your fridge is bare. Try our seasonal serving suggestions (see below left) for a quick and different taste treat all year round. Serve frozen vegetables instead of the Zucchini and Salsa Sauté for an even speedier bail-out supper! The nutrients may change but the Rainbow Balance Chart will remain the same.

1 lb	fish fillets, fresh or defrosted (bluefish, cod, haddock or sole)	500 g
1 tsp	butter or soft margarine	5 mL
2 tsp	lemon juice	10 mL
1 tbsp	chopped fresh herbs (optional)	15 mL
	Pepper	

1. Spray microwaveable 10-cup (2.5 L) baking dish with nonstick cooking spray.
2. Place fillets in dish; top with butter, lemon juice, fresh herbs (if using), and pepper to taste.
3. Cover and microwave on High for 3½ to 4½ minutes. Let stand for 5 minutes or until fish is opaque and flakes easily when tested with fork. Serve with Quicky Couscous and Zucchini and Salsa Sauté (opposite).

Makes 4 servings

Zucchini and Salsa Sauté

Substitute red or yellow pepper for the green pepper and add a chopped onion if you wish.

1 tsp	olive oil	5 mL
1	medium sweet green pepper, sliced into strips	1
2	medium zucchini, sliced (about 1 lb/500 g)	2
1 cup	prepared salsa	250 mL

1. In large nonstick skillet, heat oil over medium-high heat; add green pepper and zucchini and sauté for 3 to 4 minutes or until tender-crisp.
2. Add salsa; cook for 1 minute or until heated through.

Makes 4 servings

Quicky Couscous

2 cups	water	500 mL
2 tsp	olive oil	10 mL
1½ cups	quick-cooking couscous	375 mL
	Salt and pepper	

1. In medium saucepan, bring water and olive oil to boil. Stir in couscous.
2. Cover and remove from heat; let stand for 5 minutes. Fluff with fork. Add salt and pepper to taste.

Makes 4 cups (1 L)

Supper includes Fast Fish in the Microwave, Quicky Couscous (1 cup/250 mL) and Zucchini and Salsa Sauté

Per serving of supper

Calories	431
Protein	31g
Fat	6g
Carbohydrate	63g
Dietary fibre	6g

Excellent source of vitamin C, niacin, vitamin B6, folic acid, vitamin B12

Good source of vitamin A, thiamine, iron, zinc

Very high source of dietary fibre

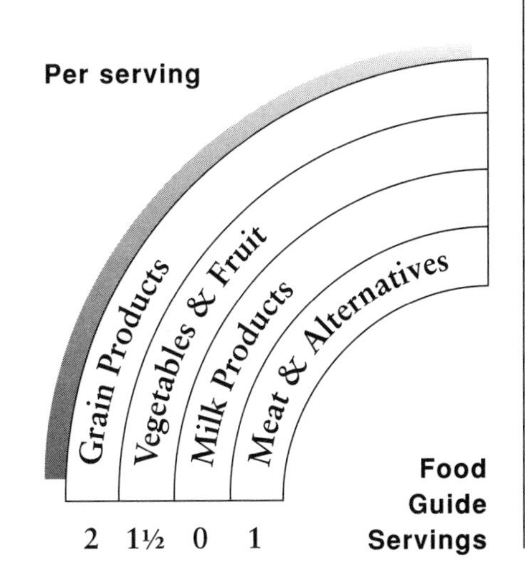

Filling in the Rainbow

Complete this meal with a serving from the Milk Products group.

French Toast with Peaches and Syrup

Our kids think we have flipped when we serve this meal for supper. They love it because it tastes great. We love it because we usually have all the ingredients on hand and because it is a completely balanced meal when served with a glass of milk.

8	large eggs	8
½ cup	2% milk	125 mL
8	slices whole wheat bread	8
2 tsp	soft margarine	10 mL
1	can (28 oz/796 mL) sliced peaches, drained	1
¾ cup	pancake syrup	175 mL

1. In shallow dish, beat eggs with milk. Add bread slices, one at a time, turning to soak completely.
2. In large nonstick skillet, melt margarine over medium heat; add bread slices and cook, turning once, until golden and set in centre.
3. Serve with peaches and syrup.

Makes 4 servings

Per serving

Calories	511
Protein	19g
Fat	14g
Carbohydrate	80g
Dietary fibre	7g

Excellent source of vitamin A, riboflavin, niacin, folic acid, vitamin B12, iron

Good source of thiamine, zinc

Very high source of dietary fibre

VARIATIONS

1. Substitute raisin or egg bread for the whole wheat.
2. Substitute fresh cantaloupe, mangoes or strawberries for the peaches.

Buy peaches packed in unsweetened juice

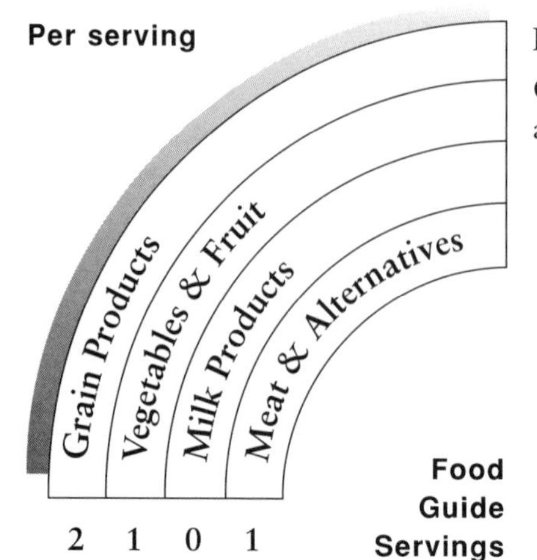

Filling in the Rainbow

Complete this meal with a glass of milk.

Spaghettini with Broccoli and Ham

Our daughters Lisa, 6 and Heather, 5 don't like tomato sauce on their pasta. We've come up with a more nutritious way for them to enjoy their pasta and cheese.

8 oz	spaghettini	250 g
3 cups	chopped fresh broccoli	750 mL
¼ cup	soft margarine	50 mL
8 oz	extra-lean ham, diced	250 g
½ cup	grated Parmesan cheese	125 mL

1. In large saucepan, cook spaghettini according to package directions, adding broccoli during last 2 minutes of cooking. Drain and return to saucepan.
2. Add margarine, ham and Parmesan cheese; toss to coat.

Makes 4 servings

Per serving

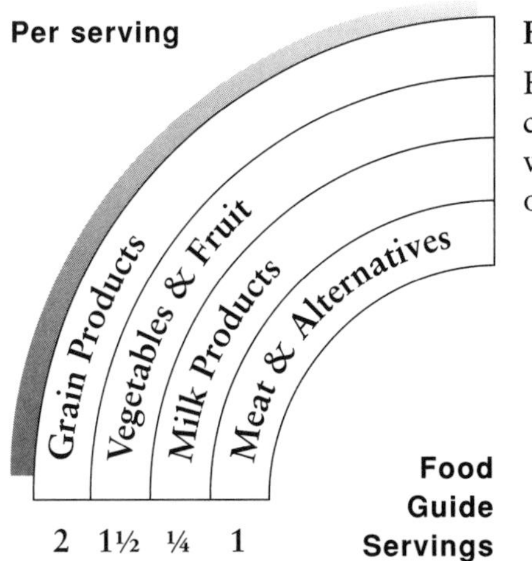

Filling in the Rainbow

Every food group is covered, but children will benefit from a glass of milk.

Shopping List
broccoli
extra-lean ham
Parmesan cheese

Per serving

Calories	461
Protein	25g
Fat	19g
Carbohydrate	47g
Dietary fibre	4g

Excellent source of vitamin A, vitamin C, thiamine, riboflavin, niacin, vitamin B12, iron, zinc

Good source of vitamin B6, folic acid, calcium

High source of dietary fibre

KID-FRIENDLY TIP

Be sure not to overcook broccoli as the taste becomes stronger and is less appealing to children.

Children may eat a smaller serving size. Check child-size servings (page 22)

Sweet Beans and Toast

This super-fast meal is the highest-fibre and lowest-fat meal in Suppertime Survival. *It's a weekly meal at Lynn's house and one of her daughter Amelia's favourites. She even enjoys it as a meal to go.*

1	can (14 oz/398 mL) beans in tomato sauce	1
2 tbsp	fancy molasses	25 mL
4	slices whole wheat toast	4
1	medium carrot, cut into sticks	1
1	medium sweet green pepper, sliced	1

1. In medium saucepan, simmer beans and molasses over low heat for 4 to 5 minutes or until bubbling. Serve over toast with carrot sticks and green pepper strips on the side.

Makes 2 adult servings

Shopping List
canned beans in tomato sauce
fancy molasses
carrot
green pepper

Per serving

Calories	422
Protein	16g
Fat	3g
Carbohydrate	93g
Dietary fibre	24g

Excellent source of vitamin A, vitamin C, thiamine, niacin, vitamin B6, folic acid, iron, zinc

Good source of riboflavin, calcium

Very high source of dietary fibre

MICROWAVE METHOD
Heat beans for 2 minutes, or until hot on Medium-High; stir.

VARIATION
Add half medium sweet green pepper, chopped, and 1 small fresh tomato, diced, to beans.

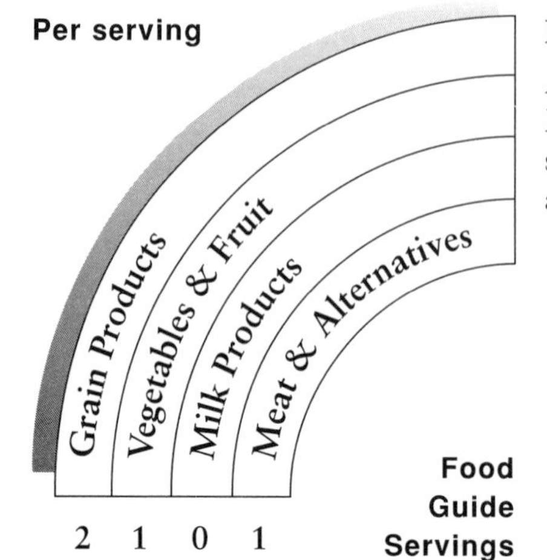

Filling in the Rainbow
Add something from the Milk Products group, such as a fruit yogurt or a glass of milk.

Tuna Salad Toss

This is made all in one bowl and can easily be doubled to serve four. If you have lettuce washed and ready to use in the fridge, dinner can be on the table in five minutes. This is a perfect late-summer/early-fall supper when tomatoes are at their best. Feel free to add chopped or sliced celery, green peppers or green onion. They make a great salad even better!

1	can (6½ oz/184 g) water-packed tuna, drained and flaked	1
4 cups	torn dark green salad greens	1 L
1	large tomato, cut into chunks	1
3 tbsp	light mayonnaise	50 mL
1 tbsp	lemon juice	15 mL
	Pepper	

1. In large bowl, toss together tuna, salad greens, tomato, mayonnaise, lemon juice, and pepper to taste.

Makes 2 servings

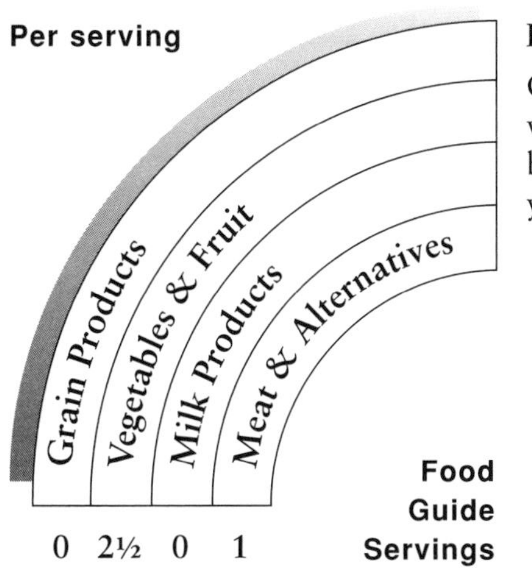

Filling in the Rainbow

Complete this meal with whole grain bread or buns and low-fat fruit yogurt.

Shopping List

canned water-packed tuna

dark green salad greens

tomato

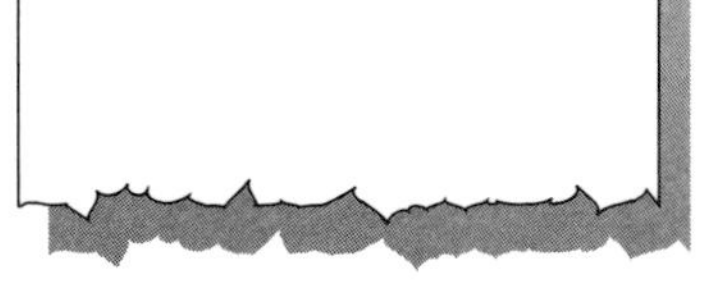

Per serving

Calories	207
Protein	24g
Fat	8g
Carbohydrate	10g
Dietary fibre	3g

Excellent source of vitamin A, vitamin C, niacin, folic acid, vitamin B12

Good source of thiamine, riboflavin, vitamin B6, iron

Moderate source of dietary fibre

VARIATION

Substitute 1 can (7.5 oz/213 g) salmon for the tuna. Leave in salmon bones for a calcium boost.

It's hard to get enough calcium without Milk Products. Including 2 to 4 servings from the Milk Products group each day is the easiest way to get your daily requirements.

Tortellini with Creamy Cheese Sauce

Shopping List
frozen meat tortellini
broccoli

KID-FRIENDLY TIP
Children may eat a smaller serving size. Check child-size servings (page 22).

For some reason, kids don't seem to like having their vegetables mixed up with the rest of their meal. We have solved this problem by serving the broccoli beside the pasta instead of mixing it in. This brightens up the dinner plate and gives kids a complete meal. If you introduce broccoli to your children when they are babies they are more likely to continue eating it as they get older. The cheese sauce goes well with the broccoli so it is even more likely to be eaten!

1	package (1 lb/500 g) frozen meat tortellini (about 4 cups/1 L)	1
2 tbsp	soft margarine	25 mL
3 tbsp	all-purpose flour	50 mL
2½ cups	2% milk	625 mL
¼ cup	grated Parmesan cheese	50 mL
Pinch	nutmeg	Pinch

1. In large saucepan, cook tortellini according to package directions; drain and rinse under hot water. Cover and set aside.
2. In same saucepan, melt margarine over medium heat; add flour and stir until blended. Whisk in milk and cook, stirring constantly, until boiling; reduce heat and simmer for 4 to 5 minutes until thickened. Remove from heat. Stir in cheese and nutmeg.
3. Return cooked tortellini to saucepan and stir to coat. (It is now the perfect temperature for kids!)

Makes 5 servings

Ravioli with Prepared Pasta Sauce

One serving provides 2 Grain Products, 1 Vegetables and Fruit, ¾ Milk Products and 0 Meat and Alternatives, 444 calories and 11 g fat.

1	package (1 lb/500 g) frozen cheese ravioli	1
1	jar (375 mL) tomato-based pasta sauce	1
¼ cup	grated Parmesan cheese	50 mL

1. In large saucepan, cook ravioli according to package directions; drain and return to saucepan.
2. Add pasta sauce and simmer over low heat for 3 to 4 minutes or until heated through.
3. Sprinkle each serving with Parmesan cheese.

Makes 4 servings

Supper includes Tortellini with Creamy Cheese Sauce and steamed broccoli (½ cup/ 125 mL)

Per serving of supper

Calories	521
Protein	25g
Fat	19g
Carbohydrate	60g
Dietary fibre	1g

Excellent source of vitamin A, thiamine, riboflavin, niacin, vitamin B12, calcium, iron

Good source of vitamin C, zinc

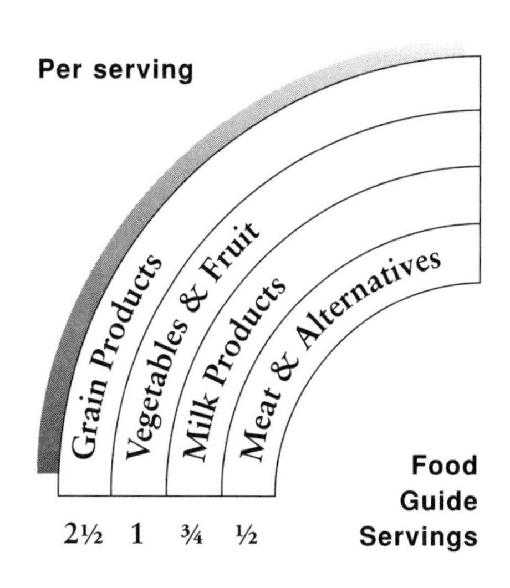

Filling in the Rainbow

This meal has something from each of the four food groups. Finish the meal with fresh fruit or berries to increase the Vegetables & Fruit servings and get more fibre, too.

Chapter 4

EATING ON THE RUN—MEALS TO GO

With today's fast paced lifestyle and busy family schedules, eating on the run is a reality. Often families find themselves away from home at mealtimes. At other times, family members may be heading out the door for other activities right in the middle of supper. Finding time to prepare or even eat supper seems impossible. It's not surprising that Canadians eat out on average about 5 times per week or that supper is the meal eaten out most often*.

Finding ways to make sure your family is eating balanced meals and getting the nutrients they need, while eating on the go, is important. This can be accomplished by incorporating home-made Meals to Go and even the occasional fast food meal into your family's schedule.

Meals to Go are meals that can be eaten on the run, in the car, or while hanging out at the arena or pool or wherever else you need to be. Home-prepared portable meals can be just as quick as fast foods but have the added benefit of being more nutritious and less expensive. When you are faced with a grueling schedule of dashing off to a meeting, going out to work or driving kids every which way but to the dinner table, the **Meals to Go** and fast food tips suggested in this book can help.

Meals to Go can be leftover from supper meals that you have already made and served. Others need to be made completely ahead of time such as Pizza Pockets (page 105) or Spinach Frittata Fingers (page 70). Prepare these meals in advance and have them ready to go whenever someone has to run out at mealtime.

---

*Canadian Restaurant and Foodservice Association, Foodservice Facts, 1995.

MEALS TO GO

Here is a list of our **Meals to Go** with suggestions for making a complete meal. Generally, these meals include a serving from at least three out of the four food groups in Canada's Food Guide to Healthy Eating.

Anytime Pizza
Fruit Cup
Milk

Asparagus Frittata
Toasted English muffin
Fruit cup
Milk

Bacon and Potato Frittata
Whole grain bun
Fruit juice

Bail-Out Bean Burrito
Fruit
Milk

Grilled Lemon Chicken on a Bun
Vegetable or fruit juice

Black Bean, Corn and Couscous Salad
Low-fat fruit yogurt
Whole grain bun

Carrot Soup
Raisin bagel
Slice of cheese

Chicken Fajita
Pudding cup
Fruit juice

Broccoli Soup
Egg salad sandwich
Milk

Crispy Chicken Fingers
Whole grain bun
Carrot sticks
Milk

Curried Turkey Salad
Bran muffin
Milk

Curried Beef in a Pita
Fruit yogurt

Greek Pasta Salad
Whole grain bun
Pudding cup

Lentil and Pasta Soup
Crackers
Cheese
Orange

Mediterranean Pizza
Fruit juice
Fig bars

Pizza Pockets
Kiwifruit
Milk

Pork Souvlaki in a Pita
Milk

Spanish Rice and Lentils
Carrot sticks and red pepper strips
Milk

Spicy Garden Gazpacho
Tuna salad sandwich
Milk

Spinach Frittata Fingers
Bagel
Pear
Milk

Sweet Beans and Toast
Carrot sticks
Fruit yogurt

Turkey Sandwich with Cranberry Sauce
Milk
Oatmeal cookies
Fruit

Zucchini and Red Pepper Frittata
Whole grain bread
Pudding cup

TIPS FOR MEALS TO GO

1. Put meals to go together ahead of time so you are not dashing about at the last minute packing food as well as sports equipment.
2. Prepare vegetable sticks and fruit pieces in advance so you'll always have something ready to go.
3. Make up a batch of muffins using low-fat bran, oatmeal or mixed grain muffin mix. Use milk instead of water to give them a calcium boost. Keep a supply of muffins in the freezer and pull them out as needed.
4. Save money by making your own pudding cups or fruit cups. The packaged varieties cost two to three times more and the packaging has to be thrown away.
5. Make environmentally-friendly meals to go. Use small reusable plastic containers for fruit, puddings, cookies, vegetable sticks, etc. Keep a set of larger plastic containers for sandwiches, pita pockets and pizza. Save plastic water bottles for beverages such as water and juice. Use a Thermos to keep milk cold.
6. Keep meals to go safe to eat. Remember to keep hot foods hot and cold foods cold. Use insulated lunch bags to maintain temperature.
   - Keep hot foods such as soups, beans and casseroles in a Thermos meant for hot foods. To keep pizza, fajitas or burritos hot, heat them up, wrap in paper towel and then wrap in aluminium foil. They should stay hot for up to one hour. Frittatas can be eaten hot or cold.
   - Whenever you pack cold food or meals to go containing meat, fish or eggs, or any food mixed with mayonnaise, always keep these foods cold and out of the danger zone by packing them with a freezer pack. You could also use a plastic water bottle filled with water or juice that has been frozen overnight.

If you know family members will be waiting around an arena or pool, take along nutrient-packed snacks and drinks to avoid having to buy something less nutritious.

FITTING FAST FOODS INTO SUPPERTIME

The occasional stop for supper at a quick serve or fast-food restaurant is a reality for many families. But if you make fast food stops a regular habit then your family may end up eating too much fat and salt, and not enough fibre

What your family eats is more important than when or where they eat it.

and important vitamins such as A, C, D and folic acid. Once you realize this, it is easier to make choices that will help your family have a healthier eating pattern.

If supper isn't going to happen at the usual time, let family members know what to expect and when they will eat.

Fast-Food Tips:

- Enjoy your fast-food stop but don't expect it to satisfy everyone's nutrient needs.
- Balance the rest of your family's day. If your family did not have any fruit or vegetables at their fast-food stop, provide these foods at other meals or snacks.
- Order sandwiches or meals that include whole-grain bread or rolls, if available.
- Choose milk instead of pop. Milk is an excellent source of calcium which is especially important for children and teens. Pop is not a good source of any nutrients. If family members are worried about the fat or calories in milk, they can choose skim or 1% milk.
- Try bean burritos or chili for something different. These meals add fibre to your family's day and are lower in fat than many other fast-food choices.
- Deep-fried foods such as French fries are high in fat. If you eat out often, choose baked potatoes, rice, and salads with low-fat dressing more often than fries.
- Salads are often surprisingly high in fat. This is mostly due to the amount of dressing added. Order salads with the dressing on the side and choose a lower-fat dressing. Salads made with tossed greens are usually lower in fat than Caesar, potato or macaroni salads.
- When choosing hamburgers, order the smaller-sized burgers without mayonnaise, sauce or bacon. Two small plain hamburgers have less fat than a larger burger with sauce and all the trimmings.
- Order pizza with lower-fat ingredients such as ham, pineapple, peppers, tomatoes, onions and mushrooms. Bacon, sausage, pepperoni and extra cheese all increase the amount of fat in a pizza.
- Choose chicken that is baked, broiled, grilled or barbecued. Deep-fried and breaded chicken (especially small pieces) are higher in fat. Have chicken with salad or rice, instead of French fries and hold the gravy.

- Try ordering foods without the extras (mayonnaise, sour cream, gravy) or have them served on the side so you can control the amount. These foods provide fat and calories to meals, but don't add nutritional value.
- Many fast-food restaurants now offer lower-fat alternatives to their traditional fare. Check out the chart "Fat and Calories in Some Popular Fast Foods" and try making choices that are lower in fat.
- Some fast-food restaurants provide nutrition information booklets to consumers. Ask for one if you want to know more about the nutrition content of fast foods or the ingredients used in preparing the foods.

FAT AND CALORIES IN SOME POPULAR FAST FOODS

Food	Fat* (grams)	Calories* (kcal)
Wendy's		
Sandwiches		
Grilled Chicken Sandwich	6.8	283
Hamburger, Kids' Meal	9.3	269
Cheeseburger, Kids' Meal	13	313
Plain Single Hamburger	16	354
Jr. Hamburger Deluxe	13	311
Breaded Chicken Sandwich	15	392
Jr. Cheeseburger Deluxe	16	355
Chicken Club Sandwich	18	432
Single with Everything	19	411
Big Classic	19	446
Jr. Bacon Cheeseburger	20	383
Big Bacon Classic	31	573
Salads		
Fresh Salads to Go (without dressing)		
Caesar Side Salad	3.3	95
Side Salad	3.8	67
Deluxe Garden Salad	7.4	128
Grilled Chicken Salad	9.6	221
Taco Salad	30	594
Salad Dressings (2 tbsp/30 mL)		
French, low-fat	0.1	30
Italian, Red, Fat and Calorie Reduced	3.2	39
French	11	127
Thousand Island	15	142
Caesar Italian	16	150
Blue Cheese	18	163
Hidden Valley Ranch	10	98
Hidden Valley Ranch, reduced fat	5.3	56

continued on next page

Food	Fat* (grams)	Calories* (kcal)
Chili		
Small (8 oz)	6.6	213
Large (12 oz)	9.9	320
Cheddar Cheese, shredded (2 tbsp/30 mL)	5.4	67
Potatoes		
Plain Baked Potato	0.3	309
Sour Cream & Chives Potato	4.3	358
French Fries (small)	15	326
Broccoli & Cheese Sauce Potato	13	465
Bacon & Cheese Sauce Potato	16	517
French Fries (medium)	17	374
Cheese Sauce Potato	22	562
Chili & Cheese Sauce Potato	23	618
Harveys		
Sandwiches		
Charbroiled Chicken Sandwich	4.7	264
Harvey's Junior Burger	9.5	236
Chicken Strips	22.0	364
- plum sauce	0	69
- sweet & sour sauce	0	49
- honey mustard sauce	0.4	78
- barbecue sauce	0.1	56
Hot Dog	11.7	313
Fish Sandwich	14.9	393
Hamburger	17.5	357
Cheeseburger	22.0	418
Superburger	27.0	506
Double Burger	38.8	609
Side Orders		
Vegetable Soup	1.2	99
Salad	6.7	103
Salad Dressings (43 mL)		
- Fat-Free Italian	0	14
- Light French	4.2	68

continued on next page

Food	Fat* (grams)	Calories* (kcal)
- Ranch	21	205
- Feta cheese	17	170
French Fries (junior)	12.9	292
French Fries (regular)	16.4	385
Onion Rings	19.9	286
French Fries (large)	22.4	526
Poutine	42.9	738
Gravy	0.7	43
Taco Bell		
Tacos & Tostadas		
Chicken Soft Taco	10	223
Soft Taco	11	220
Taco	11	180
Tostada	11	242
Soft Taco Supreme	15	270
Taco Supreme	15	230
Burritos		
Bean Burrito	12	390
Chicken Burrito	13	345
Chicken Burrito Supreme	23	520
Chili Cheese Burrito	18	391
Beef Burrito	19	432
Burrito Supreme	19	440
7 Layer Burrito	23	540
Big Beef Burrito Supreme	25	525
Specialty Items		
Pintos 'n' Cheese	9	190
Beef MexiMelt	14	262
Nachos	18	345
Nachos Supreme	18	364
Nachos BellGrande	34	633
Mexican Pizza	38	574
Taco Salad	55	860

continued on next page

Food	Fat* (grams)	Calories* (kcal)
Swiss Chalet*		
Chicken		
Quarter Chicken, white meat, no skin	8	225
Barbecue Chicken Sandwich	9	434
Grilled Chicken Breast and Rice	9	641
Chicken Strips (7)	11	319
Chalet Dipping Sauce (100g)	1	28
Quarter Chicken, white meat, skin	22	381
Chicken Pot Pie	24	494
Hot Chicken Sandwich with French fries, vegetables and gravy	41	1007
Grilled Chicken Breast and Caesar Salad	46	775
Wings/Ribs		
Wings with sauce (8)	26	526
½ Back Rib	26	405
Salads		
Chalet Salad with Low-cal Italian Dressing	1	44
Chalet Salad with House Dressing	11	161
Chicken Salad Bowl	21	444
Chicken Salad Almandine	60	868
Potatoes/Fries/Rice		
Baked potato	trace	272
Rice (142 g)	1	236
French fries (150 g)	22	302

*Average size only. Size may vary. Grams of fat are approximate due to rounding off. Information correct at time of printing and subject to change by restaurant.

Nutrition information reprinted with permission from the following sources:

"Fresh Ingredients, Quality Choices—Wendy's Nutrition Guide (1995)." Wendy's Restaurants of Canada, Inc.

"Harvey's Nutrition and Food Sensitivity Guide" (1995). Harvey's. Cara Operations Limited.

"Cross the Border ... to Good Nutrition" (1994). Taco Bell Corp Item #1685.

"Swiss Chalet's Guide to Good Eating" (1995). Swiss Chalet. Cara Operations Limited.

Curried Beef in Pita (page 36)

Photo courtesy of Beef Information Centre

Chapter 5

Feeding a Family

WHAT IS YOUR FAMILY EATING?

There is proof that healthy eating habits are associated with good health. Besides preventing nutrient deficiencies, healthy eating helps infants and children grow and develop to their full potential. Healthy eating before and during pregnancy can help develop healthy babies and improve the nutritional status of mothers. Healthy eating in the teenage years can help prevent eating disorders, promote healthy weights and prevent osteoporosis in later years. For adults, eating foods that are lower in fat and higher in carbohydrates, fibre and antioxidant vitamins can help reduce risks of developing heart disease and some types of cancers. A lower-fat, higher-fibre foodstyle can also help control diabetes, high blood cholesterol levels, high blood pressure, obesity and other chronic diseases. For seniors, a well-balanced diet that satisfies vitamin needs can help boost immunity.

Most families can achieve a healthier way of eating simply by:

- eating more whole grain and enriched products
- eating more vegetables and fruit
- choosing lower-fat milk and cheese and leaner meats
- having beans, peas and lentils more often
- using added fats like cooking oils, butter, margarine and salad dressing in smaller amounts and less frequently.

Basil Zucchini Strata (page 120)

Photo courtesy of the egg producers of Ontario

How do your family's food choices measure up?

Because of the many benefits of healthy eating, it's worth it to examine your family's foodstyle. Family members may be eating too much fat and not enough fibre. Your family may also be missing out on some important nutrients that come from vegetables and fruit. To find out for sure, complete the chart opposite.

Add up the check marks in each column. If there are more checks on the left-hand column than on the right, your family is probably eating too much fat and salt, and not enough fibre. Also, foods on the right tend to contain higher amounts of important vitamins and minerals. You may have found out that your family is using some foods more often than you thought.

Now compare your family's food choices to the suggestions made in Canada's Food Guide to Healthy Eating. Think about what various members had to eat today and ask yourself the following questions.

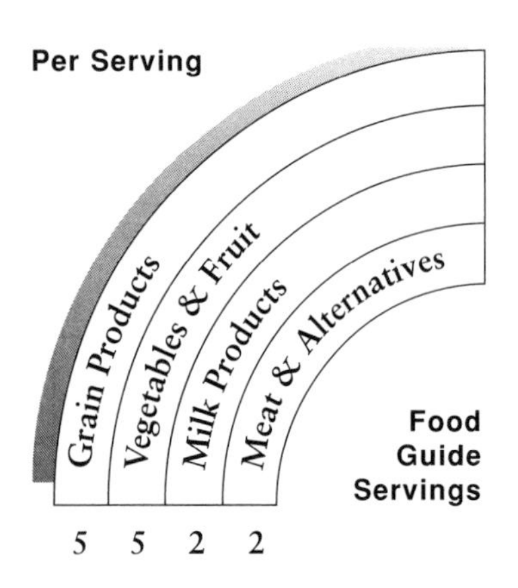

Minimum number of servings from each food group.

1. Did everyone in your family eat a variety of foods from each of the four food groups?
2. Did every family member have the minimum number of servings from each of the four food groups?
3. Did your family eat mostly lower-fat foods?
4. Did your family include whole grain and enriched bread, cereals or other grain products during the day?
5. Did your family include any dark green or orange vegetables or orange fruit in their daily intake?
6. How many Other Foods that are high in fat or calories did family members consume?

If you answered NO to questions 1 to 5 above, look for ways to help your family improve their food choices. Start by making a few small changes at a time and you may be surprised to find out how easy it is to improve your family's eating habits. Changes you make now will affect your family's health and wellness in years to come.

Eating well doesn't mean giving up your family's favourite foods

Switching to a healthier way of eating doesn't mean avoiding favourite foods or convenience foods. No single food, or day that includes too many junk foods, will destroy a healthy eating pattern. Healthy eating happens

RATE YOUR FAMILY'S FOOD CHOICES

Place a check mark next to the items your family eats most often and see how your choices measure up.

Grain Products	
❑ croissants, commercial muffins	❑ bagels, English muffins, homemade or lower-fat commercial muffins
❑ doughnuts, pastries	
❑ white bread or rolls	❑ whole-grain bread or rolls
❑ sweetened cereals	❑ whole-grain or bran cereals
❑ instant or white rice	❑ brown rice
❑ pasta with powdered sauce mix or rich cream sauce	❑ pasta with light or tomato-based sauce
❑ cream-filled sandwich type or chocolate-coated cookies	❑ oatmeal cookies, fig bars, graham wafers
Vegetables & Fruit	
❑ fruit drinks, punch, sweetened juice	❑ unsweetened fruit juice
❑ canned fruit in syrup	❑ canned fruit in juice
❑ vegetables with sauce, butter or margarine added	❑ vegetables steamed or boiled with no added fat
❑ raw vegetables with regular salad dressing or dips	❑ raw vegetables with reduced-fat salad dressing or dips
❑ pale-coloured vegetables or fruit	❑ dark green or orange vegetables or orange fruit
	❑ raisins, dried fruit
Milk Products	
❑ cream, half and half	❑ skim, 1% or 2% milk, buttermilk
❑ whole milk	
❑ regular yogurt or creamed cottage cheese (more than 2% M.F.)	❑ yogurt or cottage cheese (2% M.F. or less)
❑ regular sour cream (10% M.F.)	❑ light sour cream (5% M.F.)
❑ regular cheese	❑ reduced-fat cheese
❑ ice cream, regular or premium	❑ frozen ice milk, yogurt or sherbet
Meat & Alternatives	
❑ luncheon meats, hot dogs, bacon	❑ lean ham, beef, turkey or reduced-fat luncheon meats
❑ regular ground beef or sausage	❑ lean ground beef (10% fat)
❑ tuna packed in oil	❑ tuna packed in water
❑ deep-fried fish	❑ fresh, frozen or canned fish
❑ poultry with skin	❑ poultry with skin removed
Other Foods	
❑ potato chips, corn chips, snack crackers	❑ plain popcorn, lower-fat crackers
❑ candies, chocolates	
❑ regular mayonnaise, regular salad dressing	❑ light mayonnaise, lower-fat salad dressing
❑ pop	
__ **TOTAL check marks**	__ **TOTAL check marks**

over a period of time. What your family eats during a typical week is what matters most. A healthy diet is not made up of just one type of food or meal, but rather a whole variety of foods. Let your family enjoy favourite foods, but provide foods that are higher in fat less often and balance them out with lower-fat choices.

WHAT'S A HEALTHY WEIGHT?

If your family members have healthy weights and feel good about the way they look and feel, then your family is on the right track.

Healthy kids come in different shapes and sizes

Many parents and caregivers are concerned about the way their children grow and whether they are a normal weight. Normal growth throughout childhood includes periods of fast and slow growth. Kids may appear to be chubby or skinny, depending on the stage they are in. This is all very normal since kids vary tremendously in the way they grow and develop.

What is normal growth?

Newborn babies double their birth weight by four to six months and triple it by one year. After the first year, weight gain slows down and levels off to about 4 to 6 pounds a year (2 to 3 kg). Prior to puberty, both girls and boys gain weight. This is a perfectly normal occurrence and should not be cause for concern. Girls aged 10 to 14 will grow about 10 inches (25 cm) taller and gain 40 to 50 pounds (18 to 23 kg). Boys aged 12 to 16 will grow about 12 inches (30 cm) taller and gain 50 to 60 pounds (23 to 27 kg).[1] If you are worried about your child's weight, check his or her growth chart. Most doctors keep track of your child's weight and can tell you if your child is following a normal growth curve.

Should I put my child on a diet?

Putting children on a diet is NOT recommended. Restricted food intake can affect normal growth and

[1]Satter, E. "How to Get Your Kid to Eat But Not Too Much," Bull Publishing, 1987.

development and can cause kids to miss out on important nutrients that they need to grow properly. The stresses and pressures of dieting can also lead to poor self-esteem, further weight problems and possibly even eating disorders.

Rather than dieting, children should be provided with healthy food choices and be encouraged to get involved in enjoyable games and physical activities. Because healthy eating and activity habits begin in childhood, parents and caregivers can be great role models for a healthy lifestyle. Parents and caregivers also need to have realistic expectations for their child, since body size and shape are inherited. Parents need to accept children for who they are, show affection and attention and help children build self-esteem and positive attitudes about themselves and their bodies.

Healthy Eating and Activity Habits for Kids

- Provide meals and snacks based on foods from the four food groups. If snacks like chips, cookies, candy and soft drinks are your child's preferred foods, don't stock them as everyday foods. A treat once in a while is okay, but these foods can interfere with your child's intake of more nutrient-dense foods.
- Let your child decide when he or she is full. Parents should decide what foods kids will eat, but children know when to stop eating. Forced or restricted eating can interfere with a child's normal appetite control system. Young children have small stomachs and may need smaller portion sizes (see "What is a child-size serving?" page 22).
- Set regular times for meals and snacks to help kids feel secure about food.
- Eliminate distractions such as television at mealtimes so that kids are aware of what they are eating.
- Help your children become more physically active by establishing active playtimes, enrolling them in activity programs and by limiting the amount of time they spend watching television or playing video games.

If your child or teen has an obvious weight problem, consult your physician and ask to be referred to a Registered Dietitian for appropriate advice.

Weighty issues for teens

One of the major concerns during the teenage years is weight. Girls often worry if they gain weight while many boys are concerned if they don't gain weight. Gaining weight is a natural process of puberty and teens need reassurance that it will and should happen. Girls' bodies start to change shape as they develop hips and breasts. Boys' bodies begin to develop a little later than girls, but they eventually do gain the weight and muscle mass they so desire.

Unfortunately, many teens today are faced with great pressures about body size and shape. Magazines and advertisements that flaunt ultra-thin female models and muscle-bound males promote the message that personal image is all-important and thin is in. It's no wonder that many teens end up emotionally distressed and in an endless battle with their weight.

Some teens may end up obsessed with dieting in a futile attempt to attain a body shape they were never meant to have. Some resort to extremes such as following very rigid and nutrient-deficient diets, fasting, binge eating and using laxatives or vomiting in order to control their weight.

Since eating disorders such as anorexia nervosa and bulimia often begin in early adolescence, teens need to be advised about the perils of dieting. Parents should strongly discourage dieting, especially during the formative years and throughout puberty. Once full adult height and growth are reached, sometime at the end of the teen years, then weight control strategies may be initiated if necessary. In the meantime, teens who are worried about their weight should keep physically active and follow the Fast Food Tips (page 150) and Tips for Lower-Fat Eating (page 197). Parents can help by setting a good example, not dieting themselves, practising healthy eating habits and being active.

What is the right weight for teens?

There is no right weight and no accurate tables that give ideal weights for teenagers because growth is so variable during the teenage years.

Weigh scales can be misleading because they show total weight, not fat weight or muscle weight. A muscular person will weigh more than someone less muscular. It is normal for teenage females to have 15 to 20 percent of their total body weight as fat, while fat makes up 10 to 15 percent of a male teenager's total body weight.

AVERAGE ENERGY REQUIREMENTS OF ADOLESCENTS

Age	Average Height (cm)	Average Weight (kg)	kcal/kg	kcal/day
13-15 male	159	50	57	2800
female	157	48	46	2200
16-18 male	172	62	51	3200
female	160	53	40	2100

Source: Health Canada, Nutrition Recommendations: The Report of the Scientific Review Committee. Ottawa (1990). Reproduced with the permission of the Minister of Supply and Services Canada, 1995.

PERILS OF DIETING

- Weight gain: It has been proven that diets don't work over the long run. Ninety percent of people regain the weight that they have lost.[2] Most people even gain more weight than they started with. Few people can stay on a diet for long, because most diets are too rigid. Once dieters go back to their usual eating pattern, the weight goes back on.
- Restricted diets can harm growth and development in children and teens. When calories or foods are eliminated, kids may miss out on important nutrients such as calcium, iron and zinc.
- Most fad diets are terribly low in nutrients and simply don't work. Be wary of diets that eliminate one or more food groups. Eating grapefruit or popcorn won't make anyone skinny, over the long term, and starvation diets are dangerous. Our bodies need more than 50 different nutrients to function properly. Diet shakes and bars can't possibly deliver all the nutrients, fibre or energy that we require.
- Skipping meals early in the day (breakfast or lunch) can cause a greater food intake later in the day. It's better to try to eat smaller, healthy snacks or meals throughout the day using foods from the four food groups.

What is a healthy weight for adults?

There is no such thing as an ideal weight but there is a range for what is considered to be a healthy weight zone. People come in a wide variety of shapes and sizes and can still be healthy and fit. Size and shape are largely influenced by family history and the genes inherited from parents. Body weight is also influenced by the kinds and amount of food eaten and by physical activity.

---

[2]"Obesity—Exploding Some Myths," Healthy Bites, National Institute of Nutrition, Winter 1995.

Many people unnecessarily put themselves on a diet, with the hope of losing weight, when in fact they may already be in a healthy weight range. One-third of women diet even though they already have healthy weights.

Use the "Rate Your Weight" chart (opposite) to determine if you are in a healthy weight zone. This chart is meant to be used by adults 20 to 65 years of age. It should not be used with children, teens, pregnant or breast-feeding women, seniors, very muscular people or endurance athletes.

Body Mass Index (BMI): The BMI is a height and weight ratio, calculated by kg/m^2.

To use the Rate Your Weight chart: Select your height. Follow its vertical line until it crosses the horizontal line of your body weight.

How did the adults in your family rate?

- If you are in the "Healthy Weight" zone (BMI 20-25), that's great! Keep up the good work.
- If you cross above the dotted area but are below the broken line, you are in the "Caution" range (BMI 25-27). Further weight gain is not recommended.
- If you cross above the broken line into the "Health Risk Zone" (BMI > 27), you are too heavy and are at increased risk of potential health problems, such as high blood pressure, diabetes, heart disease, some cancers, psychosocial problems and arthritis. You should consider losing some weight.
- If you are in the "Underweight" zone (BMI < 20), you are too thin and should not try to lose more weight. Being underweight does have some health risks, such as heart irregularities, emotional distress and anemia. If you are a woman and over-exercising, you could also be at risk of depleting your body's store of nutrients such as iron.

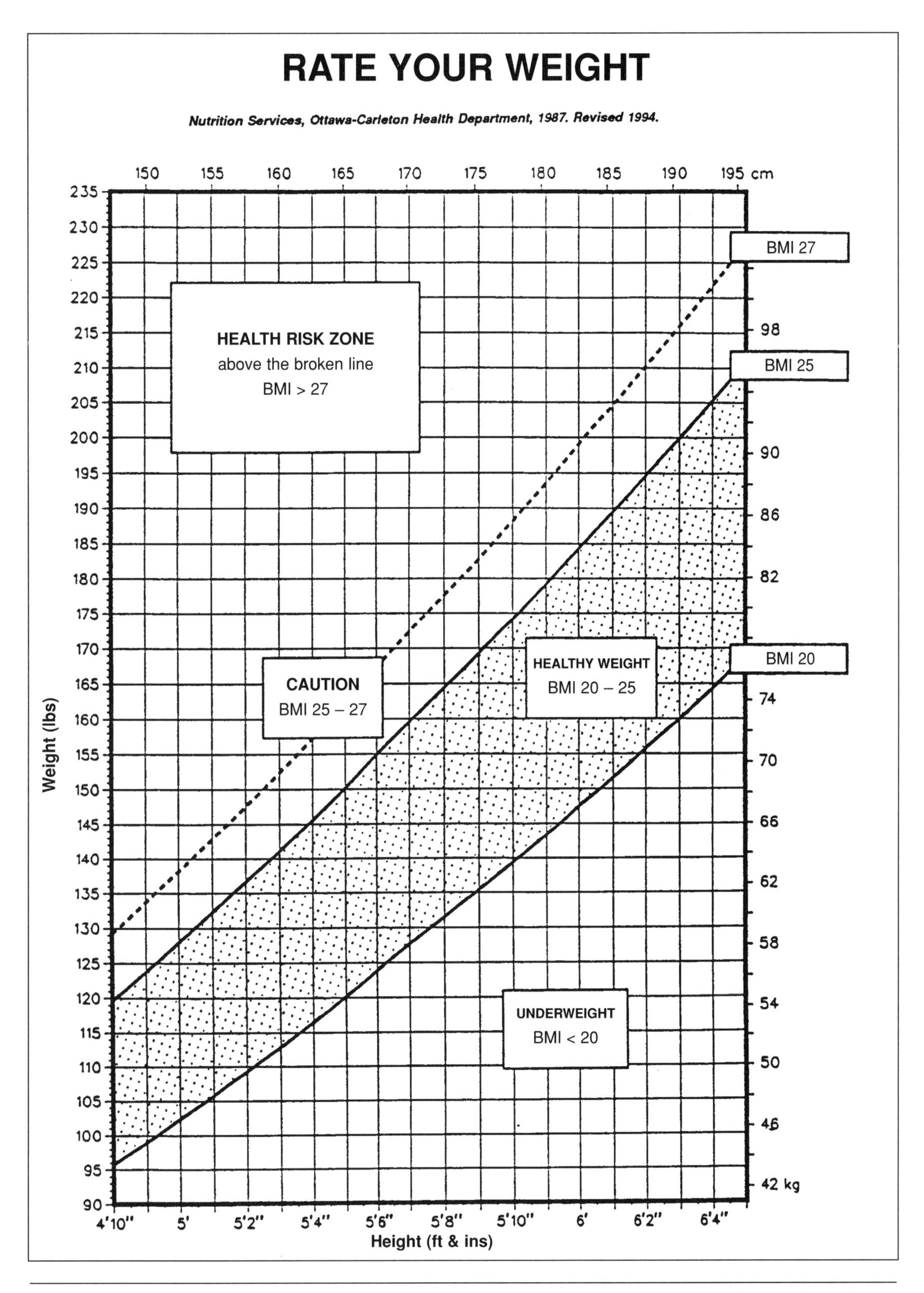

Developed by the Ottawa-Carleton Health Department, 1987. Revised 1994. Printed with permission. Nutrition Services, Ottawa-Carleton Health Department.}

How can your family achieve and maintain a healthy weight?

Instead of dieting, set healthy eating goals that your family can live with for life. Cut back on fat, include more high-fibre foods such as grains, vegetables and fruit and increase everyone's level of physical activity. Planning meals using Canada's Food Guide to Healthy Eating will help.

If weight loss is necessary, it should come off slowly, the way it was gained. One to 2 pounds (0.45 - 0.9 kg) a week should be the goal. If someone in your family needs weight control advice contact a Registered Dietitian.

Chapter 6

Managing Mealtime Madness with Young Children

Feeding a family is a tricky business. Every family includes a group of individuals all trying to live and work together as a unit. Tastes, nutritional needs and lifestyle all vary according to each family member's age and stage. Knowing how to satisfy the nutritional needs of everyone is challenging enough but becomes even more difficult when you add young children to the picture. Here are some coping strategies for some common food-related concerns of children.

For information on feeding babies and toddlers, refer to Appendix IV.

Does this kid sound familiar?

When Lynn's daughter Heather was four years old, she:

- wanted couscous or plain pasta every night for dinner;
- thought her sandwiches were edible only if cut into four triangles, with the crusts off;
- wanted only peanut butter sandwiches for lunch for an entire month, then switched to turkey sandwiches;
- had to have a red cup filled to the top with milk that she poured herself;
- insisted on whole apples with the skin off, but only ate half.

FOOD HABITS THAT DRIVE YOU WILD!

Food jags

Wanting to have the same food all the time is not unusual for children. Don't worry! They eventually move on to a new favourite food. In the meantime, round out their meal with a variety of other foods. Continue to offer different food choices at other meals and snacks during the week. If you limit the variety of meals that you provide, your child's acceptance of new or different foods will decrease.

When ketchup is a vegetable

Most children, especially Lynn's daughter Amelia, wish it was! Getting children to eat more vegetables isn't easy. Most kids will eat raw vegetables such as carrots, cucumbers and even raw cauliflower or broccoli. Try serving vegetable sticks for snacks, when kids are hungry, and you won't need to worry about getting extras in at mealtime. You can also purée vegetables and blend them into pasta sauces so that kids don't even know they are there. Try our Batch Ground Meat and Vegetables (page 88).

Playing with food

If your child dawdles or eats too slowly, check the serving sizes, which might be too big (see What is a child-size serving? on page 22). Also check the timing of snacks: too much food prior to supper will decrease a child's food intake.

Reluctance to try new foods

Often children say they don't like a food without even trying it. Simply offering a sample of food and putting it on a child's plate, whenever you eat it, can help increase the likelihood of acceptance. If you try to force your children to eat a food or even reward them with something they like, such as dessert, you decrease your chances of having them accept that food. Acceptance of a new food takes time and many repeated exposures. Sometimes a child may not accept a new food until he or she has been exposed to it 12 to 15 times.[1] Introducing new foods with peers around who like those foods can also help increase acceptance. Children may also be more willing to try new foods if they have been involved in preparing the meal.

---

[1]Birch, L. "Children's Preferences for High-Fat Foods," *Nutrition Reviews,* Vol. 50, No. 9, 249-255, 1992.

NOT EATING ENOUGH FOODS

If your child is growing properly, you probably have nothing to worry about. Children's appetites vary with growth spurts and activity patterns. On some days, children will seem hungrier than on others and will eat accordingly. A child's average intake of foods over time is what's important, not the amount of food eaten at each meal. If your child isn't eating a lot at suppertime, review what your child has eaten earlier in the day or even the day before. If your child has eaten a variety of foods from each of the four food groups, then he or she is probably doing okay. If poor intake of food continues for an extended period of time, consult your physician or a Registered Dietitian.

SUGAR AND HYPERACTIVITY

Research has proven that sugar does not cause hyperactivity.[2] Nevertheless, many parents and teachers observe a change in behaviour following the consumption of sugary foods. Most often the hyperactive behaviour is caused by nonfood factors such as the excitement associated with birthday parties, Halloween and the anticipation of a treat. This doesn't mean children should have unlimited access to sweets. Highly sweetened foods should not replace more nutrient-dense foods.

Survival at the Supper Table

Parents and caregivers do have to set some guidelines for kids at the dinner table, otherwise chaos, poor manners and possibly choking may result. Kids learn most of their social behaviour at home, so set a good example and be a positive role model. Our friend Barb McHughan posts this list in her kitchen to try to curb mealtime madness.

1. No dancing on or around the table.
2. Do not leave the table without asking.
3. Remember your manners.
4. Remember to use a knife, fork or spoon.
5. Do not bother other diners.
6. No negative comments about the food.
7. Pleasant conversation only.

[2]Does Sucrose or Aspartame Cause Hyperactivity in Children? *Nutrition Reviews*, Vol. 52, No. 5, 1994.

HEALTHY SNACKING IS ACCEPTABLE!

Snacks can actually help contribute to a child's total daily nutrient needs if the right choices are made. Snack foods should come from one of the four food groups in Canada's Food Guide to Healthy Eating. Keep a variety of these nutrient-packed snacks on hand.

- Prepare raw vegetable or fruit platters ahead of time and keep them in the refrigerator for after school snacks. Children are more likely to eat more of these foods when they are hungry. You don't need to worry so much about getting as many vegetables or fruit in the supper meal if some are eaten before dinner.
- Leave the candy, chips and pop at the store so your kids won't be tempted to eat these foods on a regular basis. Keep the cookie jar out of sight until after meals. Snacks that are high in fat and/or calories and low in nutrients fill kids up and decrease their intake of healthier foods.

Nutrient-packed snacks

- whole-grain bread, buns or bagels
- bread sticks
- whole-grain crackers
- cereals that are low in sugar
- fruit
- fruit cups
- juice popsicles
- raw vegetables
- unsweetened fruit juice instead of fruit drinks
- vegetable juice
- milk
- plain or fruit yogurt
- milk puddings
- cheese
- peanut butter
- pizza
- oatmeal, bran or whole-grain muffins

Avoid Foods that Cause Choking

Any food that is round or cylindrical in shape such as wieners, whole grapes or hard foods such as candies, popcorn, nuts and raw vegetable pieces can cause choking. Sticky foods such as soft candy (toffee type) and peanut butter (not spread on crackers or bread) can also get stuck and block airways. Kids under three are at the greatest risk of choking on these foods. In order to prevent choking, parents and caregivers should:

- avoid giving high-risk foods to children who have difficulty chewing or swallowing;
- watch children when they are eating and make sure that they are sitting upright and not laughing, jumping or running around;
- cut weiners and grapes lengthwise;
- give babies cooked vegetables.

MANAGING MEALTIME MADNESS TIPS

- Spend some time playing a game or reading with your children if you have not been with them all day. Children appreciate time to show off their school work or talk about their day.
- If you are with children all day, schedule an afternoon playtime outside or a quick walk to the park to keep them active and burn off some energy before supper.
- If your child always seems to need help with something just when you are making supper, you may need to suggest an alternative activity for them while you cook. Negotiate a more suitable time when you can help him or her with homework, crafts or other activities.
- If little ones climb up your legs while you are preparing supper, a bucket of toys on the kitchen floor and free access to the pot cupboard can help keep young ones busy and your hands free. Sometimes a hug, a quick chat or story is all children need before they let you get on with meal preparation. Try the Make and Bake meals (page 53) if you like to spend time with your child while supper cooks.

- If you can afford to, hire a teenager occasionally to help out with the children while you do a few errands or odd jobs around the house, go for a walk or simply enjoy making supper in peace.
- Encourage a quiet time prior to supper. Reading, listening to stories or music, colouring, doing homework or playing quiet games encourages everyone to settle down.
- Enjoy mealtimes together. Suppertime is a great time for sharing news and getting caught up on important events. As children get older and into more activities, continue to schedule meals together as often as possible.

Chapter 7

Supermarket Survival

STEERING SMARTLY THROUGH THE GROCERY AISLES

The nutritional quality of your meals depends on how successful you are at navigating the aisles in your grocery store. The foods that you buy and bring home are the ones that you will actually eat, so it is very important that you make wise food choices right at the store.

Here are some smart shopping tips:

- Use the *Suppertime Survival* Weekly Meal Planner and prepare a shopping list. Take the list when you go shopping so that you don't forget to buy items that you need for the meals you plan to make. Having a list will also help prevent you from buying items that you don't need.
- Check grocery store flyers for specials and use coupons for items that you normally use.
- Eat before you shop. If you're hungry, you may be more likely to impulse shop and buy extras that you don't really need.
- Have foods from each of the four food groups in your grocery cart to ensure that you can make balanced meals.
- Read food labels and try to choose the lower-fat, higher-fibre options. For example, yogurt containing 0.1% M.F. (milk fat) contains less fat than a yogurt

containing 4% M.F. A high-fibre food contains at least 4 grams of fibre per serving. For more information on reading labels, see Making Sense Of Food Labels (below).

- Skip the aisles that are stocked with pop, candy, chips and other snacks. These foods provide energy but few nutrients and many are high in fat and salt. Popcorn, sunflower seeds and unsalted pretzels are lower-fat snack choices.
- Check the "best before" date on foods and be sure that you can use them before that date. Items such as dairy products have a best-before date stamped on them. Other foods such as fresh meat, fish and poultry are labelled with their packaging date and should be eaten within a few days (see storage chart on page 181).
- Try to buy fewer convenience foods such as frozen entrées, TV dinners, snack foods, packaged desserts and baked goods. Besides costing a lot, these foods often contain hidden fats and more salt than you need.
- Get the best buy for your food dollar. Use unit prices on shelf labels to determine the best buy. Compare the cost of items per weight and choose the one with the lower cost.
- Buy in bulk when items are on sale. Soups, pasta, rice, canned and frozen goods can be stored easily for extended periods and are great to stock up on. Buying in bulk is only beneficial if you have the space to store the food properly before it spoils.
- Ask about attending a supermarket tour in your area. These are conducted by Registered Dietitians. To find out if there is one in your area, contact your local public health unit.

MAKING SENSE OF FOOD LABELS

Food labels can help you shop for foods and nutrients, but you need to read the whole label and the fine print to see if a food product is really the best choice.

All kinds of foods make claims about their nutrient content. Many of these claims can be confusing and some may even be misleading.

What's on a label?

There are three important bits of information on a nutrition label. The nutrition claim, nutrition information and the ingredient list can all help you decide if that food product is right for you.

Nutrition claims can be found in big, bold type on the front of a package. Claims are used to grab your attention about a specific nutrition concern such as fat. While claims must be truthful, they can be misleading. For example, a bag of potato chips may claim to be "cholesterol-free" and yet provides 20 grams of fat in a 2-oz (56 g) serving (about the size of a small bag of chips or 2½ cups/375 mL). That's about one-third of an average woman's daily fat limit. Sometimes "cholesterol-free" claims appear on foods that normally don't even contain cholesterol (e.g., bread). The point here is that if you use nutrition claims to make food choices, then look at the other information on the nutrition label. The claims don't tell the whole story.

Nutrition information must be provided on a food package if a nutrition claim is made about a food. For instance, if a product says "low in fat" then the number of grams of fat in one serving of the product must be stated on the nutrition information panel.

An ingredient list has to be put on every prepackaged product. Ingredients are listed in descending order based on their weight. The ingredient list can help you make healthier food choices. For example, if sugar is the first ingredient listed, that food contains more sugar than any other ingredient.

How to use food labels to make healthier choices

1. Check the list of ingredients for the type of fat used. For example, a granola cereal that contains hydrogenated vegetable oil and coconut oil, which are sources of saturated fat, has this label:

   Ingredients: Rolled oats, raisins coated with **hydrogenated vegetable oil,** brown sugar, rolled whole wheat, **coconut oil,** modified milk ingredients, dried unsweetened coconut, almonds, honey, natural flavour.

2. Look for the nutrition information panel. This label tells you that this bran cereal is low in fat (less than 3 grams fat per serving) and high in fibre (more than 4 grams per serving).

Energy	105 Cal/440 kJ
Protein	3.1 g
Fat	*0.4 g*
Carbohydrate	25 g
Sugars	3.3 g
Starch	17 g
Dietary fibre	*4.4 g*

3. Keep track of the amount of fat you eat. This macaroni and cheese dinner provides 11 grams of fat per ¾-cup (175 mL) serving. Adjust the amount of fat if you eat more or less than the stated serving size.

   Nutrition information for ¾ cup (175 mL) prepared macaroni and cheese:

Energy	278 Cal/1160 kJ
Protein	8.3 g
Fat	*11 g*
Carbohydrate	37 g

4. Trans-fatty acids act like saturated fat. Trans-fatty acids are found in foods containing partially hydrogenated fats. Currently they are not listed on food labels. To find out the amount of trans-fatty acids in these cookies, add up the amount of polyunsaturates, monounsaturates and saturates (7.4 g). Subtract this amount from the total fat content (9.4 g). The 2.0 gram difference is approximately the amount of trans-fatty acids in a serving of 4 cookies.

Energy	200 Cal
Protein	2.2 g
Fat	9.4 g
Polyunsaturates	*0.5 g*
Monounsaturates	*1.8 g*
Saturates	*5.1 g*
Cholesterol	0.1 mg
Carbohydrate	26.7 g

5. Check labels for sodium information. The amount of sodium will be listed in mg per serving. For example, look at this label for a prepared tomato pasta sauce:

   One serving (½ cup/125 mL) provides:

Energy	70 Cal
Protein	2.2 g
Carbohydrate	13 g
Sodium	*482 mg*
Potassium	537 mg

You should also look at the list of ingredients on a food label. If salt or sodium appears in connection with any ingredient, then you know that it contains sodium. Also, if sodium or salt appears at the beginning of the ingredient list, then you know that food is high in salt. For example, this ingredient list illustrates a high-sodium choice: dehydrated onions, *salt*, potato starch, *monosodium glutamate*, corn syrup solids, natural and artificial flavours, colour, hydrogenated vegetable oil, *disodium guanylate* and *disodium inosinate.*

SHOPPING FOR LOWER-FAT FOODS

- Include plenty of vegetables and fruit in your shopping cart. If they don't take up about a quarter of your groceries, go back for more. Add frozen vegetables for convenience and instant meal makers.
- Fill your cart with grain products such as bread, bagels, rolls, couscous, different kinds of pasta and rice, Italian-style flatbread rounds, pita bread and flour tortillas.
- Check the percentage of milk fat (% M.F.) or butter fat (% B.F.) on labels of milk, yogurt, cheese and ice cream. Choose the lower-fat versions such as: skim, 1% or 2% milk, yogurt or cottage cheese; or light sour cream or reduced-fat ricotta cheese.
- Don't forget meat alternatives such as eggs, light peanut butter, canned beans, peas, lentils and tofu.
- Buy fish (haddock, cod, sole, perch) without breading or sauce and choose tuna that is packed in water.
- Look for lean cuts of meat such as: sirloin, eye of the round, inside round, flank steaks and lean or extra-lean ground beef; pork tenderloin or centre cut-loin; veal; cold cuts such as lean ham, turkey or roast beef.
- Look for reduced-fat salad dressings that contain less than 3 grams of fat per serving (1 tbsp/15 mL) or fat-free salad dressings.

HOW TO MAKE SENSE OF NUTRITION CLAIMS

If the label says...	Then this is what it means...
Calorie-reduced	Contains 50% fewer calories than the same food when not calorie-reduced; it is suitable for dietary use
Low calorie	Is calorie-reduced and contains 15 calories or less per serving; this food usually contains fewer calories than a calorie-reduced food but more than a calorie-free food
Calorie-free	Contains no more than 1 calorie per 100 g
Source of energy	Contains at least 100 calories per serving as indicated on the label
Low in fat	Contains no more than 3 g of fat per serving
Fat-free	Contains no more than 0.1 g of fat per 100 g
Low in saturated fatty acids	Contains no more than 2 g of saturated fatty acids per serving and no more than 15% of energy derived from these
Low in cholesterol	Contains no more than 20 mg of cholesterol per serving and per 100 g and low in saturated fatty acids
Cholesterol-free	Contains no more than 3 mg of cholesterol per 100 g and low in saturated fatty acids
Source of dietary fibre	Contains at least 2 g of dietary fibre per serving
High source	Contains at least 4 g of dietary fibre per serving
Very high source	Contains at least 6 g of dietary fibre per serving
Low in sugar	Contains no more than 2 g of sugar per serving
No sugar added or unsweetened	Has no sugar added although it may contain naturally present sugar
Sugar-free	Contains no more than 0.25 g of sugar per 100 g and no more than 1 calorie per 100 g; this food usually contains the least amount of sugar and often the fewest calories; it is suitable for dietary use
Low sodium or low salt	The food contains 50% less sodium than the regular product and not more than 40 mg of sodium per 100 g*; and no salt has been added. It is a food suitable for dietary use
No added salt or unsalted	No salt is added to the food and none of the ingredients contains a large quantity of salt
Salt-free or sodium-free	The food does not contain more than 5 mg of sodium per 100 g; foods bearing this claim are usually those containing the smallest amount of salt or sodium
Source of, contains Vitamins and Minerals	Contains at least 5% of the recommended daily intake
Good source, high in Vitamins and Minerals	Contains at least 15% of the recommended daily intake (in the case of vitamin C 30%)
Excellent source, very high in, rich in Vitamins and Minerals	Contains at least 25% of the recommended daily intake (in the case vitamin C 50%)

*2 exceptions: Cheddar cheese may contain up to 50 mg of sodium per 100 g. Meat, poultry and fish may contain up to 80 mg of sodium per 100 g

Source: Guide to Nutrition Labelling. Consumer and Corporate Affairs. Minister of Supply and Services Canada, 1991.

Chapter 8

The Safe Kitchen

PREVENTING FOOD-RELATED ILLNESS

Preparing tasty and nutritious meals for your family is everyone's goal. But making sure the food is safe to eat is even more important. We've all heard about people who get sick when eating away from home, but even home-prepared food can cause food poisoning. Symptoms include diarrhea, vomiting, nausea, stomach cramps, fever, dizziness and headaches. Food poisoning may cause discomfort for a day but it can also be more serious and lead to death in some cases, especially very young or old people and those with weak immune systems.

Food poisoning occurs when bacteria that have come into contact with food are allowed to multiply to levels that can cause illness when that food is eaten. Bacteria are everywhere and they multiply rapidly, especially in high-protein foods. Meat, fish, poultry, eggs, dairy products and food mixtures containing mayonnaise could be unsafe to eat if they are not handled or stored properly.

Bacteria are too small to be seen and in some instances foods containing high levels of bacteria look, smell and taste normal. Therefore it is important to practice safe food handling techniques when preparing and storing foods.

KEEP FOODS OUT OF THE DANGER ZONE

Bacteria can't grow at or below 40°F (4°C) and are destroyed at or above 140°F (60°C).

To keep bacteria from multiplying:

Keep cold foods cold below 40°F (4°C).
Keep fridge set at 40°F (4°C).
Keep freezer set at 0°F (–18°C).
Keep hot foods hot above 140°F (60°C).

FOOD SAFETY TIPS

Here's how you can prevent food-related illness in your home:

Choose wisely:

- Select clean eggs with no cracks.
- Buy items that you will use before the best-before date expires.
- Don't buy tins that are bulging or badly dented or packages that are open.
- Buy frozen foods and meat, poultry, fish and dairy products at the end of your shopping trip and store promptly.

Prepare carefully:

- Always wash hands with soap and hot water before and during food preparation and especially after handling raw meat.
- Cover your mouth and nose and turn away from food when sneezing or coughing. Wash your hands again before handling food.
- Avoid letting any raw eggs or drippings from raw meat, fish or poultry come into contact with prepared (cooked) foods, or raw vegetables or fruit that you are intending to eat because this is how bacteria can travel between foods. For example, do not put the cooked turkey back on the same cutting board that the raw

turkey was sitting on. Sanitize anything that has touched raw meat, before using it again, to avoid contaminating other foods. Cutting boards, knives, countertops, sinks and dishcloths should be all be washed in hot soapy water then rinsed in chlorinated water. To sanitize, add a capful of bleach to a sink full of clear water, rinse utensils and air-dry.

- Don't stuff your turkey or chicken the night before you cook it. Raw poultry should be stuffed just prior to cooking to prevent bacterial growth.
- Use a clean spoon each time you test foods to avoid spreading germs from saliva.

Defrost safely:

- Don't leave foods to thaw on the counter because bacteria multiply quickly on warmer outside surfaces, making food unsafe to eat. The safest way to thaw foods is in the refrigerator, allowing five hours per pound (10 hours per kilogram) of food. You can use a microwave to thaw foods quickly. Remove food from packaging and thaw on a clean microwaveable plate. Cook microwave-defrosted food immediately since outer edges of the food can be in the danger zone (40°F/4°C to 140°F/60°C).

Can I thaw turkey in my garage?

No! Thawing poultry properly takes about five hours per pound (10 hours per kilogram) in the fridge. If you must, you can thaw a whole chicken or turkey by placing in a leak-proof plastic bag and immersing it in cold water. This method takes about one hour per pound (two hours per kilogram). The water should be changed often to keep the outside of the poultry cold.

Cook appropriately:

- Use a meat thermometer to ensure that meat or poultry is cooked to the correct internal temperature. Insert thermometer in the centre or fleshy part of meat, not touching any bone. For turkey, insert thermometer into inner thigh, just above and not touching the bone.

- Cook all poultry until it is no longer pink and juices run clear when pricked with a fork.
- Thoroughly cook all ground meat until it is no longer pink. In particular, hamburger patties should be checked in the middle before serving to make sure that they are cooked through.

E. coli bacteria can be present in undercooked hamburger meat and in some instances has caused food poisoning and even death. This has often been called hamburger disease, but other foods such as unpasteurized milk, ham, turkey, cheese and water can also contain E. coli.

Store properly:

- Keep hot foods hot (meat, poultry, fish, and combination dishes such as lasagna and casseroles). Leaving foods to sit on the counter at room temperature will cause bacterial growth. If someone is coming home late for dinner, put that portion on a clean plate, cover and refrigerate. He or she can heat it up later in the microwave.
- Keep cold foods cold until ready to serve, especially milk, soft cheese and foods containing mayonnaise such as meat, fish, egg or poultry salad.
- If in doubt, throw it out! Forgotten leftovers, mouldy cheese, and foods past their expiry date can all be a source of bacteria and should not be eaten. Foods that have thawed, and been refrozen before being cooked are also unsafe to eat.
- Check labels on packaged fresh meat. If it says that the meat has been previously frozen, do not refreeze. Previously frozen raw meat can be frozen after it has been cooked thoroughly.
- Refrigerate foods after opening if the labels tell you to (mayonnaise, salad dressings, etc.)
- Best-before dates don't apply once a container is opened. Milk, cream, cottage cheese, sour cream and yogurt should be used as quickly as possible after

opening. Salad dressing and mayonnaise keep six months unopened but should be refrigerated and used within two months after opening.

- Rewrap and freeze any raw meat, fish and poultry that you will not be using within two days.
- Proper refrigeration and freezer storage of all fresh and frozen meat, fish, poultry, eggs and prepared dishes such as lasagnas, casseroles, chili and soups is very important.
- Use the following chart to keep foods safe to eat and to maintain good food quality.

FOOD STORAGE CHART

Food	**Refrigerator 40°F (4°C)**	**Freezer 0°F (-18°C)**
Deli and Vacuum-Packed Foods:		
Bacon (side)	7 days	1 month
Corned Beef, in pouch with pickling juices	5-7 days	drained, wrapped 1 month
Hot dogs, opened package	1 week	1-2 months in
Hot dogs, unopened package	2 weeks	freezer wrap
Lunch meats, opened package	3-5 days	1-2 months in
Lunch meats, unopened package	2 weeks	freezer wrap
Egg, chicken, tuna, ham or macaroni salads	2-3 days	don't freeze well
Commercial vacuum-packed dinners	2 weeks, unopened	don't freeze well
Store-cooked convenience meals	1-2 days	don't freeze well
Stuffed pork and lamb chops, stuffed chicken breasts	1 day	don't freeze well
Eggs:		
- fresh, in shell	3 weeks	don't freeze
- raw yolks, whites	2-4 days	4 months
- cooked, hard	1 week	don't freeze well
- egg substitutes, liquid, opened	3 days	don't freeze
- egg substitutes, liquid, unopened	10 days	4 months
Mayonnaise, commercial, refrigerated, after opening	2 months	don't freeze
Fish, seafoods and shellfish	1-2 days	4-6 months
Ham:		
- canned	6-9 months	don't freeze
- fully cooked, whole	7 days	1-2 months
- fully cooked, half	3-5 days	1-2 months
- fully cooked, slices	3-4 days	1-2 months
Hamburger and stew meats	1-2 days	3-4 months
Ground turkey, lamb, pork, veal	1-2 days	3-4 months
continued on next page		

Food	Refrigerator 40°F (4°C)	Freezer 0°F (-18°C)
Meat, fresh:		
Beef steaks	3-5 days	6-12 months
Pork chops	3-5 days	4-6 months
Lamb chops	3-5 days	6-9 months
Roasts, beef	3-5 days	6-12 months
Roasts, lamb	3-5 days	6-9 months
Roasts, pork and veal	3-5 days	4-6 months
Organ meats	1-2 days	3-4 months
Meat leftovers:		
Cooked meat and meat dishes	3-4 days	2-3 months
Prepared frozen dinners, casseroles, keep frozen until ready to serve		3-4 months
Poultry, fresh:		
Chicken or turkey, whole	1-2 days	1 year
Chicken or turkey pieces	1-2 days	9 months
Poultry, cooked		
Chicken nuggets, patties	1-2 days	1-3 months
Fried chicken	3-4 days	4 months
Chicken or turkey pieces, plain	3-4 days	4 months
Cooked poultry dishes	3-4 days	4-6 months
Sausage, raw from pork, beef, turkey	1-2 days	1-2 months
Sausage, hard, pepperoni, jerky sticks	2-3 weeks	1-2 months
Soups and Stews	3-4 days	2-3 months

Adapted from: Safe Food Handling, Ontario Ministry of Health. Reproduced with permission. Queen's Printer for Ontario, 1993.

Appendix I

Vitamins and Minerals

VITAMINS—IS YOUR FAMILY GETTING ENOUGH?

If your family does not eat many vegetables and fruit, then they may be missing out on some important vitamins. We need vitamins to help us function properly. Vitamins play a vital role in regulating chemical reactions in our bodies, protecting cells from destruction and converting food into energy. Some vitamins (A, D, E, K) are fat soluble and are stored in the body. The rest (B vitamins and C) are water soluble, so we need a regular supply of these in our diet.

Vitamins play an essential role in keeping everyone healthy. Without vitamins, nutrient deficiencies such as scurvy, rickets and anemia can result. Some vitamins, especially vitamins C, E and beta-carotene, may help protect against heart disease and some forms of cancer. Folic acid has been shown to help reduce birth defects such as spina bifida. And research has shown that the elderly can boost their immune systems if they increase their vitamin intakes.

What are antioxidants?

Antioxidants are chemical substances that help trap and prevent the formation of free radicals. Free radicals are unstable molecules that form as a result of chemical reactions in our bodies. If these free radicals aren't destroyed by an antioxidant, they can damage cell membranes and the genetic makeup of cells.

Vitamins C, E and beta-carotene (the plant form of vitamin A) are called antioxidants because they help make free radicals harmless. By acting in this manner, these nutrients have been found to have a role in preventing cell damage, which contributes to the development of some diseases.

Antioxidant vitamins, heart disease and cancer

There is growing evidence that vitamins C, E and beta-carotene can help protect against heart disease and cancer. Vitamins C, E and beta-carotene appear to protect against heart

Recommended Daily Nutrient Intake of Vitamins A, C, E and Folic Acid

Vitamin	Male		Female	
	25-49	50-74	25-49	50-74
Vitamin A (RE)*	1000	1000	800	800
Vitamin C (mg)**	40	40	30	30
Vitamin E (mg)	9	7	6	6
Folic Acid (µg)***	230	230	185	195

*There is no RNI for beta-carotene.

**Smokers should increase vitamin C by 50%

***Pregnant women should have 200 additional mg, breast-feeding women 100 additional mg daily

Source: Health Canada, Recommended Nutrient Intakes for Canadians. Nutrition Recommendations: The Report of the Scientific Review Committee. Ottawa (1990). Reproduced with the permission of the Minister of Supply and Services Canada, 1995.

disease by lowering the risk of atherosclerosis (fatty buildup in arteries). Vitamin E, particularly in a supplement form, has shown the most impact on reducing the risk of coronary heart disease.[1,2,3] Eating vegetables and fruit rich in vitamin C or beta-carotene is linked with a reduced risk of all cancers.[4,5,6]

The best way to get vitamins is to get them directly from food sources such as vegetables and fruit. Research on antioxidant vitamins is not conclusive but clearly shows that we need to get more of these nutrients in our diet and that vegetables and fruit are the best sources. Vegetables and fruit also contain non-nutritive substances (i.e., flavones, indoles, isothiacyantes and phenols) that have a protective role against chronic diseases. Because antioxidant vitamins work best when they are eaten in combination with one another, offer your family a variety of dark green or orange vegetables and dark orange fruit.

Folic acid and birth defects

Folic acid is a B vitamin that is very important to women considering pregnancy. Research has shown that adequate intakes one month prior to pregnancy until the end of the first trimester can prevent neural tube birth defects such as spina bifida.[7] Some vegetables and fruit are good sources of folic acid (see Vitamin Functions and Food Sources chart, page 187), but many women have trouble getting enough folic acid to satisfy the recommended amount. Women need 400 µg of folic acid per day prior to and during pregnancy[7]. Pregnant women and women who are considering pregnancy should speak to their physician or Registered Dietitian about folic acid supplements.

Boosting immunity in seniors

People with nutrient deficiencies, such as the elderly, may have a higher rate of infections due to immune systems that are not working effectively. Increasing nutrient intakes to adequate levels can improve immunity in nutrient-deficient seniors, resulting in less infections.[8]

These *Suppertime Survival* meals are an excellent source of folic acid (they contain at least 25% of the Recommended Daily Intake for folic acid).

Asparagus Frittata*
Bail-Out Bean Burritos
Baked Fish with Oven-Fried Potatoes
Basil Zucchini Strata
Black Bean, Corn and Couscous Salad**
Broiled Minted Lamb Chops with Rosemary Potatoes
Barbecued Salmon Supper **
Chili and Cornbread
Easy on Ya Lasagna
Family Tuna Noodle Casserole
Fast Fish in the Microwave
Flake and Bake Chicken
French Toast with Peaches and Syrup
Fusilli with Vegetarian Pasta Sauce
Lentil and Pasta Soup
Marinated Beef and Vegetable Kabobs
Mediterranean Pizza
Pizza Pockets
Roast Turkey Breast and Vegetable Supper
Spanish Rice with Lentils **
Speedy Vegetable and Chicken Stir-Fry with Rice
Spinach Frittata Fingers
Spinach Salad with Honey-Orange Dressing
Sweet Beans and Toast
Tangy Barbecue Chicken with Rice
Tangy Barbecue Ribs with Rice
Three-Bean Chili *
Tuna Salad Toss*
Vegetarian Lasagna
Warm Taco Salad

* supplies over 60% of Recommended Daily Intake of folic acid for adults
** supplies over 90% of Recommended Daily Intake of folic acid for adults

Who needs supplements?

Most people can get the recommended amount of vitamins they need from eating a well-balanced diet based on Canada's Food Guide to Healthy Eating. However, certain groups in the population can benefit from supplements. Before you consider a supplement for someone in your family, *it's important to discuss his or her needs with a Registered Dietitian or your physician.*

Infants may need a vitamin D supplement while they are being exclusively breast-fed. Infants taking formula should not be given supplements since formula already has vitamins added to it.

Children who cannot eat foods from an entire food group can benefit from a supplement. For example, children who can't eat milk products may need to take a calcium supplement. If parents are worried about their child's food intake, a single multivitamin pill can assure them that their child is getting added nutritive value to their diet. However, pills can't replace food and don't provide carbohydrate, protein or fat, which are all important to give children energy and to help them grow. Parents must still provide their child with a variety of healthy food choices.

Vitamin overdoses are a serious concern with children. Don't treat vitamins or other pills as candy or give a child more than the recommended amount. Store vitamins safely out of sight and reach of children.

Pregnant women should get an adequate amount of folic acid at the time of conception. Since half of all pregnancies are unplanned, women in their childbearing years who could become pregnant should try to consume adequate amounts of folic acid. An effective intake is about 400 µg (0.4 mg) per day of folic acid. Most women don't get close to that amount with their food choices, so supplements are beneficial. Pregnant women may also need a multivitamin to ensure that they get adequate amounts of other vitamins and minerals such as calcium and iron.

Adults who don't eat enough vegetables and fruit might benefit from a multivitamin supplement. However, you are better off getting your nutrients from foods rather than a bottle. Vegetables and fruit provide antioxidant nutrients, trace nutrients, fibre and other non-nutritive substances that act as protective agents against cancer and heart disease. You also don't get pep or energy from vitamin supplements.

Older people with marginal or low nutrient intakes and those who get a lot of infections may require a multivitamin supplement to improve their nutritional status.

If you do take supplements, be sure to follow the recommended dosage. More does not mean better. There are potential toxic effects from taking nutrients such as vitamins A and D and the minerals iron, zinc and selenium in high doses. You can also get side effects from too much vitamin B6 and fluoride.

MINERALS: WHO NEEDS THEM?

Minerals are inorganic substances such as sodium, iron, calcium, phosphorus, magnesium and potassium. We need minerals for a variety of purposes such as keeping our muscles working, our blood healthy, maintaining fluid balance and for growth and development. Minerals are important to every structure in our body from bones and teeth to nerves and muscles. We need some minerals in large amounts, for example calcium, phosphorus and magnesium. We get some minerals, like sodium, in quantities greater than we need. Other minerals, such as iron, fluoride and zinc, are needed in much smaller amounts.

Minerals are not made in our bodies so we need to eat certain amounts to stay healthy.

VITAMIN FUNCTIONS AND FOOD SOURCES

Vitamin	Functions	Good Food Sources
A	– maintains good vision – keeps skin and eyes healthy – promotes normal growth and development – maintains immune system	liver, dark green and orange vegetables (spinach, broccoli, carrots), apricots, cantaloupe, eggs, milk, margarine
Beta-carotene	– converts to vitamin A in body – antioxidant, combats adverse effects of free radicals	dark orange vegetables and fruits and dark green leafy vegetables such as sweet potatoes, carrots, spinach, kale, yellow squash, broccoli, apricots, papaya
B's	– releases food energy to cells – keeps eyes, mouth and skin healthy – promotes normal brain and nervous system function – promotes normal growth and development	whole-grain and enriched breads and cereals, meat, eggs, legumes, nuts, milk and milk products
C	– promotes wound healing – keeps gums and teeth healthy – helps body absorb iron – maintains strong blood vessel walls – antioxidant, combats adverse effects of free radicals	citrus fruits and juices, strawberries, leafy green vegetables, sweet peppers, kiwifruit, broccoli, brussels sprouts, cauliflower, melons, tomatoes, potatoes, sweet potatoes, guavas, mangoes
D	– helps build strong bones and teeth – ensures proper functioning of muscles, nerves, cell growth, blood clotting and energy utilization	fortified milk, eggs, liver, fish, fish liver oils, you also produce vitamin D when your skin is exposed to sunlight
E	– antioxidant, combats adverse effects of free radicals – preserves cell membranes – protects body's supply of vitamins A and C	margarine, vegetable oils, whole-grain cereals, wheat germ, nuts, seeds, leafy green vegetables, dried apricots
Folic acid	– helps form blood cells and nervous tissue – reduces risk of neural tube birth defects such as spina bifida when consumed in adequate amounts by women at time of conception	dark leafy green vegetables spinach, broccoli, green peas, Brussels sprouts, oranges, orange juice, cantaloupe, dried peas, beans and lentils, wheat germ, yeast
K	maintains normal blood clotting	dark green leafy vegetables (spinach, turnip greens), broccoli, Brussels sprouts, peas, liver, ham, whole-grain breads and cereals

The best way for your family to get minerals is from foods. In some cases, supplements may be necessary for certain family members and they should discuss their needs with a Registered Dietitian or physician.

Why is iron important?

Iron is needed to form hemoglobin in red blood cells. Hemoglobin picks up oxygen and carries it through the bloodstream to every cell in the body. Oxygen is needed to release energy that we need to keep our heart beating, our lungs breathing and our bodies working. Iron is also needed to prevent iron deficiency anemia, which can lead to fatigue and a lack of energy.

Adequate iron intakes are especially important for women, teens and children. Getting enough iron is also a concern for very athletic women and for vegetarians.

Recommended Daily Nutrient Intake for Iron

Age	mg iron per day
Children age 1-12	6-8
Teen males 13-18	10
Teen females 13-18	12-13
Adult males 19+	9
Adult females 19-49	13
Adult females 50+	8
Pregnancy (additional) 1st trimester	0
2nd trimester	5
3rd trimester	10

Source: Health Canada. Recommended Nutrient Intakes for Canadians. Nutrition Recommendations: The Report of the Scientific Review Committee. Ottawa (1990). Reproduced with the permission of the Minister of Supply and Services Canada, 1995.

FOOD SOURCES OF IRON

- Meats (especially red meat), wild meat, poultry, liver, some fish, eggs
- Beans, peas and lentils
- Whole-grain and enriched breads, iron-fortified cereals
- Dried fruit (apricots, prunes and raisins)
- Vegetables that are dark green (spinach, broccoli, Brussels sprouts and green peas)
- Nuts, seeds and sunflower seeds

TIPS TO BOOST IRON INTAKE:

- Choose iron-fortified cereal with juice for breakfast. Vitamin C helps your body absorb more iron from cereals.

- Combine citrus fruit or juices with vegetable sources of iron to increase iron absorption. Try a spinach salad with mandarin oranges, tomatoes or an orange juice-based dressing.
- Add blackstrap molasses to baked beans or muffins.
- Serve more bean dishes such as baked beans, chili con carne and salads made with kidney beans or chick-peas.
- Have dried fruit on cereal, in salads, muffins, fruit breads, and rice pudding, or just grab a handful.

These *Suppertime Survival* meals are an excellent source of Iron (They contain at least 25% of the Recommended Daily Intake for Iron, for adults).

Anytime Pizza
Bail-Out Bean Burritos
Barbecued Steak Supper
Beef Stroganoff with Noodles
Black Bean, Corn and Couscous Salad
Broiled Minted Lamb Chops with Rosemary Potatoes
Chicken Fajitas
Chili and Cornbread
Curried Beef in a Pita
Easy on Ya Lasagna
Extra-Speedy Spaghetti Supper
Family Tuna Noodle Casserole
Flake and Bake Chicken
French Toast with Peaches
Fusilli with Vegetarian Pasta Sauce
Ground Beef Stroganoff with Noodles
Harvest Vegetables with Chicken and Penne
Homemade Spaghetti Supper
Spaghettini with Broccoli and Ham
Marinated Beef and Vegetable Kabobs
Spanish Rice with Lentils
Spinach Frittata Fingers
Sweet and Sour Pork with Vermicelli
Sweet Beans and Toast
Szechuan Beef and Mandarin Orange Stir-fry with Rice
Three-Bean Chili with Couscous
Tortellini With Creamy Cheese Sauce

Concerned about calcium?

If someone in your family avoids milk or milk products or if you are worried about osteoporosis, then you should be concerned about calcium. Calcium is an important mineral that your body does not make. We need calcium to build strong bones and teeth, to keep our heart beating normally, to help our muscles contract and relax, for proper nerve functioning and to help wounds heal by clotting blood.

A lack of calcium in prime bone-building years (childhood, adolescence and young adulthood) can reduce bone density and put you at risk for osteoporosis (brittle bone disease) later in life. High-risk candidates for osteoporosis are mostly, but not limited to, lightweight inactive women with light skin colouring, especially those with low-calcium diets.

How much calcium is enough?

Calcium is important for everyone, so you should make sure your family members are meeting the minimum recommended amounts shown in the chart below. People who are at risk for osteoporosis may need to eat even more calcium (1000 mg/day for people aged 19-49 and 1000-1500 mg/day for those over 49).[9] An active lifestyle is also important to help store more calcium in bones.

Food Sources of Calcium

- Milk and milk products such as cheese and yogurt
- Fish such as salmon and sardines with bones
- Vegetables and fruit such as beet greens, bok choy, figs, kale, oranges, rhubarb and spinach
- Almonds, baked beans, chick-peas, chili con carne, red kidney beans, sesame seeds, soybeans, tofu (made with calcium sulphate), white beans

Recommended Daily Nutrient Intake for Calcium

	Age	mg calcium per day
Children aged	1	500
	2-3	550
	4-6	600
	7-9	700
males	10-12	900
females	10-12	1100
males	13-15	1100
females	13-15	1000
males	16-18	900
females	16-18	700
males	19+	800
females**	19-49	700
females	50+	800

**Pregnant and breast-feeding women need an additional 500 mg of calcium per day.

Source: Health Canada. Recommended Nutrient Intakes for Canadians. Nutrition Recommendations: The Report of the Scientific Review Committee. Ottawa (1990). Reproduced with the permission of the Minister of Supply and Services Canada, 1995.

These *Suppertime Survival* meals are an excellent source of calcium (they contain at least 25% of the Recommended Daily Intake for Calcium).

Anytime Pizza
Bail-Out Bean Burritos
Basil Zucchini Strata
Creamy Macaroni and Cheese
Easy on Ya Lasagna
Family Tuna Noodle Casserole
Mediterranean Pizza
Ravioli with Prepared Pasta Sauce
Spinach Frittata Fingers
Tortellini with Creamy Cheese Sauce
Vegetarian Lasagna
Warm Taco Salad
Zucchini and Red Pepper Frittata

What if Someone in Your Family Can't Eat Milk Products?

Food allergies or lactose intolerance may prevent a family member from eating milk products. Therefore the person may have difficulty getting all the calcium he or she needs from foods. The best source of easy-to-absorb calcium is milk and milk products. There are other food sources of calcium, such as vegetables (collards, kale, bok choy, broccoli), nuts and seeds (almonds, sesame seeds), tofu made with calcium and beans (chick-peas, kidney beans). However, the calcium from these foods is not fully absorbed and larger amounts of these foods need to be eaten. You may want to speak to a Registered Dietitian for advice about a balanced diet or supplements.

Is there too much sodium in your family's diet?

We all need to have some sodium in our diet for maintaining proper water balance and for regulating blood volume and pressure. The amount we actually need is very small (about 80 mg per day for a 70 kg man). Many people, in Western countries, consume much more than that, ranging from about 2300 mg to 6700 mg per day.[10] High intakes of sodium are associated with high blood pressure, a major risk factor for heart disease and strokes. Because of this it's important for families to look for ways to eat less sodium and salt.

How did all that sodium get in my family's diet?

Sodium is naturally present in many foods. Extra sodium gets into our foods when they are processed. Much of the sodium we eat comes from sodium chloride, which we know as table salt, and other things that we add to our foods such as soy sauce, seasoning salts, ketchup and other condiments.

High-sodium foods include:

- pickled foods such as pickles, relish, sauerkraut
- salted foods such as chips, nuts, crackers
- canned vegetables, soups, stews, pasta dishes
- packaged or dried goods such as soups, pasta, rice mixes
- processed or salt-cured meats such as hot dogs, bacon, bologna, sausages, ham

How much sodium can my family eat?

There is no recommendation for the amount of sodium to eat because most people eat more than their basic requirements. Family members who are on sodium-restricted diets will have to be careful about how much sodium they eat and should discuss their limits with their physician or a Registered Dietitian.

Tips to reduce your family's salt intake:

- Use fresh foods more often than processed foods.
- Have smoked, cured and pickled foods less often.
- Use highly salted snacks and crackers in moderation.
- Try fresh chopped basil, parsley, mint, coriander, dill or chives to liven up salads.
- Perk up foods with a squeeze of lime, lemon zest or orange juice.
- Use fresh garlic or garlic powder instead of garlic salt, celery seed instead of celery salt, and onions instead of onion salt.
- Omit the salt in recipes and experiment with different flavours: dried basil, bay leaves, cumin, coriander, curry powder, ginger, nutmeg, oregano, parsley and many more.
- Look for foods that are lower in salt—use food labels as your guide (see page 174).

---

[1]*Lederle Letter*. "Antioxidant vitamins and coronary heart disease." Volume 2 (5), October 1993.

[2]Stampfer M.J., Hennekens C.H., Manson J.E., et al. "Vitamin E consumption and the risk of coronary heart disease in women." *New England Journal Medicine*. Vol. 328:1444-1449, 1993.

[3]Rimm, E.B., Stampfer, M.J., Ascherio, A., et al. "Vitamin E consumption and the risk of coronary heart disease in men. *New England Journal of Medicine*. Vol 328:1450-1456, 1993.

[4]Weisburger, J. "Nutritional approach to cancer prevention with emphasis on vitamins, antioxidants and carotenoids." AJCN 53:226s-237s, 1991.

[5]*University of California at Berkeley Wellness Letter*. "Our vitamin prescription: the Big Four." Vol. 10 (4), January 1994.

[6]*Mayo Clinic Health Letter*. "Antioxidants." Vol. 11(8), August 1993.

[7]Picciano M.F., Green T., O'Connor D., "The folate status of women and health. *Nutrition Today*, Vol. 29, No. 6, 1994.

[8]Chandra, R. "Effect of vitamin and trace-element supplementation on immune responses and infection in elderly subjects." *Lancet* 340:1124, 1992.

[9]Osteoporosis Society of Canada recommendation based upon the 1993 Consensus Statement on Calcium Nutrition.

[10]Health Canada. Nutrition Recommendations. The Report of the Scientific Review Committee. Supply and Services Canada, 1990.

Appendix II

DO WE NEED TO EAT FAT?

Yes! Everyone needs to include some fat in his or her diet because it is essential to health. Fat helps satisfy energy needs and is a source of essential fatty acids and fat-soluble vitamins (A, D, E and K). It also helps support growth, maintenance and functioning of many body tissues including nerves and skin. We also need fat to protect vital organs and maintain body temperature.

Why the concern about fat?

Today, most adults eat too much fat, which puts them at increased risk for health problems such as heart disease, certain types of cancer, diabetes and obesity. One of the most important changes to our eating habits that we should make is to eat less fat.

How much fat is okay?

We need to get at least 15 percent of our calories from fat. The problem is that most people in Canada get closer to 40 percent of their calories from fat. Therefore, Health Canada recommends that adults try to get less than 30 percent of their total calories from fat.[1] If you translate that into grams of fat, a healthy limit for an average woman (25 to 49 years old) is about 65 grams of fat per day and about 90 grams of fat per day for an average man (aged 25 to 49).

What about fat and kids? Should I restrict their fat intake?

The fat limits suggested above do not apply to children. While children are growing and developing, they require more fat in their diets. Their need for fat decreases gradually from infancy, when they get about 50 percent of their calories from fat (breastmilk, formula) to the time when they realize their adult height in late adolescence. At that time, teens should look for ways to eat less fat and keep their fat intake at about 30 percent of total calories.

If parents are cutting back on fat, younger children can still eat the same meals and enjoy some higher-fat foods at other meals and snacks. Children can get the extra fat they

---

[1]Health Canada. Nutrition Recommendations: The Report of the Scientific Review Committee. Supply and Services Canada, 1990.

need from 2% or whole milk, peanut butter, higher-fat cheeses and ice cream. Foods such as deep-fat fried and breaded foods (chicken nuggets, fish sticks, French fries) that add fat without adding extra nutrients should be used in moderation.

What foods contain fat?

The obvious sources of fat in our diet are fats that we add to our foods. Butter, margarine, vegetable oils, salad dressing, mayonnaise and lard are some of those visible fats. Many other foods contain fat that we cannot see. Hidden fats are found in meats, dairy products, deep-fat fried foods, nuts and baked goods such as croissants, doughnuts, muffins and cookies. Some fat-containing foods are important sources of nutrients, such as meats that provide iron and zinc, and milk products that are high in calcium. If we eliminate these kinds of foods, we may decrease our intake of these and other important nutrients.

It is important to keep your family's fat intake in perspective and to focus on cutting back on fat without sacrificing nutrients. Take a look at the foods your family eats to see which foods contribute most of the fat they eat. It may very well be breakfast on the run: a take-out muffin can sometimes contain 12 grams of fat and a tablespoon (15 mL) of coffee cream adds another 2 grams of fat. Look for ways to cut down your family's total intake of fat. Provide lower-fat foods more often and have foods that are high in fat but low in nutrients less often.

How much fat does your family eat?

There are two ways to find out how much fat your family eats: fat gram charts and food labels. Use both methods to see how much fat (grams) is in your family's meals, snacks and beverages. Keep track of how much fat your family eats over a few days. After that, make some changes to their food choices by incorporating some of the "Tips for Lower-Fat Eating" (see page 197). Check fat intake afterwards to see if your family is eating less fat than before.

Here's how to monitor your family's fat intake for one day.

1. Keep a list of all the foods your family eats in a typical day. Set up a column for grams of fat beside it (see example below).

Foods Eaten	*Fat (grams)*
bagel	2
cream cheese	15
orange juice	0
apple	0
hamburger	9
2% milk	5

2. Use the *Fat Content of Some Common Foods* chart (page 199) or the *Fat and Calories in Some Popular Fast Foods* chart (page 151) to find out how much fat is in the foods eaten. Check that the serving size matches the amount of food eaten. If not, adjust the amount of fat (e.g. if 2 hamburgers were eaten, then double the fat grams).

3. Check labels on food packages. Food labels show how much fat is in a product and this is printed as grams (g) of fat.

Finding out how much fat by using a food label.

Look for the nutrition information panel on the food package. For example, the amount of fat in one low-fat oatmeal muffin is indicated on this sample food label.

Nutrition Information Panel for Low-Fat oatmeal muffins	
1 muffin (50 g)	
energy	137cal/570 kJ
protein	2.7 g
fat	**1.8 g**
polyunsaturates	0.7 g
monounsaturates	0.6 g
saturates	0.2 g
cholesterol	0 mg
carbohydrate	27 g
dietary fibre	0.8 g

This muffin contains 1.8 grams of fat. Some muffins can contain as much as 12 grams of fat. Check labels or ask for information about the fat content when choosing a muffin at a take-out stand or muffin shop.

4. Add up the total amount of fat you have eaten for the day. If total fat intake for one day was more than 65 grams (for a woman aged 25 to 49 years) or 90 grams (for a man aged 25 to 49), then look for ways to reduce fat intake using the Tips for Lower-Fat Eating (page 197).

How much fat is in your lunch?

Here's a sample lunch meal to show how easy it is to cut fat intake using some lower-fat choices.

Regular choices	**Fat (g)**	**Lower-fat choices**	**Fat (g)**
Tuna sandwich		Tuna sandwich	
- brown bread (2 slices)	trace	- bread	trace
- tuna, oil-packed (½ cup/125 mL)	7	- tuna, water-packed	1
- mayonnaise (reg., 1 tbsp/15 mL)	11	- light mayonnaise	5
Dill pickle	trace	Dill pickle	trace
2% milk (1 cup/250 mL)	5	Skim milk	trace
Banana	trace	Banana	trace
Potato chips (15 chips 1 oz/30 g)	10	2 cookies	4
Total fat	33	Total fat	10

We cut the amount of fat in this lunch by choosing lower-fat choices such as tuna packed in water, light mayonnaise, skim milk, and cookies (digestive type) instead of potato chips.

What is cholesterol?

Cholesterol is a fatlike substance found in your body that is essential for digesting food and producing hormones and vitamin D. There are two types of cholesterol: dietary cholesterol and blood cholesterol.

Dietary cholesterol comes from foods of animal origin such as meat, fish, poultry, eggs and dairy products. The cholesterol in your blood is called blood cholesterol, and most of that cholesterol got there because your body produced it.

Is cholesterol a concern?

Cholesterol is only a concern if your doctor has told you that you have high blood cholesterol levels that need to be controlled. Otherwise, most healthy people can eat foods containing cholesterol.

For most people, cholesterol from foods has little effect on blood cholesterol levels, because your body tries to maintain a balance. If you eat more cholesterol than you need, your body will produce less. Eating too much fat, especially saturated fat, has a greater influence on increasing blood cholesterol levels than eating dietary cholesterol.

High blood cholesterol levels are a risk factor for heart disease. If you want to keep your blood cholesterol at a normal level, the best strategy is to limit your intake of all fats, especially saturated fat, eat more complex carbohydrates and fibre and increase your level of physical activity.

Confused about the different types of fat?

The fat that we get from foods is made up of a combination of the following different types of fat.

SATURATED FATS are found in meats, dairy products and many processed foods that contain lard or hydrogenated palm or coconut oil. A diet that is high in saturated fats increases blood cholesterol levels, which is a heart-health concern.

TRANS-FATTY ACIDS act like saturated fats and increase blood cholesterol levels. They are found in foods that contain partially hydrogenated fats. Hydrogenation is a process that turns liquid vegetable oils into more solid forms of fat at room temperature. Shortening, some margarines, doughnuts, French fries, cookies, crackers, chips and other processed foods contain hydrogenated fats.

MONOUNSATURATED FATS are found mostly in canola, olive and peanut oils and foods made with these oils. These fats appear to be neutral in terms of lowering blood cholesterol levels.

POLYUNSATURATED FATS are found in safflower, sunflower, corn, soybean, flaxseed and sesame oils. Polyunsaturated fats have been found to decrease blood cholesterol levels.

> When choosing a margarine, select a soft margarine made from canola, corn, safflower or olive oil. Check to make sure that your margarine has a high amount of polyunsaturated and monounsaturated fat (six grams or more per 10 gram serving). When cooking, try an oil that is high in polyunsaturated fat or monounsaturated fat such as safflower, sunflower, corn, canola or olive oil.

TIPS FOR LOWER-FAT EATING

EVERY DAY:

- Include more grain products such as cereal, bread, bagels, pasta, rice and couscous at every meal. If you add butter or margarine, try smaller amounts.
- Have five to 10 servings of vegetables and fruit each day. Try them without sauces, breading or added fats. Microwave or steam vegetables or stir-fry them in small amounts of oil.
- Choose skim, 1% or 2% milk. Try cheese that has a milk fat content of less than 15%. Use yogurt or cottage cheese that has a milk fat content of less than 2% (e.g. 0.9% M.F. yogurt). Use milk in coffee instead of creamers or nondairy powders.
- Choose leaner meat, fish or poultry and meat alternatives. Trim excess fat from meats, remove skins from poultry and use fish canned in water.

STARTERS AND SNACKS

- Serve unbuttered popcorn, pretzels, mini pita bread, fruit or vegetables for snacks. Have higher-fat snacks such as cookies, snack crackers and chips less often.
- Bagels, whole wheat buns and English muffins contain less fat and more fibre than doughnuts and croissants.
- Have low-fat muffins or better yet make them yourself using packaged low-fat muffin mixes. Try homemade recipes that include no more than ¼ cup (50 mL) fat for 12 muffins.
- Several different cereals combined together without milk are great nibblers for kids.
- Try fresh or frozen fruit mixed with low-fat yogurt.
- Fat intake adds up quickly when you're munching on potato or corn chips, so have them less often. Instead, try raw vegetables plain or dipped into calorie-reduced or fat-free salad dressing, or salsa and light sour cream or low-fat yogurt dips.
- Make cream soups with 2% milk or whole milk instead of cream. To thicken soup, add puréed cooked vegetables (carrots, potatoes, squash, eggplant), pasta, rice or barley.
- Choose reduced-fat or low-calorie salad dressings or make your own with flavoured vinegars, orange juice, honey or sugar and a small amount of olive oil.

Main Meals

- Plan meals around grains, pasta, rice, vegetables and fruit. Picture a dinner plate: three-quarters of the plate should be taken up with grains, vegetables and fruit; one-quarter should include meat, fish, poultry, eggs, beans, peas or lentils.
- Keep Canada's Food Guide to Healthy Eating serving sizes in mind when dishing up meals. For example, the following meal would be appropriate for an average female: 1 cup (250 mL) of rice, ½ cup (125 mL) of steamed broccoli, 1 medium broiled tomato and 2 to 3 oz (50 to 100 g) of fish (about the size of a deck of cards).
- Use smaller amounts of meat and larger quantities of vegetables in spaghetti sauces, chili, stews and casseroles.
- Have more meals made with dried or canned beans, peas and lentils. One serving of beans is 1/2 to 1 cup (125 to 250 mL). Try Black Bean, Corn and Couscous Salad (page 136), Spanish Rice with Lentils (page 42), Sweet Beans and Toast (page 142) or Basil Zucchini Strata (page 120).
- Choose lean chicken, turkey, ham, roast beef or reduced-fat luncheon meats for sandwiches. For sandwich fillings (egg, tuna, salmon) use "light" reduced-fat mayonnaise in place of regular mayonnaise and replace half the mayonnaise with low-fat plain yogurt.
- Bake, broil, microwave, poach or steam foods instead of frying. Use a nonstick pan for cooking eggs, pancakes and French toast.
- Use smaller amount of fats and oils in recipes. Stir-frying requires only 2 tsp (10 mL) of oil. For extra flavour in stir-frys, add sesame oil (up to 1 tsp/5 mL) or hoisin sauce (2 tbsp/25 mL).
- Try lemon juice, herbs, spices, salsa, mustard, ketchup and garlic for extra flavour without adding fat.
- Instead of gravy, try cranberry sauce, relish, chili sauce chutney, salsa or flavoured mustards.
- Choose low-fat pizza toppings such as mushrooms, peppers and pineapple. Use less pepperoni, sausage, bacon, anchovies, salami and double cheese, which all add extra fat.

Desserts

- Keep oatmeal or whole-grain cookies, fig and dried fruit bars on hand.
- Have fruit, fruit crisps, banana and other fruit breads.
- Try sherbet, sorbet, frozen yogurt, ice-milk and low-fat ice cream.
- Choose low-fat yogurt and pudding made with 2% milk

FAT CONTENT OF SOME COMMON FOODS

	Approximate fat in grams
Grain Products	
Bagel (1)	2
Bread, pita bread	1
Bread, white, whole wheat	trace
Buns, hamburger or hot dog (1)	3
Cake, iced (1 piece)	8
Cereal, cold (30 g)	trace
Cereal, cooked oatmeal (1 cup/250 mL)	2
Cookies, chocolate chip (2)	5
Cookies, social tea, arrowroot (2)	2
Cookies, sandwich-type with icing (2)	5
Crackers, saltines (4)	1
Croissant (1)	12
Danish pastry (1)	15
Doughnut (1)	11
Fig bars (2)	2
Granola (½ cup/125 mL)	17
Muffin, homemade	4
Noodles, cooked egg (1 cup/250 mL)	2
Noodles, fried chow mein type (1 cup/250 mL)	11
Pancake, small (4 in/10cm)	2
Pasta (1 cup/250 mL): macaroni, penne, spaghetti	1
Pie, fruit (⅙ of 23-cm diam. pie - 2 crust)	18
Rice, cornmeal	trace
Rolls, commercial, hard (1)	2
Tortillas, corn (1)	1
Tortillas, flour (1)	trace
Vegetables & Fruit	
Most fruits and vegetables	trace
Avocado, ½ medium	15
Milk Products	
Milk (1 cup/250 mL)	
Buttermilk	2
Goats milk	11
Skim	trace
1%	2.5
2%	5
3.3% whole (homogenized)	9
Cheese (1½ oz/45 g)	
Cheddar, processed Cheddar	15
Gouda, Gruyère, Muenster	15
Feta, mozzarella	10
Swiss	12
Mozzarella, partly skimmed milk	7

	Approximate fat in grams
Cheddar, processed with skim milk	3
Ricotta, made with whole milk	6
Ricotta, made with part-skim milk	4
Cottage cheese, 2% M.F. (½ cup/125 mL)	2.5
Cottage cheese, dry curd 0.4% M.F. (½ cup/125 mL)	trace
Cream cheese (1 tbsp/15 mL)	5
Parmesan, grated (1 tbsp/15 mL)	2
Cream	
Half and half, 10% M.F. (1 tbsp/15 mL)	1.5
Light sour cream, 5% M.F. (1 tbsp/15 mL)	0.7
Sour cream, 14% M.F. (1 tbsp/15 mL)	2
Table/coffee cream, 18% M.F. (1 tbsp/15 mL)	2.7
Whipping cream, 35% M.F. (1 tbsp/15 mL)	5.2
Yogurt	
Fruit flavour, 1.4% M.F. (125 g)	2
Plain, 1.5% M.F. (125 g)	2
Frozen Desserts (½ cup/125 mL)	
Ice cream, vanilla, hard, rich, 16% M.F.	12
Ice cream, vanilla, hard, 10% M.F.	8
Light ice cream, vanilla 7.2% M.F.	5
Frozen yogurt, fruit, 6.3% M.F. (125 g)	5
Ice milk, vanilla, soft	4
Sherbet, orange	2
Meat & Alternatives	
Alternatives	
Dried beans, lentils, split peas, cooked (1 cup/250 mL)	1
Chick-peas (garbanzo beans), cooked (1 cup/250 mL)	4
Egg (1 large)	5
Nuts: peanuts, almonds, mixed nuts (½ cup/125 mL)	40
cashews (½ cup/125 mL)	33
Peanut butter (1 tbsp/15 mL)	8
Peanut butter, reduced-fat (1 tbsp/15 mL)	6
Seeds: sunflower, sesame (½ cup/125 mL)	40
Soybeans, cooked (1 cup/250 mL)	16
Tofu (3 x 2.5 x 1 inch/7 x 6 x 2 cm)	4
Fish (3 oz/90 to 100 g):	
Fish sticks, breaded, frozen (3)	8
Haddock, breaded fried (1 fillet)	7
Halibut, broiled with butter or margarine	6
Sole, cod, haddock, lobster, scallops	1
Salmon, broiled or baked with butter or margarine	7
Salmon, canned (½ cup/125 mL)	10
Tuna, packed in water (½ cup/125 mL)	1
Tuna, packed in oil (½ cup/125 mL)	7

	Approximate fat in grams
Meat (3 oz/90 to 100 g) lean, cooked:	
Beef:	
Ground, lean, drained	13
Prime rib	10
Inside round	3
Sirloin steak	6
Rump roast	7
Lamb:	
Leg, roasted	6
Chop, broiled	7
Pork:	
Spareribs	23
Leg, roasted	7
Loin centre cut chop, broiled	7
Tenderloin, roasted	4
Veal, loin, cutlet or chop, broiled	12
Poultry (3 oz/90 to 100 g)	
Chicken, roasted, no skin (½ breast)	3
Chicken, roasted, with skin (½ breast)	8
Turkey, roasted, dark meat	6
Turkey, roasted, light meat	3
Deli and packaged meats	
Bacon, fried (2 slices)	6
Bologna, beef and pork (1 slice/22 g)	6
Bologna, turkey (1 slice/22 g)	3
Cooked ham (1 slice/30 g)	3
Salami (1 slice/30 g)	4
Sausage small (1/15 g)	5
Pepperoni (1 oz/ 30 g)	13
Pork or beef wiener (1)	11
Chicken or turkey wiener (1)	7
Other Foods	
Fats & Oils (1 tbsp/15 mL)	
Butter and margarine	11
Lard	13
Mayonnaise, regular	11
Mayonnaise, reduced fat	5
Salad dressing, French, regular type	6
Salad dressing, French, calorie-reduced	2
Vegetable oils (canola, corn, olive, peanut, soybean, sunflower)	14
Condiments: ketchup, mustard, pickles, relish, vinegar	trace
Snack Foods	
Chocolate bar (30 g)	7
Chocolate-coated peanuts, 15 (30 g)	12
Gum drops, jelly beans, hard candy, mints	trace
Jams, jellies, honey, sugar, syrup	trace

Popsicles, fruit-flavoured	0
Popcorn, air-popped, plain (1 cup/250 mL)	trace
Popcorn, popped with oil and salt (1 cup/250 mL)	3
Popcorn, microwave light (1 cup/250 mL)	1
Popcorn, microwave with butter (1 cup/250 mL)	3
Potato chips, small bag (55 g) or (2½ cups/625 mL)	20
Pretzels	trace
Soft drinks	0
Tea, coffee, plain	0

Source of Fat Values: Nutrient Value of Some Common Foods, Minister of Supply and Services Canada, 1988, supplemented with data from Canada Nutrient File 1991.

Appendix III

Fibre

Eating more fibre and complex carbohydrates is something most families should focus on as a healthy eating goal. Dietary fibre is an important component of our diets that has long-term benefits. Because it provides bulk to the diet and slows down digestion, fibre helps promote regularity and plays a role in preventing bowel disorders such as hemorrhoids, diverticulitis and cancer. Eating more fibre can help with weight control and lower blood cholesterol levels, which are important strategies for preventing heart disease. Dietary fibre can also help control blood sugar levels in people with diabetes.

WHAT IS DIETARY FIBRE?

Fibre is the part of plant foods that is not digested. Because we don't digest it, fibre does not provide energy in the form of calories. There are two different kinds of fibre: soluble and insoluble. Every plant contains both types of fibres, but in different amounts. We need both types of dietary fibres to maintain health.

- Soluble fibres dissolve in water and are found in dried peas, beans and lentils, barley, oats and some vegetables and fruit (green beans, cabbage, squash, apples, citrus fruit). This type of fibre helps reduce blood cholesterol and controls blood sugar levels.
- Insoluble fibres are very useful at keeping bowels regular and preventing bowel disorders and rectal and colon cancer. Wheat, wheat bran and other whole grains, many vegetables (broccoli, carrots, peas) and skins of fruits contain insoluble fibres.

How much fibre should we eat?

Nutrition experts say that adults should eat anywhere from 25 to 35 grams of dietary fibre each day. Unfortunately, most people don't get nearly half that amount due to low intakes of vegetables, fruit, grains and legumes. Foods that are high in fibre include whole-grain and bran-containing breads and cereals, vegetables and fruit, beans, peas and lentils, nuts and seeds.

You can monitor your family's intake of fibre by looking at food labels on packaged foods and using the chart "Fibre Content of Some Common Foods" (page 206).

Here's what 30 grams of fibre a day looks like:

Food Choices	**Dietary Fibre (grams)**
Breakfast	
½ cup (125 mL) orange juice	0.4
¾ cup (175 mL) bran flakes	6.3
2 tbsp (25 mL) raisins	0.8
½ cup (125 mL) milk	0.0
1 slice whole wheat toast	1.6
1 tsp (5 mL) soft margarine	0.0
Snack	
Bran muffin	2.5
Coffee/milk	0.0
Lunch	
Sandwich, any filling, using 2 slices whole-wheat bread	3.2
Tomato slices (½ medium)	1.5
Pear	5.1
Low-fat plain yogurt	0.0
Supper	
Fast Fish in the Microwave	0.0
1 cup (250 mL) brown rice	3.3
½ cup (125 mL) steamed carrots	2.0
½ cup (125 mL) steamed broccoli	2.0
1 cup (250 mL) fresh strawberries	3.2
Total for the day	30.0 grams

Meat, fish, poultry, eggs and milk products do not contain fibre. To get more fibre, eat more foods from the Grain Products and Vegetables & Fruit groups and include meals made with dried beans, peas and lentils, more often.

HEALTHY WEIGHT TIP

A high intake of foods high in fibre and complex carbohydrates can help you feel full faster and help you eat less. For example, if you eat a high-fibre breakfast including whole-grain or bran cereal and fruit rather than a highly refined cereal and juice, you will feel full longer and be able to skip a mid-morning snack.

ARE CARBOHYDRATES IMPORTANT?

Absolutely! Carbohydrates are your body's most efficient source of energy. Foods that are high in carbohydrates can be grouped into two categories: simple and complex. Simple carbohydrates are foods such as sugar, honey, jam and candy. Complex carbohydrate foods take longer to digest and are also a source of important vitamins, minerals and fibre. They include breads, cereals, grains, pasta, rice, vegetables, fruit, dried beans, peas and lentils.

Most families can benefit from eating more carbohydrates than they currently eat. Ideally, carbohydrates should account for 55 percent of our total daily energy intake, with most of them being complex carbohydrate foods.

55% of the calories we eat should come from carbohydrate
30% of the calories we eat should come from fat
15% of the calories we eat should come from protein

Quick fibre fixes: tips to help your family eat more fibre

- Follow the Canada's Food Guide to Healthy Eating and eat 5 to 12 servings of Grain Products and 5 to 10 servings of Vegetables & Fruit each day.
- Choose cereals that contain 4 or more grams of fibre per serving such as bran flakes, all-bran type cereals, corn bran, oatmeal, shredded wheat and Shreddies-type whole wheat cereal. Use bran cereal in breading mixes for chicken or fish or to add to chili, soups, ground meat dishes or hamburger patties.
- Eat a variety of whole-grain breads, rolls, bagels and pita bread. Look for 100% whole wheat, mixed grains, pumpernickel, rye, oat and corn breads.
- Experiment with different grains such as brown rice, barley, bulgur and whole wheat pasta, in casseroles, salads and soups. Substitute whole wheat flour for some of the all-purpose flour in recipes for breads, muffins, pancakes and pizza dough.
- Have fruit instead of juice. One cup (250 mL) of orange juice has about the same amount of calories as 2 oranges, but the oranges will help fill you up and provide more fibre.
- Eat the skins of fruit and vegetables. One baked potato with its skin has nine times more fibre and less fat than 10 large French fries.
- **Fruit Smoothie: Put fresh fruit and frozen yogurt in a blender to make a fruit shake. Or try fresh fruit (1 cup/250 mL), fruit yogurt (1 cup/250 mL) and ice cubes (1 cup/250 mL) in a blender for a smoothie.**
- Use dried fruit in cereals, baked goods and salads.
- Add extra vegetables to casseroles and pasta dishes. One cup (250 mL) of green peas can add 7 grams of fibre to macaroni and cheese.
- Try canned chick-peas, kidney beans, lima beans, yellow or green beans in salads, casseroles and soups.
- Purée leftover cooked vegetables (broccoli, carrots, cauliflower), and add chicken or vegetable broth or milk to make a speedy soup.
- **Canned refried beans mixed with ½ cup (125 mL) low-fat plain (1 to 2% M.F.) yogurt and 1 tsp (5 mL) chili powder make a great dip. Use carrot sticks, green pepper and celery as dippers.**

Increase the amount of fibre your family eats gradually. Too much fibre all at once may cause bloating, gas and stomach discomfort. You should also encourage your family to drink plenty of fluids to help their bodies use fibre properly.

These *Suppertime Survival* meals are a very high source of fibre (they contain at least 6 grams of dietary fibre per serving).

Bail-Out Bean Burritos
Baked Fish with Oven-Fried Potato Cubes
Black Bean, Corn and Couscous Salad (11 grams)
Chili and Cornbread (10 grams)
Curried Beef in a Pita
Extra-Speedy Spaghetti Supper
Fast Fish in the Microwave
Flake and Bake Chicken
French Toast with Peaches
Fusilli with Vegetarian Pasta Sauce
Harvest Vegetables with Chicken and Penne
Homemade Spaghetti Supper
Marinated Beef and Vegetable Kabobs
Pork Tenderloin with Roasted Sweet Potatoes
Roast Turkey Breast and Vegetable Supper
Spinach Frittata Fingers
Spanish Rice with Lentils
Sweet Beans and Toast (24 grams)
Tangy Barbecue Chicken with Rice
Three-Bean Chili with Couscous (13 grams)
Warm Taco Salad

FIBRE CONTENT OF SOME COMMON FOODS

	Approximate fibre in grams
Grain Products	
Bagel (1/60 g)	0.2
Bread, 100% whole wheat (slice)	1.6
Bread, white (slice)	0.5
Bread, white pita (16.5 cm diam./60 g)	0.3
Bread, whole wheat pita (16.5 cm diam./60 g)	4.4
Cereal, cold (check fibre content listed on package labels of your favourite cereals)	
All-Bran type (½ cup/125 mL)	11.7
Bran flakes, with raisins (¾ cup/200 mL)	4.6
Bran flakes (¾ cup/200 mL)	6.3
100% Bran (½ cup/125 mL)	11.9
Corn Bran (¾ cup/200 mL)	5.3
Corn flakes, (1 cup/250 mL)	0.8
Rice Krispies (1 cup/250 mL)	0.3

	Approximate fibre in grams
Puffed rice (1 cup/250 mL)	trace
Shredded wheat (1 biscuit)	3.3
Shreddies type (¾ cup/200 mL)	4.8
Cereal, cooked oatmeal (1 cup/250 mL)	3.7
Muffin, bran	2.5
Pasta (1 cup/250 mL)	2.2
Rice	
Brown rice, cooked (1 cup/250 mL)	3.3
White, long-grain, cooked (1 cup/250 mL)	0.8
White, instant, cooked (1 cup/250 mL)	1.3
Wheat bran (1 tbsp/15 mL)	1.5
Vegetables (½ cup/125 mL)	
Asparagus, cooked, 4 spears	1.0
Bean sprouts,	0.6
Beans, green, cooked	1.3
Broccoli, cooked	2.0
Brussels sprouts, cooked	4.9
Cabbage, cooked	1.3
Cabbage, shredded, raw	0.6
Carrots, cooked	2.0
Carrots, raw (1 medium)	1.9
Cauliflower, cooked	0.3
Celery, stalk, raw	0.6
Corn, sweet, boiled (one 8 in/20 cm cob)	4.4
- cooked, niblets, canned	2.1
Cucumber, sliced, raw	0.4
Eggplant, cubed, cooked	1.2
Mushrooms, pieces, raw	0.5
Onions, raw (1 medium)	1.8
Peas, snow peas, cooked	2.2
Peas, green, frozen, cooked	3.5
Peppers, sweet green, raw (1 medium)	2.2
Potatoes, 1 medium with skin	2.5
- mashed with milk	2.1
Spinach, raw	0.7
- cooked	2.4
Squash, acorn, cooked (1/4)	2.6
- zucchini, cooked	1.9
Sweet potatoes, cooked (1 medium)	5.4
Tomato, raw (1 medium)	1.5
- canned	1.2
- juice	0.8
Turnip (rutabaga), cooked	1.8
Fruit (½ cup/125 mL)	
Apple	
- raw, 1 medium with skin	2.6

	Approximate fibre in grams
- applesauce, unsweetened	1.8
- apple juice	0.1
Banana, 1 medium	2.0
Blueberries	1.9
Cantaloupe, ¼	2.4
Cherries, sweet	0.8
Dates, pitted, chopped (¼ cup/50 mL)	3.8
Grapefruit, ½	2.1
Grapes	1.0
Kiwifruit, 1 large	3.1
Mango, peeled	1.7
Orange, 1 medium	2.4
- orange juice	0.4
Peach, 1 medium, peeled	1.7
Pear, 1 medium with skin	5.1
Pineapple, canned cubes	1.1
Plum, 1 medium	1.1
Prunes, 5 dried, uncooked	3.1
Prune juice	1.3
Raisins, seedless (2 tbsp/25 mL)	0.8
Raspberries	3.0
Rhubarb, diced	1.1
Strawberries	1.6
Watermelon, 1 slice	1.5
Milk Products	
Cheese	0.0
Cream	0.0
Ice cream	0.0
Milk	0.0
Yogurt	0.0
Meat & Alternatives	
Meat, poultry, fish and eggs	0.0
Dried beans, peas and lentils	
Baked beans with tomato sauce (1 cup/250 mL)	19.6
Navy beans, cooked, drained (1 cup/250 mL)	13.8
Red kidney beans, cooked, drained (1 cup/250 mL)	16.5
Lentils, cooked (1 cup/250 mL)	8.8
Chick-peas (garbanzo beans), cooked (1 cup/250 mL)	6.7
Split peas, cooked (1 cup/250 mL)	9.4
Nuts	
Almonds, whole (½ cup/125 mL)	5.1
Peanuts, dry-roasted (½ cup/125 mL)	6.5
Peanut butter (1 tbsp/15 mL)	1.0
Tofu (7 x 6 x 2 cm)	1.1

Source: Canadian Nutrient File, 1991. Data prepared by Info Access Inc. 1995.

Appendix IV

Feeding Babies and Toddlers

Breastmilk is the best source of nutrients for babies in the first six months of life. Between six and 12 months of age, breastmilk is still the ideal choice for milk feedings. When breastfeeding is not possible, an iron-fortified infant formula is recommended until babies are 12 months old. Whole milk (homogenized) can be introduced at one year of age. Skim, 1% and 2% milk are not recommended for children until after two years of age.

Infant cereals are an important source of iron and contain a form of iron that is easily absorbed. Continue to offer infant cereals until babies are 18 to 24 months of age.

WHEN CAN I START MY BABY ON SOLIDS?

Four to six months of age is the ideal time to introduce solid foods. By this time, a baby's digestive system is ready to accept food, and mouth reflexes have changed so that they won't be pushing food constantly out of their mouth. Babies can be introduced to infant cereal on a spoon once they have good head control and can sit unsupported.

WHEN BABIES WANT TO JOIN THE FAMILY TABLE

When babies are nine or 10 months old, they are ready to leave puréed foods behind in favour of sampling the family fare. Around this time, babies are ready to try new textures. They are also ready to test their coordination and independence with finger foods. Introducing family foods is a gradual process and babies should continue to eat some soft, mashed foods as well as family foods for a few months.

Even if babies have eaten before the rest of the family, it is important to include them at the family table. They can be offered small samples of what the rest of the family is eat-

Too much juice?

Too much juice may cause diarrhea and interfere with baby's intake of other foods. Delay the introduction of juice until your baby is able to drink from a cup. Juice should be diluted, half juice and half water. Two ounces (60 mL) of juice (undiluted) is all babies need to satisfy their vitamin C requirements.

Introducing Solid Foods to Babies

Foods should be introduced slowly in small quantities, a teaspoon at a time. Introduce one new food at a time every four to five days.

4-6 months	Iron-fortified infant cereals: start with rice cereal then barley, oats and wheat. Introduce mixed-grain cereals last.
6-9 months	Begin with puréed vegetables and fruit. Start with orange vegetables such as carrots or sweet potatoes. Offer yogurt (3.5% M.F.) or creamy cottage cheese. Introduce puréed meat, fish or poultry and puréed or mashed cooked beans, peas and lentils. Egg yolks are okay at this stage but egg whites should not be introduced until after the first year, due to the possible development of food allergies. Teething babies can chew on dry toast.
9-12 months	Gradually introduce textured foods. Mash foods at first, then move on to larger pieces. Let babies experiment with finger foods such as peeled pieces of soft fruit, cooked vegetable pieces, dry toast, breadsticks or crackers (low-salt types) and mild shredded cheese.

ing, such as cooked vegetables, pasta and rice. The foods won't make a great contribution to their nutrient intakes, but the act of eating with the family and feeding themselves is an important learning process.

Family favourites for babies 12 months and older

- Try grains such as rice, couscous and barley, adding whatever you want to round out a meal. Make a quick casserole: start with rice or barley, add a little tuna or chicken and mix in some cooked or frozen vegetables.
- When baby will no longer eat infant cereals, try cream of wheat or oatmeal. When making hot cereals, substitute whole milk for all or part of the water. Add some stewed prunes, apricots or other fruits if desired.
- Try French Toast with Peaches (page 140), pancakes, and plain muffins.
- Offer pasta dishes such as Creamy Macaroni and Cheese (page 34), Family Tuna Noodle Casserole (page 62), Tortellini with Creamy Cheese Sauce (page 144), Ravioli with Prepared Pasta Sauce (page 145), Extra-Speedy Spaghetti Supper (page 92), and Spaghettini with Broccoli and Ham (page 141).
- Cook, mash coarsely or use fresh or frozen vegetables as finger foods (see note on choking, page 169). Boil and mash or bake sweet potatoes, white potatoes, squash.
- Offer fresh or canned fruits packed in fruit juice or light syrup. Remove skins, coarsely mash at first then move on to chunks.
- Try Carrot Ginger Soup (page 117) or Broccoli Soup (page 116) made with whole or homogenized milk.

- Try plain yogurt (3.5 % M.F.) mixed with raspberries, finely chopped strawberries or applesauce.
- Try creamed cottage cheese with seedless oranges or canned mandarin oranges stirred in.
- Cut meat or poultry into small bits and serve with vegetables, pasta or rice. Try Roast Turkey Breast and Vegetable Supper (page 108), Tangy Barbecued Chicken with Rice (page 72), Pork Tenderloin with Roasted Sweet Potatoes (page 168), and Batch Ground Meat and Vegetables (page 88) mixed with rice.
- Some babies will eat spicy foods, although you may want to cut back on the spices at first. Try Cabbage Roll Casserole (page 58) and Chili and Cornbread (page 96).
- Offer egg dishes such as scrambled eggs, Zucchini and Red Pepper Frittata (page 50), Spinach Frittata Fingers (page 70) and Basil Zucchini Strata (page 120).
- Offer bean dishes such as Sweet Beans and Toast (page 142), Lentil and Pasta Soup (page 118), Spanish Rice with Lentils (page 42) and Three-Bean Chili with Couscous (page 122).

Appendix V

Nutrient Analysis

Nutrient analysis of these meals was performed by Info Access (1988) Inc., Don Mills, Ontario, using the nutritional accounting component of the CBORD Menu Management System. The nutrient database was the 1991 Canadian Nutrient File, supplemented when necessary with documented data from reliable sources.

Nutrient values were rounded to the nearest whole number. Non-zero values less than 0.5 appear as "trace."

The analysis was based on:

- imperial weights and measures except when the food specified is normally packaged in a metric quantity
- the average number of servings when there was a range
- the smaller quantity when there was a range
- the first ingredient listed when there was a choice of ingredients.

Optional ingredients and garnishes in unspecified amounts were not included in the calculations.

VITAMINS, MINERALS AND DIETARY FIBRE

The complete supper meals were evaluated as sources of vitamins, minerals and dietary fibre according to the criteria for food labelling outlined in the Guide for Food Manufacturers and Advertisers, 1988 (Consumer and Corporate Affairs Canada). A meal supplying 15 percent of the Recommended Daily Intake (RDI) of a vitamin or mineral (30 percent for vitamin C) is described as a good source of that nutrient: one supplying 25 percent of the RDI (50 percent for vitamin C) is described as an excellent source. A meal containing 2 grams of dietary fibre is described as a moderate source, one containing 4 grams of dietary fibre as a high source, and one containing 6 grams of dietary fibre as a very high source.

RAINBOW BALANCE CHART VALUES

In consultation with the authors, Info Access used customized software to derive the rainbow chart values. The values were based on the serving sizes specified in Canada's Food Guide to Healthy Eating.

Milk Products servings in the rainbow balance charts were rounded to quarter servings, and servings from the other food groups to half servings. The nutrient contribution of the specific foods was considered when rounding the rainbow values.

WHAT COUNTS AS A SERVING?

Canada's Food Guide to Healthy Eating displays portion sizes for typical choices from each of the four food groups. For the Meat & Alternatives group, 2 to 3 oz (50 to 100 g) of meat, fish or poultry, ⅓ to ⅔ of a can of tuna, 1 to 2 eggs, and ½ to 1 cup (125 to 250 mL) canned or cooked dried beans, peas or lentils were each counted as one serving. Numerous ingredients (e.g., dry bread crumbs, cornmeal, cornflake crumbs and flour, condensed soups and light sour cream) are not specifically mentioned in the Food Guide but they do fall into one of the four food groups. Serving sizes for such items were approximated according to the nutrient contribution of comparable foods in the same groups. In addition, 1 cup (250 mL) of couscous counts as two servings from the Grain Products group, two, 8-inch (20 cm) flour tortillas count as 3½ servings from the Grain Products group and one cup (250 mL) of tortilla chips count as one serving from the Grain Products group. One cup (250 mL) of cottage cheese and ¼ cup (50 mL) of feta cheese and light ricotta cheese all count as half a serving from the Milk Products group. Two tablespoons (25 mL) of Parmesan cheese counts as ¼ serving from the Milk Products group.

INDEX